Implementing Security for
ATM Networks

For quite a long time, computer security was a rather narrow field of study that was populated mainly by theoretical computer scientists, electrical engineers, and applied mathematicians. With the proliferation of open systems in general, and of the Internet and the World Wide Web (WWW) in particular, this situation has changed fundamentally. Today, computer and network practitioners are equally interested in computer security, since they require technologies and solutions that can be used to secure applications related to electronic commerce. Against this background, the field of computer security has become very broad and includes many topics of interest. The aim of this series is to publish state-of-the-art, high standard technical books on topics related to computer security. Further information about the series can be found on the WWW at the following URL:

http://www.esecurity.ch/serieseditor.html

Also, if you'd like to contribute to the series by writing a book about a topic related to computer security, feel free to contact either the Commissioning Editor or the Series Editor at Artech House.

Recent Titles in the Artech House Computer Security Series

Rolf Oppliger, Series Editor

For a listing of recent titles in the *Artech House Computing Library,* turn to the back of this book.

Implementing Security for ATM Networks

Thomas D. Tarman
Edward L. Witzke

Artech House
Boston • London
www.artechhouse.com

Library of Congress Cataloging-in-Publication Data.
Tarman, Thomas.
    Implementing security for ATM networks/Thomas Tarman, Edward Witzke.
    p. cm.—(Artech House computer security series)
    Includes bibliographical references and index.
    ISBN 1-58053-293-4 (alk. paper)
    1. Computer networks—Security measures.   2. Asynchronous transfer mode.
    I. Witzke, Edward.   II. Title.   III. Series.
TK5105.59 .T37 2002
005.8—dc21   2001053535

British Library Cataloguing in Publication Data
Tarman, Thomas.
    Implementing security for ATM networks.—(Artech House computer security series).
    1. Asynchronous transfer mode   2. Telecommunication systems—Security measures
    I. Title   II. Witzke, Edward
    621.3'8216
    ISBN 1-58053-293-4

Cover design by Igor Valdman

© 2002 ARTECH HOUSE, INC.
685 Canton Street
Norwood, MA 02062

International Standard Book Number: 1-58053-293-4
Library of Congress Catalog Card Number: 2001053535

10 9 8 7 6 5 4 3 2 1

To our families:

Dawn and Riley Tarman
and
Kären and Eric Witzke

Contents

Foreword

The news continually reminds us of the need for increased protection of our information, systems, and communications networks from malicious activities. No one is immune: Threats are directed at the public sector, private corporations, and our personal lives. Stories every week describe thousands of daily attacks against government computers, compromises of major corporate Web sites at the rate of several per hour, and identity theft as our most rapidly increasing crime statistic. Reports and summaries of security incidents indicate that the situation may be getting worse, even as our reliance on information systems and networks increases. As our networks are pressed to handle interactive, multimedia information and to provide quality of service assurances, high-speed transport end to end, and seamless connectivity with wireless devices, ATM continues to play an essential, if often behind-the-scenes, role in our rapidly evolving communications infrastructure. Today, voice over packet telephony and wireless data services loom on the horizon without offering us any strong reason to hope they will be secured in an appropriate and timely manner.

How do we then account for the fact that, paradoxically, there is no apparent lack of research papers, conferences, standards, books, training courses, trade shows, and products addressing information security? Several experts have pointed out why security is difficult to specify, to implement correctly, to sell, and to use. Security analysis and design are often superficial; many products contain flaws; piecemeal solutions do not work; testing is inadequate; and one weak link breaks the chain. Standards are often incomplete and sometimes ineffectively weak. Some "solutions" leave the hard part as an exercise for the user. Widespread popular misunderstanding of the depth and intricacy of the problem persists.

The authors of *Implementing Security for ATM Networks* demonstrate their understanding of these issues. By comprehensively applying their knowledge and experience with ATM security, they break new ground. They describe for us the foundations, the model, the applications, the methods, and the rationale. Finally, they give us a glimpse of the future. They make a persuasive case for comprehensive ATM network security, treat the subject systematically, and dispel many misconceptions.

Properly designed and implemented cryptographic systems, services, protocols, and algorithms can provide a secure connection between already secured endpoints, but they can do nothing to secure these endpoints in the first place. Improperly designed or implemented, cryptography provides merely a false sense of security and an attractive target. The authors, there-fore, do not limit themselves to cryptographic protocols but treat the entire subject of ATM security.

One unfortunate trend today is the appearance of protocol specifica-tions with incomplete, overly constrained, or oversimplified security solu-tions. Effective security solutions must be comprehensive; they must span the spectrum from the end user to the low-layer communications infrastructure; they must provide flexibility and extensibility. By covering all these aspects of ATM security, the authors demonstrate that such comprehensive solutions are achievable.

The authors address the questions of implementing efficient, high-speed encryption, integrating security within the constraints of existing sig-naling protocols, and providing security functionality at several protocol lay-ers. They describe a full range of security services together with key management, negotiation, nesting, proxy servers, and user-defined exten-sions. To accomplish all of this, they bring together a rare combination of talents indeed: knowledge of networking and security, experience with specification and implementation, skills with hardware and software. The reader will appreciate their thorough understanding of ATM networking and security, from the big picture to the fine-grained details. This volume reflects the years they have spent improving ATM security technology and demon-strating the practical implementation of these ideas.

This book will be an invaluable guide to anyone implementing or deploying secure ATM networks. Also, it will help service providers and enterprises make better-informed decisions about the security functionality they need, and it will help users of these networks find clear, understandable explanations of the available security services and options. Finally, it will help all of us better appreciate the challenge of providing comprehensive, high-assurance security solutions for the networks upon which we increasingly rely. I trust that all readers will have an enjoyable and worthwhile experience.

Richard F. Graveman
Morristown, New Jersey
November 2001

Preface

Asynchronous transfer mode (ATM) technology is quietly making a major contribution to the evolution of voice, video, and data networking. The evidence to support this statement is quite remarkable. At the beginning of the millennium, more than 75% of all global Internet backbone data traffic is running over ATM. High-speed data access for business and the home, via xDSL technology, is predominately based on ATM, and native ATM protocol support is integrated into the most widely distributed personal computer operating systems, Windows 2000 and Windows 98. Additionally, all vendors of carrier grade network switching equipment provide native ATM interfaces on their product offerings, and virtually all WAN multiservice switching products for voice and data networking support ATM interface options. More importantly, at the beginning of the new millennium, much of the core voice telephony network is running over ATM.

Why ATM Security?

The widespread adoption of ATM in the public network infrastructure has been a widely anticipated event, primarily because ATM was specifically designed as the Broadband Integrated Services Digital Network (B-ISDN) transport facility for SONET networking. The expectation that ATM would become a future network transport to support high-performance, mission-critical applications such as broadcast quality video and voice compelled organizations such as the U.S. Department of Defense to invest in developing security technology for ATM. As a result of this investment, research in

ATM cryptographic technology has demonstrated that ATM had properties that could support very high performance security mechanisms.

But the principal reason for ATM security today is to support the use of ATM in the public telephony and data networks. With the potential for widespread adoption of ATM in the core voice telephony network, ATM's ability to support public network reliability and security becomes very important. Within the United States alone, there is a national interest in public network reliability and security; having been the principal concern of organizations like the President's National Security Telecommunications Advisory Committee (NSTAC), the Network Reliability and Interoperability Council (NRIC) of the Federal Communications Commission, the Network Reliability Steering Committee of the Alliance for Telecommunications Industry Solutions, and the National Research Council, to name just a few. These organizations have all recognized that technological change is one of the fundamental sources of unforeseen threats to the current reliability of the public telephone network. In order for ATM networking technology to successfully contribute to the next generation of public telephone network architecture, integrated security protection strategies are highly desirable.

In response to these and other concerns, the ATM Forum formed a security working group in 1995 to develop an interoperability specification for the fundamental security services that can be applied to ATM virtual circuits. These mechanisms include access control, and the cryptographically based security services, confidentiality, authentication, and integrity. Since these mechanisms were designed to be implemented on ATM virtual circuits, they can be applied to user data flows and most ATM network control flows. The ATM Forum approved this specification, the ATM Security Specification Version 1.1, in March 2001.

Intended Audience and Organization of This Book

This book is intended for readers who wish to understand more about ATM security (other than what is currently written in standards and research papers). It should aid network architects who wish to enforce security policies within their ATM infrastructures, ATM security device implementers who would like to understand the background and philosophy behind the mechanisms in Security 1.1, and researchers who wish to understand the current and future state of ATM security. Although this book does not cover all of the details contained in the ATM Forum Security Specification, there are topics where some detail is presented in order to illustrate fundamental concepts (e.g., security agent addressing and nesting of security services).

Part I contains chapters that provide background information on network security and ATM. Part II contains chapters that will help network architects who wish to understand how existing traditional ATM functions can be used to implement security. In addition, Part II also provides information to network architects and ATM security device implementers regarding how the ATM security services defined in Security 1.1 can be implemented in ATM networks. Part III provides additional details for the ATM security device implementer who wishes to understand the philosophy behind the mechanisms of Security 1.1. Finally, Part IV provides the researcher with a view of the current state of ATM security and describes topics of continuing and future research.

Since this book is intended as a companion to the ATM Forum's ATM Security Specification Version 1.1, the reader is urged to obtain a copy of this specification at http://www.atmforum.com.

Acknowledgments

This book represents a compilation of years of work in the development of specifications and research in ATM security, and the authors are grateful to a number of individuals and groups who have made substantial contributions to this book and to ATM security in general. Specifically, the authors would like to thank Carter Bullard for his technical input and his effort in the early development of this book, the members of the ATM Forum Security Working group for their technical contributions and discussions, and Richard Graveman and Wolfgang Klasen, the chair and vice-chair (respectively) of the Security Working Group, for their technical input and leadership over the years. Finally, the authors would like to express their gratitude to Lyndon Pierson, Doug Brown, and Sumit Ghosh for reviewing portions of this book, and to the anonymous reviewer for his constructive technical input, which improved the quality of this book.

Part I:
Fundamentals

1

Introduction to Network Security

A general discussion of network security is in order before describing security approaches and mechanisms specific to asynchronous transfer mode (ATM) networks. This chapter provides a description of security concepts generic to any network, large or small, ATM or otherwise. It also introduces concepts that will be described in much greater detail later in the book. Finally, it covers some of the trade-offs associated with network security design.

1.1 Up-Front Security Analysis

It is vitally important to perform up-front security analysis. Without this step, one will not know where they are trying to go or what they are trying to achieve, let alone, where they have been! Some security methodology should be used so this can be approached in a methodical manner and, hopefully, ensure completeness. A number of computer network security methodologies have been developed and documented in the literature.

One methodology, published by Graft, Pabrai, and Pabrai [1], lays out three phases: specification, design, and implementation. In the specification phase, the security system requirements are determined and the design constraints are identified. The design phase defines the security architecture, locates the required functionality within the architecture, defines the needed service primitives, selects the underlying mechanisms to implement the services, and defines the service protocols. The third phase, the implementation

3

phase, covers activities such as the development of required hardware and software, testing and verification, performance analysis, and certification and accreditation.

Another methodology published by Pierson and Witzke [2] consists of two phases. They cover design, review, and accreditation in the first phase, and operations in the second phase. The design, review, and accreditation phase encompasses:

- Definition of protected resources;
- Security policy;
- Statement of threat;
- Protection measures;
- Risk analysis;
- Incident detection mechanisms;
- The security plan;
- Certification and accreditation.

By defining the resources or assets to be protected and the statement of threat, the scope and granularity of all succeeding elements is bounded. The statement of threat is derived through a process of nonoverlapping decomposition, which starts with the universal set of all hazards. This set is divided and redivided in a tree fashion, until eventually each subtree ends with a specific threat or a nonspecific category such as *other events or methods*. This nonspecific category contains threats that, for one reason or another, are not being addressed at that time in the methodology.

Because the second phase of this methodology is the operational phase and deals with items such as event investigation and loss mitigation, interested readers are referred to the paper [2].

Neither of these network security methodologies is entirely adequate or complete, but they are a place to start. Other methodologies and tools (design and process outline (DEPO), failure-mode analysis, fault trees, attack trees, and adversary sequence diagrams), some possibly adapted from the physical security or engineering disciplines, may help to fill in the gaps.

1.1.1 Threats and Assets That Require Protection

Each asset or resource that requires protection must be well defined before one can assemble a statement of threat. After the assets or resources have been identified, they can be matched with threats, their desired protection levels can be determined, and protection measures can be developed. A *definition of protected resources* or *statement of protected assets* should identify and characterize the resources or assets that require protection. For example, in an ATM network, the statement of protected assets may include the following:

- Confidentiality of user data on ATM virtual circuits;
- Integrity of switch configuration data;
- Authenticity of network control signaling messages.

This characterization should include the location, nature, replacement cost, costs associated with displaced service and loss or compromise of data, and a narrative description of costs that are intangible or cannot be estimated.

A *threat* is an event or method that can potentially cause the theft, destruction, corruption, or usage denial of either service, information, resources, or materials. It must be emphasized that a threat is a "what" (earthquake, flood, voltage surge) or a "how" (TEMPEST attack, packet insertion, Trojan horse), not a "who." Perpetrators (hackers, terrorists, information warriors, disgruntled employees) are the "who" elements. Perpetrators may be characterized by motivations, levels of funding, and weapons or equipment.

Different kinds of perpetrators may use the same method, and one perpetrator may use many different methods. For network security planning, categorizing threat events or methods is of greater importance than categorizing perpetrators, because protection measures are based on the damaging events and methods, not who happens to be employing them. One can assume that perpetrators will use whatever methods, as appropriate, that they have at their disposal.

The *statement of threat* should define the types of threat events or methods that pertain to the network being examined. Examples of threats in ATM networks that may be incorporated by the statement of threat include the following:

- Unauthorized capture of ATM cell traffic in a public network;
- Unauthorized access to, and modification of, switch configuration data;

- Injection of false routing information in a private network.

  (Note that these threats correspond to the example ATM network assets listed earlier.)

The definition of protected resources and the security policy (described below) are the components that drive the statement of threat. Countermeasures are developed specifically, and only, for those threats defined in the statement of threat.

To develop the statement of threat, the authors use nonoverlapping decomposition. One begins with the universal set of all hazards, and typically divides it into natural and nonnatural (man-made) events or methods. Eventually each subtree's decomposition ends with a general category such as other events or methods, which, as stated earlier, are not being addressed at this time. (Future revisions or updates to this statement of threat may further break out or consolidate hazards, thus changing the scope of the "other" category.) An example threat decomposition that illustrates this concept is shown in Figure 1.1. The granularity of this statement of threat also governs the granularity of the documented countermeasures and other security methodology elements.

The resulting threat list should not contain overlap, except for the general "other" category. All threats map into a specific item identified in the statement of threat or into a nonspecific item identified as "other." After more experience is gained with the communications network to be secured, planners can add more detail to the items in the statement of threat and improve the countermeasures.

Once the protected resources or assets are defined and the threats are identified, then the threats can be mapped to the assets, providing a threat-asset mapping. Countermeasures can then be developed for each of the threat-asset pairs. Continuing the example for ATM networks, the list of countermeasures may include:

- Encryption of ATM cells at the private-public network boundary;

- Strong user authentication and access control lists for switch management access;

- Control message authentication and secure routing message processing mechanisms.

Any risk analyses (described later) can also be performed based on the threat-asset pairs.

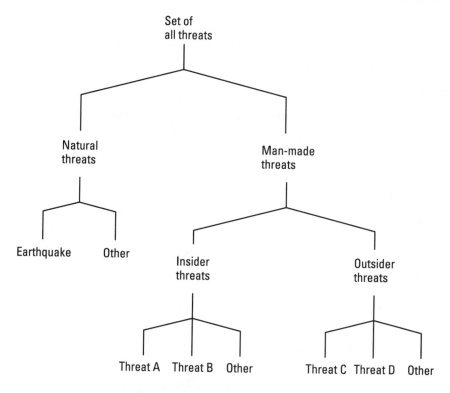

Figure 1.1 Nonoverlapping threat decomposition.

1.1.2 Usage Policies

Usage policies lay out the ground rules for usage of the network. This simply deals with who is authorized to do what on the network (e.g., nodes that can establish ATM connections with each other, administrators who are authorized to configure ATM switches, etc.). This is part of the *network security policy*, which also includes a statement of management intent about protecting computing or communication resources. This statement identifies to what extent important classes of resources are to be protected from a broad class of perpetrators. A security policy should briefly describe the appropriate use of the computing and communication resources. It should also describe the intent of protections against compromise of need-to-know, privacy, corporate security, national security, or other applicable losses perpetrated by insiders or outsiders or caused by natural hazards. (Insiders are personnel authorized to enter physical security boundaries, while outsiders are those who are not.)

A security policy need not be formalized with a mathematical model of security, although formal computer security models may aid in the development of countermeasures for certain resources. (A system security model defines the security rules that every implementation must enforce [3].) Computer or communication resources and threats vary widely; therefore, it is unlikely that a single formal model and associated formal security policy can be used to plan adequately for all aspects of computer and communications security or for all networks.

1.1.3 Attack Methods

The goal of most attacks is to steal or corrupt information, deny access to information or network resources, or make unauthorized use of the network resources. This can be accomplished in many ways, too numerous to list here. A sample of these is:

- Attacks on the software such as Trojan horses, viruses, and time bombs;

- Operations security attacks such as dumpster diving and data aggregation;

- Personnel security attacks such as social engineering, bribery, and blackmail;

- Limit and boundary probe attacks, such as buffer overflows, exceeding transaction rates, and entry of out-of-bounds values;

- Radio frequency attacks, such as TEMPEST (RF emanations from computers and communication lines) and Van Eck observation (reception of emissions from video displays), jamming, and electromagnetic pulse (EMP) bombs;

- Network attacks, such as sniffing, packet insertion, and connection takeover.

These attack methods and many others are detailed in the book by Dr. Cohen [4].

1.1.4 Determining Countermeasures

Protection measures are countermeasures that defeat or help to defeat one or more threats. A given protection measure may partially negate several threats, but to fully negate a threat, multiple protection measures may be necessary. This introduces the concept of multiple barriers or providing *protection in depth*. Because many protection measures (barriers) have inherent vulnerabilities, several measures that overlap (in the sense that they are protecting the same, rather than different threat-asset pairs) may be necessary to effectively counter a threat against a specific asset. A more detailed analysis of multiple barrier theory can be found in the work of Cooper [5].

Incident or event detection mechanisms are another type of countermeasure. These are somewhat analogous to intrusion detection measures in the physical security environment. Physical security intrusion detection can be viewed as perimeter entry detection, room entry detection, and surveillance. In network security, these analogues can be viewed as detection of a breach of the perimeter of the network, detection of a breach at specific compartments (nodes, switches, etc.), and general network surveillance. The detection mechanisms should note an event or incident that is unusual and may be an indication that a threat event has occurred or is occurring, or that a threat method was attempted or is being attempted. The detection mechanism may also be triggered by attempts to circumvent the various protection measures that have been put into place in a network. Detection mechanisms should duly signal and log anomalies as appropriate, and do so in a secure fashion so perpetrators cannot easily cover their tracks.

Countermeasures, whether they are protection measures or detection mechanisms, should not be chosen and implemented randomly because they are cheap and readily available or because they are popular and in vogue. The selection of countermeasures should be driven by the statement of threat and the assets to be protected. If it is not an asset you are worried about protecting, or a threat with which you are concerned, do not spend valuable resources protecting it.

The selection of countermeasures should be driven by the statement of threat and the assets to be protected. (This is an example of how the statement of threat limits the scope and granularity of other elements.) For each threat-asset pair, one or more countermeasures should be developed to afford protection.

1.1.5 Trust in Countermeasures

It is imperative that the countermeasures (both protection measures and detection mechanisms) that are deployed be trusted in their operational correctness. Sometimes this means putting parts of the logic in hardware such as application-specific integrated circuits (ASICs) where an implementation cannot be modified. Oftentimes countermeasures, whether implemented in hardware or software, need to be designed and developed by trusted personnel. The personnel security environment, including background investigations and separation of duties, is described in Cooper's book [5].

1.1.5.1 Implementation Correctness

In some schools of thought, validation generally ensures that each item functions and contains the features as prescribed by its requirements and specifications at the corresponding level in the design. Others feel that validation is concerned with a system's logical correctness in a given external environment (as opposed to verification, which they feel deals with system's logical correctness in the test environment) or probability of system failure based on sufficient quantitative information about past behavior of the system. In any of the cases, validation is attained by unit and system testing.

In a theoretical sense, software, and maybe some hardware, can be viewed as a theorem. A formal proof might then be constructed to prove the correctness of the theorem, and hence the software or hardware module. In practice, this is labor intensive and therefore cost prohibitive. A more practical approach is to develop confidence in a (combined hardware and software) system through accumulated experience on a controlled set of test cases [6]. From the results of the unit and system tests on the specified cases, correct functioning of the complete system is inferred.

1.1.5.2 Configuration Control

Configuration control is the set of procedures, activities, and tools used to ensure that the design and actual units (hardware devices, software modules) of a system or network are well defined and their function not changed without a review of the reasons for, and implications of, the change, and documentation of any such changes. Configuration control is necessary to prevent unauthorized modification of network devices (e.g., ATM switches and servers), and additions to or deletions from a communications network.

From a software point of view, changes to programs must be controlled so that authorization and authentication routines are not bypassed, so that malicious code is not introduced, and to generally maintain integrity of the software operating within the network. The network hardware must be controlled so that pieces (like cryptographic devices and intrusion detection sensors) are not bypassed and surreptitious nodes are not introduced.

1.1.6 Balancing Acceptable Risk with Cost of Countermeasures

Part of network security planning is *risk analysis*. Risk analysis is an analytical technique for estimating the expense caused or loss incurred by a successfully exploited vulnerability. Because many of the factors going into the risk calculations are estimates, the resulting numbers produced by the risk analysis contain uncertainty. The risk analysis, however, is usually quite useful to illustrate relative weaknesses, that is, where one item is more or less vulnerable than another. This brings into focus the areas for which further countermeasures are required.

The first thing to quantify for each threat-asset pair is the annual frequency of occurrence (AFO), or how often a certain threat will be successful against a particular asset or resource. As indicated by its title, this quantity is normalized to an annual basis. (Note that in some forms of risk analysis, this can be further broken down to how frequently a certain threat is *attempted* against a particular resource or asset, multiplied by the probability the threat event or method will be successful. This is especially useful in force-on-force attacks, such as a group of well-armed perpetrators physically attacking a building that houses a network control center.)

The next thing to quantify is the estimated loss per occurrence. In cases where human lives (e.g., remote medical imaging applications) or national security are at stake, it becomes difficult to assign a dollar value to the loss. Other metrics can be used in place of dollars, as long as the metric is consistent throughout the risk analysis. (For example, one could place the value of a lost human life at 1.0 and everything else, such as the value of a lost router or switch in a research network, to be something less.)

Once these two things are quantified as well as possible/practical, the annual loss expectancy (ALE) can be calculated by multiplying the AFO by the estimated loss per occurrence. The ALE needs to be calculated for each threat-asset pair, defined earlier in the network security analysis. To help clarify the analysis, the numbers may be expressed in terms of exponents (by their logarithms).

For each threat-asset pair analyzed, management must review the ALE to determine if the level of risk is acceptable. If the level of risk is unacceptable, countermeasures must be added and the situation reanalyzed to determine the residual risk. *Residual risk* is the portion of risk that remains after the security countermeasures have been applied. *Acceptable risk* is the level of residual risk that will be tolerated—that management is willing to accept. Various references [5, 7, 8] discuss risk analysis in detail.

For example, suppose one threat-asset pair is that a naturally occurring (not intentionally set) fire will burn down a network switching facility. It may happen once in 100 years for an AFO of 10^{-2}. The damage caused by a fire, rounded to an order of magnitude, may be $1,000,000 or 10^6 dollars. This would yield an annual loss expectancy of $10,000 or 10^4 dollars. For ease of comparison with the ALE of other threat-asset pairs, the logarithm (base 10) of the ALEs may be used as simple shorthand, in this case giving a value of 4.

In another example, suppose a certain denial of use attack will be used approximately once a month. This would have an AFO of 10^1 or 10 to 12 times a year. If the lost productivity due to this attack is 10^2 ($100), then the ALE is $1,000 per year ($10^3$) or a 3 in the log shorthand.

A balance must be achieved between the risk and the cost of the countermeasures. In the second example above, it is clearly not economically feasible to spend $100,000 on countermeasures, but it would be wise and prudent to spend $100 to $1,000 to implement measures that could counter the threat. In the first example, a fire protection system costing $10,000 would pay for itself in one year, while one costing $100,000 would have a payback period of 10 years.

In the end, management must examine the risks, the available countermeasures, and the cost of such countermeasures, and determine how much should be spent on putting what countermeasures in place, to reduce the residual risk to a level with which they are comfortable and can accept.

1.2   Protection Countermeasures

Once the initial security planning has been accomplished, the countermeasures that have been specified by that planning exercise need to be implemented. Some of those countermeasures are discussed here.

1.2.1   Encryption

Cryptography is "the art or process of writing in or deciphering secret code" [9]. Encryption is the process of enciphering or encoding a plaintext message into ciphertext. Decryption is the inverse operation—deciphering or decoding a ciphertext message back into its corresponding plaintext. In the context here, we will speak of encryption, but it is assumed there is a corresponding decryption process. (This is not always the case; for example one-way encryption, used to encrypt passwords in a user authentication file.)

Encryption breaks down into two distinct types: *public-key* and *secret-key*. Each of those will be described in the following sections.

1.2.1.1 Public-Key Encryption

Public-key or asymmetric encryption algorithms use two keys: one private and one public (one for secrecy and one for authentication). In a system such as Rivest-Shamir-Adleman (RSA), the secrecy key is made public, while the authentication key is kept private. In this manner, a certain party (party A) can encrypt a message or token in such a manner that anyone is allowed to decrypt it using party A's public key. This provides an authentication property, as in order to be properly decrypted with party A's public key, the message *must* be encrypted using party A's private key, which only A possesses. This also provides nonrepudiation, that is, the property of being able to definitively tie a message to a specific user or key holder. In other words, the owner of a certain key cannot deny that a message, operated on by that key, originated from him, because only he possesses the private key that signed the message.

Secrecy is obtained by encrypting with party A's public key. If someone wishes to send a secret message to party A, they can encrypt the message with party A's public key. Now, the only key that can properly decrypt this message is party A's private key, so only party A can see the plaintext message. This is possible because the two keys are mathematically related. Either of the keys (private or public) can encrypt a message, as long as the other key of the pair is used to decrypt the message. Not only can public key cryptosystems provide both secrecy and nonrepudiation, but also key distribution and management for public key systems tends to be easier than with secret key/symmetric systems.

A major disadvantage to public-key encryption systems is the encryption/decryption rate or throughput. Because public-key cryptosystems are based on mathematical problems that are easy to compute in one direction but difficult to compute in the other direction (such as factoring or discrete logarithm problems), the encryption and decryption operations, even when accompanied by the proper keys, are computationally intensive, and hence slower.

1.2.1.2 Secret-Key Encryption

Secret-key or symmetric-key encryption algorithms use one key for both encryption and decryption, and this key must be kept secret. For a secure message exchange, party A uses the shared secret key to encrypt the plaintext message into ciphertext. After party B receives the message, he decrypts the ciphertext using the shared secret key. Although symmetric key encryption systems are much faster than public-key systems, because the symmetric key systems are usually based on logical or simple arithmetic operations, they present their own set of problems with key management and distribution

Key Exchange

Key exchange for secret key encryption poses several potential problems. One problem is that of interdependence (or the lack of perfect forward/backward secrecy). If party A wants to change keys from key A1 to key A2, and if he encrypts key A2 with key A1 before sending it through the communication channels, then breaking key A1 not only gives the attacker all the information encrypted with key A1, but also key A2 and all the information encrypted with key A2, including possibly the next key (A3). Because of this, keys must be exchanged via different methods (out of band), such as using a courier or a separate key-exchange key.

The other problem with key exchange for symmetric encryption systems is scalability. Each pair of communicating parties must have at least one shared key, resulting in an order n^2 key distribution problem. Each of these pairs of communicating parties can also have multiple simultaneous sessions, which may require different keys. If encryption is simultaneously present at several network layers, a separate key may be required at each layer where encryption is present. When combining multiple simultaneous layers and sessions with the n^2 key exchange problem (especially when one is forced to use out of band methods), the number of keys that must be managed becomes very large.

The ATM Security Specification Version 1.1 [10] indicates that a secret *master key* is exchanged (often coupled to an authentication service) between security agents. This exchange can be performed using either symmetric (secret-key) or asymmetric (public-key) encryption algorithms. Placing this master key when the connection is negotiated enables subsequent session key exchanges and updates as long as the master key has not been compromised. Therefore, perfect forward secrecy with respect to *session keys* alone is maintained, but compromise of a master key will compromise the secrecy of the session keys.

Key Update

Not only is key exchange a huge problem as the size of the cryptosystem scales (as ATM networks are well suited for), but also getting all the keys changed or updated at the same time can be a nearly impossible task. If out-of-band distribution channels are used, an agreed upon key changeover time can be specified, but in the previous section we saw how out-of-band key distribution solutions do not scale well. Key updates, like any key exchanges, should provide perfect forward secrecy.

In the context of ATM security, key update for a specific session is performed in two phases. In the *exchange phase*, the new session key is randomly generated (providing perfect forward/backward secrecy), exchanged, and prepared for use. The new key is then put into use in a *changeover phase*.

1.2.1.3 Hybrid Encryption Schemes

Hybrid encryption systems, a combination of public-key and secret-key encryption, address some of the problems with strictly symmetric or asymmetric encryption systems exposed in the previous sections. Hybrid encryption combines the key management advantage of public-key systems with the speed of secret-key systems. The public-key algorithm is used for communication of a session key, while the secret-key algorithm provides bulk encryption for the session.

When using a hybrid encryption system, each communicating party should have a public-key/private-key pair in place, which serves as a key-exchange key. When party A wishes to initiate a session, he creates or selects a session key for use with a secret key traffic encryption algorithm. This session key should be signed for authentication by party A, and then encrypted using party B's public encryption key and the system's public-key encryption algorithm (such as RSA or Diffie-Hellman, described in [11]). Now this key can be transmitted to party B over an insecure channel.

When party B receives the key message, he decrypts it using the private key of his public-key encryption pair and the system's public-key algorithm. Next he verifies party A's signature to ensure authenticity. Various key exchange protocols may require further exchanges to ensure the session key has been properly exchanged.

With the session key successfully exchanged and authenticated, private communication can now take place between the two parties using the speedier bulk encryption algorithm. Each transmitted message is encrypted using the exchanged session key and the symmetric encryption algorithm. The received message is decrypted with the session key and symmetric algorithm.

Each communicating session can exchange keys in this manner to support multiple concurrent communication sessions using the high-speed symmetric encryption algorithm included in the hybrid encryption system. Hybrid encryption not only allows for dynamic generation and exchange of session keys as shown here, but even allows for flexibility or agility of bulk encryption algorithms.

1.2.2   Authentication

Authentication is establishing *who* someone is, as opposed to authorization, which is determining *what* that person or process is allowed to do or access. (Authorization is briefly discussed later in this chapter.) Authentication involves possessing or knowing something and using it to prove your identity.

1.2.2.1   Data Origin Authentication/Integrity

Data integrity can be assured by providing a checksum over the message. Frequently this is calculated using a hash function. These checksums can aid in detecting intentional manipulations by a third party (when used with encryption) and unintentional modifications, such as bit errors caused by communication line noise. Data origin authentication, or authentication of the data and its source, can be added by introducing a cryptographic key, thus ensuring that only authorized parties can generate the correct hash code over the blocks of the message. Data integrity protections range from simple parity checks (probabilistic protections from random natural modifications) to keyed hash functions (almost certain protection from malicious modifications).

Hash Algorithms

Generically, a hash function takes values and manipulates them to place them over a (typically smaller) range of values, or as Schneier [11] puts it, converts variable length values into fixed length values. The hash algorithm should produce a uniform distribution of collisions; that is, all hash chains should be approximately equal in length.

Hashing functions are often used to help organize, for example, keyed records of a file. If each record in a 1,000-record data set was appended to a file, it would take an average of 500 reads to find a specific record. More optimal methods of indexing and ordering are available, but records might have to be shifted around and rewritten as each new record is added to the data set. By hashing an index into a value spanning a smaller range, the number of reads required to retrieve a given record is reduced.

For this example, a hash function might map record keys into a range of 1 to 100. A good hash function might generate 100 *hash chains* of 10 records each. Now, to retrieve a specific record, the key is hashed to a value.

(The 100 values produced by the hash function may or may not be consecutive.) In a nonrandom access type of memory (such as a sequential access disk file), it could take an average of 50 reads to find the head of the matching hash chain. Searching the hash chain for the desired record will take an average of another 5 reads. By using a hash function on the record key, the average number of reads required to retrieve a specific record has been reduced from 500 to 55; in the worst case, the number of read functions is reduced from 1,000 to 110.

For hash functions used with files, the number of items to be hashed is much greater than the range of the hash function. When hash functions are used in the context of data authentication, the opposite is true. For data authentication, additional properties are desired. There should be no collisions of the hashed values; it would be difficult to find another message that hashes to the same.value. It should be easy to compute the hash of a value, but it should be hard to go the other way, computing the original value from the hashed value. This way, the hash function can do its job without adding overhead and, it is difficult to engineer an input value or set of values that when hashed, will produce an output equal to an existing hash value.

A subtle point here is that in a language such as English, many combinations of letters or characters are nonsense. Another way of looking at this is that, considering every possible combination of characters, there are relatively few valid messages. This makes it comparatively easy to produce a reasonably unique, short hash value from a long message. In a situation involving binary data, under conditions where each value is equally likely, producing a shorter, reasonably unique hash value requires more effort.

The authenticity of a message can be verified through manipulation detection codes (MDCs) and message authentication codes (MACs), which make use of hashing algorithms. A manipulation detection code such as the Quadratic Congruential Manipulation Detection Code Version 4 (QCMDCV4) can be computed over an entire message, which "hashes" the whole message down to a relatively small number of bits (in this case, 128). Only this value, then, needs to be encrypted to provide authenticity of the entire message. This generally saves considerable time, as encryption is usually a computationally intensive function. If an unauthorized entity modifies the message, the MDC value will not verify the integrity of the message. Because the MDC is encrypted, the bogus party performing the manipulation of the message cannot insert a new, recomputed MDC at the proper location, since he doesn't have the encryption key. Only the authorized party possessing the encryption key can create an authentic message that will have the correct MDC.

Keyed MACs

A message authentication code is similar to an encrypted MDC. MACs are not only used to detect manipulations to the message, but also to demonstrate authenticity by virtue of the fact that a MAC has a key associated with it.

A MAC is calculated by a hash function that is controlled by a key. Again the hash function for a MAC should be easy to compute, difficult to reverse, and produce few, if any, collisions. In this way, MACs not only detect unauthorized modifications, whether intentional (as by a party tampering with the message) or accidental (as by communication line noise), but also authenticate the origin of the message. Only an authorized party should possess the key necessary to control the hash function and form the MAC.

The ATM Security Specification Version 1.1 describes seven methods to compute MACs. Four of them are based on symmetric block encryption algorithms; the other three are based on one-way (nonreversible) hash functions.

The four symmetric, block encryption–based functions are Data Encryption Standard (DES), cypher block chaining (CBC)MAC, DES40/CBC MAC, Triple DES/CBC MAC, and fast data encipherment algorithm (FEAL)/CBC MAC. These use the specified symmetric block cipher (DES with a 56-bit key, DES with a 40-bit key, Triple DES, or FEAL) on the message, in cipher block chaining mode. This builds a dependency relationship between the blocks of the message; that is, one cannot change part of the input message without expecting a change in the final output. The last block that is encrypted, which contains feedback from the previous blocks, is used as the MAC. The details of these encryption algorithms can be found elsewhere [11–13], as can details of the CBC mode of operation [14].

The three methods based on one-way hash functions are MD5, SHA-1, and RIPEMD-160, and each of these hash functions uses the HMAC algorithm for generating keyed message authentication codes. MD5, SHA-1, and RIPEMD-160 hash the message blocks with constants and employ chaining to build a hash value that can then be encrypted by a symmetric cipher or a public-key (asymmetric) cipher. MD5, SHA-1, and RIPEMD-160 provide the manipulation detection aspects, and the hashed message authentication code (HMAC) algorithm supplies the authentication function. For a further discussion of this, see the "Digital Signatures" section below. Again, details of the algorithms (HMAC, MD5, SHA-1, and RIPEMD-160) can be found elsewhere [11, 15–17].

1.2.2.2 Initial Authentication

Initial authentication is authenticating the parties wishing to communicate, rather than message authentication, where the authenticity of each message is determined. In the ATM Security Specification, this initial authentication is referred to as *user plane authentication* or *entity authentication.* At the beginning of a connection this service determines that the identities of the calling and/or called parties are genuine. Authentication is performed using either secret (symmetric) key algorithms or public (asymmetric) key algorithms.

Secret Key Protocols

When using symmetric/secret key algorithms (such as DES) for initial authentication, two nodes, entities, or security agents need to have shared secret keys in place before the authentication can proceed. For the ATM Security Specification 1.1, these keys are preplaced through manual configuration. In general, other symmetric encryption algorithms such as the new Advanced Encryption Standard (AES) algorithm, Rijndael, may be used to carry out the authentication exchange.

Protocols based upon secret key algorithms are not significantly slowed by the encryption, but these will not provide nonrepudiation, and will have order n^2 key management problems.

Public Key Protocols

In the case where the security agents are using asymmetric/public key algorithms (such as RSA), the agents need to know each other's public keys. Again, this can happen through preplacement of the public keys, or dynamically by obtaining public key certificates. Certificates contain the party's name, its public key, some additional information, and a signature generated by a trusted party (certification authority). The public key certificates can be retrieved from a public key directory or exchanged directly during security negotiations. Regardless of how the certificate is obtained, it needs to be validated to ensure that no tampering or corruption has occurred, and that the certificate itself is still valid. This certificate verification process may also require the retrieval and verification of chains of certificates and policy checking.

Protocols based upon public key algorithms do provide nonrepudiation and have only order n key management problems, but are slowed significantly by the encryption algorithm.

Digital Signatures

The digital signature process, whether used for initial authentication, certificate verification, or elsewhere, first reduces the message to be signed using a hash algorithm (such as SHA-1). Next, the hash value is encrypted by the signer using his RSA private key or his digital signature algorithm (DSA) private key with the corresponding algorithm. This minimizes the amount of data that must be encrypted by the computationally intensive public key algorithm.

Note that when using public key encryption algorithms for both secrecy and authentication, different keys are used. As shown in Figure 1.2, when a message is being signed, the signer's private key is used to encrypt the message or a digest of the message. This shows that only the possessor of that key could have signed the message, although anyone can verify the signature by using the signer's public key. When secrecy is desired, the message is encrypted with the receiver's public key. At that point, the only one able to properly decrypt the message is the one possessing the receiver's private key.

Certificate Infrastructure

Since certificates are important in many implementations of public-key cryptography, a certificate infrastructure must be in place. Certificate

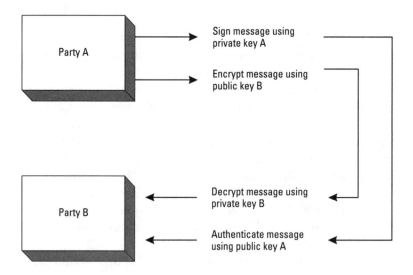

Figure 1.2 Use of public and private keys.

infrastructures may take two forms: hierarchical and distributed. In the hierarchical model, a hierarchy of certification authorities is constructed. A master certification authority (CA) can issue certificates, thereby extending or transferring trust to a number of CAs under him. These CAs can then issue certificates to other CAs, and so on. At some level a CA certifies individuals. A certificate containing a public key can then be verified back through the chain of certificate authorities to determine the validity of the key, prior to the key's use.

Distributed certification, used with Pretty Good Privacy (PGP), makes use of *introducers*. Users generate their own public key, have various introducers sign the public key for them, and distribute their own public key. When users receive a new public key, they examine the list of introducers who have signed the key. If they recognize one of the introducers as someone they trust, and the introducer's signature is verified, this new public key can be added to their "key ring."

1.2.3 Authorization

In general, authorization is to grant power to do something or permission to access something. As mentioned earlier, in the context of security, authorization is determining what a person or process is allowed to do or access. The authorization rights or privileges are based on access controls and security policy.

1.2.4 Access Control

Whereas authorization is an administrative control that is implemented by policy, access control is the technical implementation of authorization rights and permissions. Effective access control requires proper authentication of the entity requesting the access. This means the requesting entity authenticates itself, or proves who it is, to the system. Once the entity has been authenticated (such as at the time of login), access can be controlled in several ways, using access control lists and security labels.

1.2.4.1 List-Based Access Control

An access control or authorization list is a list of subjects that are allowed access to a given object. In the physical world this might be a paper list, posted in the guard shack, of people allowed to enter a certain area. A subject-object mapping example in the cyber world might be a disk file access system where the subjects may be users, roles, or groups. The object may be UNIX file access permissions.

1.2.4.2   Label-Based Access Control

Information transfer security labels transport information used by protocol elements in the network to determine how to handle messages communicated between systems. This security label information can be used to control access, specify protections, and determine handling restrictions as the messages move through the network. FIPS PUB 188 [18] lays out the format for these labels.

The labels describe the sensitivity level of the messages passing through the network. A sensitivity level may be made up of two components: a hierarchical level, which is an ordered set; and a group of access categories, which is a containment set. Because the hierarchical set has linear ordering, "greater than" and "less than" relationships can be defined. The containment set defines relationships differently. One element of a containment set is greater than another only if the second element is a subset of the first.

An example of this could be a hierarchy of sensitivity levels such as confidential, secret, and top secret. Compartments could be restricted, formerly restricted, and others. To completely specify the allowed access, both components (sensitivity and compartment) are needed (e.g., secret restricted).

Carrying this hierarchical level and containment set information with each data message, or even only with connection setup messages, allows network components to make access control decisions and enforce rules.

1.2.5   Auditing

Auditing can take two forms. The first form includes reviews, assessments, and tests of hardware, software, and procedures, to determine operational correctness or compliance with law and policy. Internal or external teams trained to exploit vulnerabilities and uncover anomalies can do this.

The second form is the examination of audit trails and activity logs. Many activities, both intrinsic to a computer's operating system and layered as networking or user applications, are recorded in log files. These audit trails, that is, the records in these log files, can be examined visually or with log file processing software to detect unusual activity that may be indications of potential security problems.

1.3 Trade-Offs and Optimizations

The most secure computer is not plugged in to any power source! The most user-friendly and versatile systems will have very few security restrictions and therefore, few protections. Trade-offs are always necessary, especially between security and usability. Examining the residual risk can aid in determining whether more money and effort should be spent to counter a certain threat.

A major trade-off is whether to use a public-key or secret-key cryptosystem. Key management for public-key cryptosystems is easier than for secret-key systems, but public-key systems suffer in performance due to the exponentiation operations it must conduct.

Other trade-offs include the use of public keys or secret keys for message authentication. Using a MAC or MDC with a public-key cipher to produce a digital signature provides nonrepudiation capability. Only the person whose key signed the message could have originated that message. Using a secret key-based MAC may be easier in terms of implementation and other factors, especially if one is trying to create synergy between MAC keys and encryption keys. However, this does not provide nonrepudiation.

Implementers must pay close attention to trade-offs, but at the same time look for optimizations and areas of synergy. The hybrid encryption (described above) attempts to walk an optimal path between public-key and private-key encryption. It takes advantage of the strengths of each type of encryption and minimizes the weaknesses.

References

[1] Graft, D., M. Pabrai, and U. Pabrai, "Methodology for Network Security Design," *IEEE Communications*, Vol. 28, No. 11, 1990, pp. 52–58.

[2] Pierson, L. G., and E. L. Witzke, "A Security Methodology for Computer Networks," *AT&T Technical Journal*, Vol. 67, No. 3, 1988, pp. 28–36.

[3] Landwehr, C. E., "The Best Available Technologies for Computer Security," *Computer*, Vol. 16, No. 7, 1983, pp. 88–100.

[4] Cohen, F. B., *Protection and Security on the Information Superhighway*, New York: John Wiley & Sons, 1995.

[5] Cooper, J. A., *Computer and Communications Security*, New York: McGraw-Hill, 1989.

[6] Deutsch, M. S., *Software Verification and Validation*, Englewood Cliffs, NJ: Prentice-Hall, 1982.

[7] Cooper, J. A., *Computer Security Technology*, Lexington, MA: D. C. Heath, 1984.

[8] National Bureau of Standards, *Guidelines for Automatic Data Processing Risk Analysis (FIPS PUB 65)*, 1979.

[9] Berube, M. S., *The American Heritage Dictionary, 2nd College Edition*, Boston: Houghton Mifflin, 1982.

[10] ATM Forum, "ATM Security Specification Version 1.1," af-sec-0100.002, March 2001.

[11] Schneier, B., *Applied Cryptography*, New York: John Wiley & Sons, 1996.

[12] National Institute of Standards and Technology, *Data Encryption Standard (FIPS PUB 46-3)*, 1999.

[13] American National Standards Institute, *Triple Data Encryption Algorithm Modes of Operation (ANS X9.52)*, American Bankers Association, 1998.

[14] National Bureau of Standards, *DES Modes of Operation (FIPS PUB 81)*, 1980.

[15] Rivest, R., *The MD5 Message Digest Algorithm*, Internet Engineering Task Force RFC 1321, 1992.

[16] National Institute of Standards and Technology, *Secure Hash Standard (FIPS PUB 180-1)*, 1995.

[17] International Standards Organization, *Hash Functions—Part 3: Dedicated Hash Functions (ISO/IEC 10118-3)*, 1997.

[18] National Institute of Standards and Technology, *Standard Security Label for Information Transfer (FIPS PUB 188)*, 1994.

2

ATM Networking Fundamentals

ATM is a connection-oriented networking technology; that is, it switches packets of data (ATM cells) very quickly along a preestablished virtual circuit from the source to the destination. Cell-switched networking is advantageous in that it minimizes end-to-end transit delay (after connection establishment), allows flows to be routed so as to load-balance the network (i.e., traffic engineering), and supports appropriate allocation of network resources at connection establishment to provide requisite quality of service. Cell-switched networks also have security advantages because only the connection's endpoints and switches can see the user data (unlike shared Ethernet segments, where all nodes can view traffic on the segment, including traffic meant for other nodes).

However, making connectionless higher-layer protocols such as IP (where each packet is routed independently without a preestablished circuit) work on connection-oriented protocols like ATM is complex. Because ATM does not provide a broadcast service as other network technologies do (e.g., Ethernet), devices such as broadcast servers and address resolution servers are required. These may add central points of failure to the network and introduce additional configuration complexity, which is prone to configuration errors. Nevertheless, ATM is widely used today, particularly in the Internet core and in the enterprise backbones of many organizations.

The primary purpose of this chapter is to set the stage for ATM security by briefly introducing ATM networking concepts and basic security issues with ATM. ATM is rich in protocol specifications, so a single chapter treatment of ATM is not nearly adequate for readers who want the protocol details. Interested readers who wish to learn more should consult texts such as [1–4] for more authoritative coverage of ATM networking.

2.1 ATM Reference Model

ATM is a connection-oriented network technology that asynchronously switches data along a virtual circuit that is established prior to data transfer. An ATM network is composed of two types of equipment: ATM switches that forward data units along the virtual circuit, and ATM endpoints that terminate the virtual circuit (e.g., hosts, IP routers, and ATM video codecs). The functions that are present in each device, and the protocols that each device uses to perform ATM functions are framed in the context of two reference models: the ATM protocol reference model and the ATM interface reference model. The ATM protocol reference model is shown in Figure 2.1.

The protocol reference model consists of three planes: the user plane, control plane, and management plane. The user plane supports the transfer of data traffic between ATM endpoints along a permanent virtual circuit

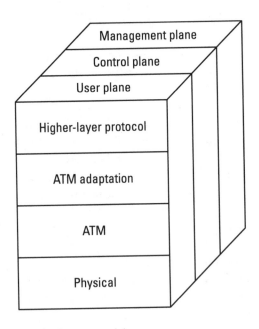

Figure 2.1 ATM protocol reference model.

(which is configured manually) or a switched virtual circuit (which is configured automatically via a signaling protocol). This traffic may be from a higher-layer protocol such as IP, or may come directly from a *native* ATM application. In addition, traffic associated with other mechanisms that adapt higher-layer protocols to ATM (e.g., ATM address resolution for classical IP over ATM and connections between elements in a local area network emulation (LANE) network) is also considered user plane traffic.

The ATM control plane is responsible for the establishment of switched virtual circuits. The signaling protocols (e.g., Q.2931 [5]) that perform dynamic connection establishment are part of the control plane. In addition, the routing protocol traffic (e.g., PNNI 1.0 [6]) that distributes network topology and state information to ATM switches is also considered (by many) to be control plane traffic.

Finally, the ATM reference model includes the management plane. This plane is responsible for two things: allowing peer devices to pass layer-specific management information (e.g., alarms and configuration parameters), and allowing remote configuration and status monitoring of ATM network elements. Examples of the first management function are operations and management (OAM) and the integrated layer management interface (ILMI). An example of the second management function is remote management of ATM switches and interfaces via the Simple Network Management Protocol (SNMP) and the ATM management information base (MIB) [7].

Each plane consists of four layers: the physical layer, ATM layer, ATM adaptation layer, and the higher-layer protocols or applications. The physical layer is the layer that provides the physical links between the ATM network elements. ATM enjoys a rich number of physical layer specifications, covering rates from T1 (1.5 Mbps) to synchronous optical network (SONET) OC-3 (155 Mbps) to SONET OC-48 (2.4 Gbps), with more being developed. Except for the bandwidth provided by the physical link, the type of physical layer connection that is used has little impact on the user plane or control plane functions, due to the abstraction provided by layering. The variety of physical layer connections, however, has a greater effect on the management plane because each connection type has different management properties (e.g., OAM information and MIBs).

The ATM layer is the layer that is responsible for switching cells on a virtual circuit. (The concept of cell switching and the ATM cell format are described in Section 2.2.) Depending on the type of user plane virtual circuit (e.g., constant bit rate, variable bit rate, available bit rate, or unassigned bit rate), traffic management functions such as flow control and cell-policing mechanisms may also be performed. These mechanisms are also considered part of the ATM layer. For control plane traffic, the identifiers associated with their virtual circuits are specified as well-known values, which allow automatic bootstrapping of signaling when two devices are connected. For management plane traffic, ATM specifies special OAM cells that allow ATM devices to communicate management information within the user plane virtual circuit.

The ATM adaptation layer (AAL) provides the interface between higher-layer applications or protocols that typically use variable length frames and the ATM layer, which transfers data in small, fixed-length data units. A variety of AAL types is specified in the ATM standards, with each type designed for different types of data traffic. Table 2.1 describes the key attributes of each AAL.

Control plane and ATM network element management plane traffic uses AAL 5 because it provides an efficient mechanism for transferring control messages. In addition, the virtual circuit signaling protocols such as Q.2931 use the service specific connection oriented protocol (SSCOP), which resides between AAL 5 and the signaling protocol and provides reliable, in-order delivery of signaling messages. The combination of SSCOP and AAL 5 is called the signaling AAL, or SAAL.

The higher-layer applications and protocols use the services provided by the AAL. For the user plane, protocols such as IP are included in this layer along with native ATM applications that access the AAL directly via ATM applications programmer's interfaces (APIs). For the control plane, this layer includes the control plane protocols such as Q.2931 and PNNI 1.0. For the management plane, this layer includes the network element management protocols and the ILMI.

Table 2.1
ATM Adaptation Layer Attributes

AAL Type	Constant or Variable Bit Rate Traffic	Clock Recovery at Destination?	Example Application
1	Constant	Yes	Pulse-code modulated voice
2	Variable	Yes	Compressed voice and video
3/4	Variable	No	Data
5	Variable	No	Data (more efficient than AAL 3/4)

The ATM interface reference model is used to describe the different kinds of connections and the signaling protocols that occur over each connection type. The various ATM interfaces are shown in Figure 2.2.

The interfaces defined by ATM are as follows:

- *User to network interface (UNI):* This interface connects an ATM end system (host or IP router) to an ATM switch. The UNI signaling protocol (e.g., UNI 3.1 [8]) allows an end system to request a connection to another end system.

- *Private network to network interface (PNNI):* This interface connects two switches that belong to the same private network. The PNNI 1.0 signaling protocol [6] allows switches to exchange network routing information and propagate connection requests toward the destination end system.

- *ATM internetwork interface (AINI):* The AINI connects two switches that belong to different organizations. Therefore, complete network state information (e.g., topology information as provided by PNNI) is typically not transferred across this interface; only basic reachability information and virtual circuit signaling is transferred. This signaling protocol is found at the private network's attachment

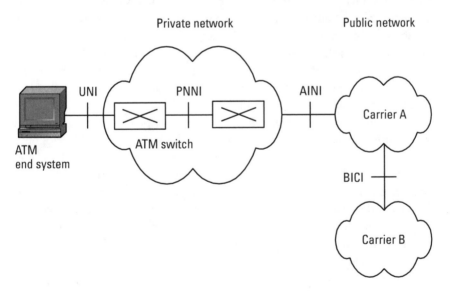

Figure 2.2 ATM interfaces.

to the public network and allows sites to establish dynamic connections to each other through the public network.

- *Broadband intercarrier interface (BICI):* This interface connects two public carriers' ATM networks. The signaling protocol that operates across this interface also permits end-to-end virtual circuits on-demand, but it does not permit transfer of other information (e.g., network topology and management information) that carriers may consider proprietary.

Security issues are present in both types of reference models. Certainly, in the protocol reference model, ATM user plane traffic may need to be protected, depending on the data's sensitivity to unauthorized disclosure or modification. In addition, control plane traffic may also require protection, depending on the consequences that may result if protocol message traffic were maliciously altered or injected into the network. Finally, management plane flows (particularly for remote management) may require extra protections to restrict access to only authorized remote managers to mitigate the risks of unauthorized network configuration or disclosure of configuration data.

Likewise, security issues vary depending on the location in the interface reference model. For example, the set of security threats that apply to PNNI networks are different from the set of threats that apply to the AINI because the set of attacks that originate inside the private network are different from the set of attacks that originate from the public network. In addition, UNI security considerations differ from AINI and PNNI security because the UNI is the endpoint's attachment to the network; therefore, end-to-end security services are likely to be found at the UNI.

The mechanisms available for protecting user plane, control plane, and management plane traffic vary according to the layer being considered and the outcome of the threat-asset analysis described in Chapter 1. Physical layer protections can be provided via mechanisms such as protection of the cable plant from unauthorized connections and protection of network devices from unauthorized physical access. ATM and AAL connection protections may be provided via careful configuration of network components (as described in Chapter 3) or through special security mechanisms such as encryption and data integrity (as described in Chapter 4). Security for higher-layer protocols is afforded by application- and protocol-specific security mechanisms such as Secure Sockets Layer (SSL) encryption and IP Security (IPSEC). The control plane protocols are also protected by careful configuration (e.g., address filtering) or special security mechanisms such as the control plane integrity mechanism in the ATM Security 1.1 Specification [9].

2.2 Cell Switching

ATM is a virtual circuit-switched network technology that uses small, fixed-length cells to carry data between the endpoints of a virtual connection (VC). ATM cells contain exactly 5 bytes of header information and 48 bytes of payload. The ATM cell header is shown in Figure 2.3.

The cell header contains the following fields:

- *Generic flow control (GFC):* This 4-bit value is only used on the UNI. This field is not currently used, but was specified to allow an ATM network to throttle the rate at which an end system transmits cells into the network.

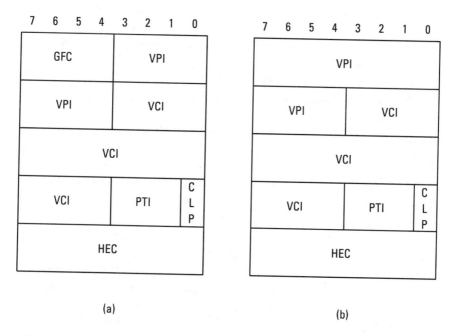

Figure 2.3 ATM cell header formats: (a) UNI format and (b) NNI format.

- *Virtual path identifier (VPI):* This field consists of 8 bits for a UNI cell and 12 bits for an NNI cell. This field allows cells to be switched as part of a virtual path, which aggregates virtual circuits.

- *Virtual channel identifier (VCI):* For a given port on an ATM switch or end system, VPI/VCI combination uniquely identifies the virtual circuit to which the cell belongs.

- *Payload type identifier (PTI):* The PTI discriminates different cell types for a given VPI/VCI combination. One function provided by the PTI is to distinguish user data cells from operations and management cells (which are described in Section 2.7).

- *Cell loss priority (CLP):* The network uses this bit to mark ATM cells that do not conform to the traffic contract set for the VC. These cells are more likely to be discarded by switches that are experiencing congestion.

- *Header error check (HEC):* This field is used to detect header errors and correct single bit errors. HEC is also used for cell delineation.

Virtual circuit switching requires a VC to be established between the two endpoints before they can communicate. This VC is defined by the contents of switching tables contained in each ATM switch in the end-to-end connection. An example showing the role of switch tables in switching ATM cells on a virtual circuit is shown in Figure 2.4.

When an ATM cell arrives at switch A on port = 0, VPI = 0, and VCI = 123, switch A looks through its table for the row that corresponds to the arriving cell. When the table entry is found, the cell is switched to the corresponding output port and the cell's VPI and VCI values are translated to new values as specified by the switching table. In this case, the cell is switched to port 1, and the VPI and VCI values are modified to 1 and 100, respectively. When the cell arrives at switch C, the same process occurs to switch the cell to the destination host on VPI = 0, VCI = 130.

The switch tables are populated according to the type of virtual circuit that is established. For permanent virtual connections (PVCs), the switch tables are configured via management access to the switch (e.g., through a remote terminal session, using a Web browser [with an HTTP server running on the switch], or using SNMP). For large networks, however, this quickly becomes unmanageable. For example, in a network of 100 nodes, the number of bidirectional, point-to-point (Pt-Pt) connections required to provide full connectivity is $n(n-1)/2$, or 4,950 PVCs, which grows $O(n^2)$ with

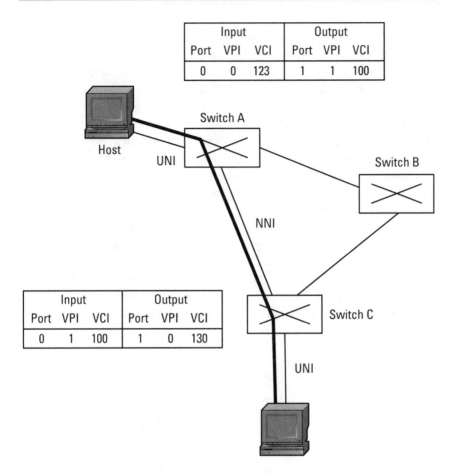

Figure 2.4 Cell switching on a virtual circuit.

the number of nodes in the network. Given the number of switches required to support these connections and the amount of time required to configure a switch table entry in each switch, the amount of work required to configure a large, fully connected network via PVCs makes the task impossible.

Fortunately, the switch tables can be configured automatically via signaling protocols that establish switched virtual connections (SVCs). These signaling protocols, which are described in more detail in Section 2.4, establish SVCs on-demand by taking a connection request (which contains a globally unique address of the desired end system) originated by the requesting end system, and routing the request through the network of switches to the destination. At each hop along the way, the switches allocate VPI/VCI values and automatically configure their switching tables. Of course, the requesting end system must know the address of the required destination. However, mechanisms such as ATM Address Resolution (described in Section 2.9.1) and ATM Name Services [10] can be used to automate the delivery of ATM addresses to requesting endpoints.

So why use PVCs at all? In the early days of ATM networking before signaling standards were widely adopted, multivendor networks could not be used without PVCs. Today, this is no longer true. For ATM networks that are connected via ATM service providers, however, PVCs are often the only service that is available, and permanent virtual paths (PVPs) are still frequently used to interconnect sites in a virtual mesh, as shown in Figure 2.5.

In this example, the virtual path tunnels connecting sites A, B, and C form a virtual mesh. These tunnels originate and terminate at the border switches at each site, and they allow each site to signal each other through these tunnels as if each of the sites were directly connected. All SVCs that result from signaling between these logically adjacent switches are carried in these PVP tunnels. This allows SVCs between the sites without signaling

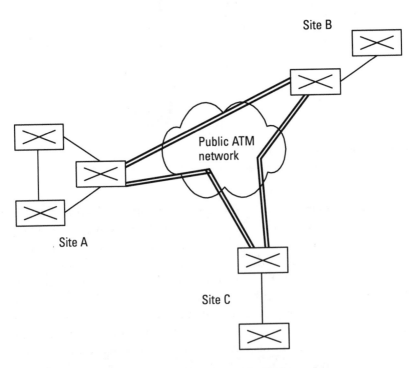

Figure 2.5 Using PVPs to interconnect sites via public ATM network.

directly to the ATM service provider's network. This provides some security protections, as SVC requests originating outside the mesh (i.e., from other customers attached to the public network) do not enter these tunnels and are not propagated to these sites. The use of PVPs to implement simple virtual private networks is described in Chapter 3.

In addition to the Pt-Pt PVCs, SVCs, and PVPs described above, ATM also allows point-to-multipoint (Pt-Mpt) connections. Pt-Mpt connections originate from a single source called the *root*, branch at appropriate switches, and terminate at multiple destinations called *leaves*, as shown in Figure 2.6.

As with Pt-Pt connections, Pt-Mpt connections (multipoint VCs) can be PVCs or SVCs. However, since multipoint connections are used primarily for multipoint applications such as videoconferencing, members join and leave multicast groups frequently. Therefore, multipoint VCs are usually signaled.

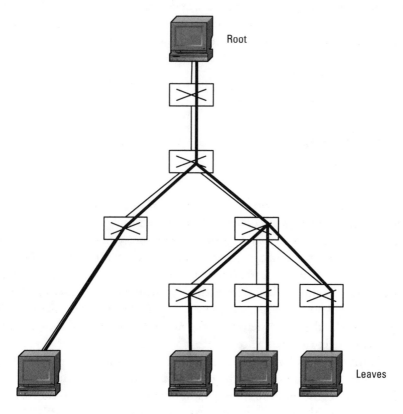

Figure 2.6 Pt-Mpt virtual circuit.

Signaled multipoint VCs can be initiated from the root (e.g., a conference moderator) or by the leaves (e.g., the conference attendees). When the leaves initiate such connections, the leaf can be added to the multipoint VC automatically by the network, or the network can notify the root and allow the root to add the leaf. The ATM signaling mechanisms required to implement these scenarios are described in more detail in Section 2.6.

2.3 ILMI

The integrated layer management interface [11] allows adjacent ATM switches and end systems to exchange layer-specific information with each other. These ATM devices may be physically adjacent (i.e., connected via a physical link) or logically adjacent (i.e., connected via a virtual path connection). ILMI uses the SNMP Version 1 protocol, and includes its standard operations such as get, get-next, set, and trap. The protocol allows the exchange of information that is stored in each device's ILMI management information base, which includes the following attributes:

- Physical layer;
- ATM layer;
- Virtual circuit;
- Address registration;
- Service registry.

ILMI is mostly known as the mechanism that performs address registration when an end system or a switch connects to another switch. When an end system connects to a switch, it provides its end system identifier (ESI) to the switch. The ESI is analogous to the media access control address found in Ethernet adapters in that it is a 6-byte value, which consists of two fields: an organizationally-unique identifier (3 bytes) identifying the manufacturer of the device, and a unique number that is assigned by the manufacturer. The switch provides the end system with the network's prefix, and the combination of the prefix and the ESI comprises the end system's address.

ILMI also allows adjacent devices to exchange other information about each other. Information regarding the ATM-specific capabilities of the devices includes the maximum number of bits in the VPI and VCI fields that is supported by the device and the version information for the ILMI and signaling protocols (UNI and PNNI). In addition, ILMI allows devices to provide information about virtual circuits that are carried by their interfaces and can send traps to peer ILMI devices when virtual circuits are created or destroyed. Finally, ILMI can instruct peer devices of network services such as the address of the LAN emulation configuration server (LECS), which is described in more detail in Section 2.9.2. The MIB information (including other MIB attributes not described here) is accessible not only by ILMI peers but also by remote management stations through a proxy SNMP agent running on the device.

As stated earlier, ILMI uses the SNMP Version 1 (SNMPv1) protocol for retrieving and setting information in the ILMI MIB and propagating asynchronous trap events. However, since SNMPv1 does not provide security mechanisms such as confidentiality and authentication, neither does ILMI. Therefore, since ILMI traffic is not encrypted, ILMI could reveal configuration information to an eavesdropper. In addition, if a malicious end system M learns the ESI of another end system A, M could connect to the switch and appear to the rest of the network (and to any ATM address filters placed in the network) as end system A. (Of course, if M attaches to the switch while A is attached, the switch should detect the existence of duplicate addresses.) In this case, address filters should be configured on the ATM network UNIs to physically control where an ESI may be used, as described in Chapter 3.

2.4 ATM Virtual Circuit Signaling

ATM signaling protocols are used to allow ATM endpoints to request and accept SVCs, as well as to allow switches in a network to propagate the request to the destination. The UNI 3.1 [8] and UNI 4.0 [12] signaling protocols, which are asymmetric protocols (i.e., each end of the link implements different procedures, depending on whether the device is a user or network device), are derived from the ITU's Q.2931 B-ISDN signaling protocol [5]. These protocols establish virtual circuits using a two-way end-to-end handshake, as shown in Figure 2.7.

When a calling end system wishes to establish an SVC with a called end system, it sends a SETUP message over its UNI to the switch to which it is attached. The switch examines the called party addressing information contained in the SETUP message (described further below), and forwards the SETUP message out the port that is closer to the destination (as determined by the PNNI routing protocol, which is briefly described in Section 2.5).

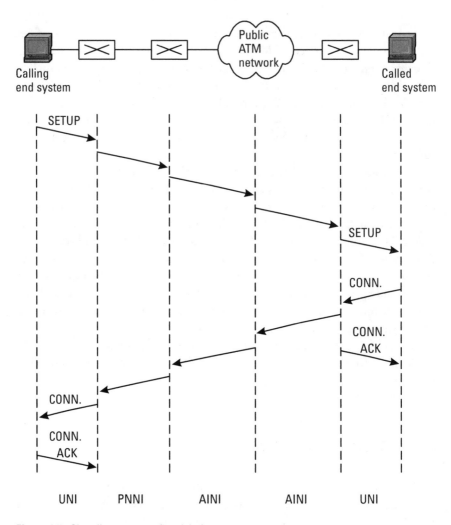

Figure 2.7 Signaling two-way handshake.

Every other switch (including those in the public network) performs similar operations, until the SETUP message reaches the called end system.

If the called end system wishes to accept the connection, it issues a CONNECT message to the switch to which it is attached. The switch activates the new virtual circuit, and forwards the CONNECT message to the next switch along the same path that the SETUP message took. When the CONNECT message reaches the calling end system, the virtual circuit is established end-to-end.

As the CONNECT message reaches each hop, the device processes the CONNECT, and it sends a CONNECT ACKNOWLEDGE back to the previous hop to indicate that it is configured and ready to switch cells on the virtual circuit. This acknowledgement is only a local acknowledgement, and does not constitute a third end-to-end flow.

Information about the connection request and the connection as established is contained in information elements (IEs) that are encapsulated by the signaling message. Addressing information for the calling and called end systems are contained in the calling and called party IEs, respectively (though the calling party IE is optional). In addition, other virtual circuit parameters such as quality of service (QoS) information, AAL type information, and information about higher-layer protocols may also be present in the message.

When a connection is no longer required, the calling party, called party, or any switch along the virtual circuit's path may issue a RELEASE message. This message may contain a *cause* IE that describes the reason for the connection release, and may also provide other diagnostic information.

The ATM Forum's UNI 3.1 specification [8] provides establishment of Pt-Pt SVCs according to the Q.2931 protocol [5]. In addition, UNI 3.1 also defines procedures for Pt-Mpt connections initiated by the root of the connection (as described in Section 2.6). In UNI 4.0 [12], a number of new features were added, including the following:

- *Leaf-initiated join* (described in Section 2.6).

- *Anycasting:* This capability allows a calling party to initiate a connection to any one of a number of servers that provide the same service. These servers share the same anycast address, and the network decides (e.g., based on load-balancing considerations) which server receives the connection request.

- *Available bit rate (ABR):* UNI 4.0 supports the information transfer and call acceptance procedures associated with ABR connections, which are described further in Section 2.8.

- *Security:* UNI 4.0 defines an information element and call processing procedures for supporting security negotiation in SVC signaling. This capability is described further in Chapters 4 and 5.

Security is an important consideration for signaling because the signaling protocol affects the network configuration, which affects the availability, confidentiality, and integrity of ATM connections. Furthermore, a switch's decision to propagate a connection request, and an end system's decision whether to accept a connection may be based on information contained in the message (e.g., the calling party IE). Clearly, in situations where address spoofing is a credible threat, strong *caller identification* is required to determine the acceptability of a connection request. Chapters 4 and 5 go into more detail about how security information is transported in signaling (security signaling), and Chapter 10 describes mechanisms for protecting signaling messages themselves (signaling security).

Another security consideration with signaling is the fact that signaling is both a hop-by-hop and an end-to-end protocol. Signaling is end-to-end in the sense that certain information elements (e.g., called party address) are not usually modified as the signaling message traverses the network. However, other information elements (e.g., the QoS parameters information element) are likely modified hop-by-hop, as part of SVC signaling. This complicates the protection of signaling messages, as there is no way to determine if a message is modified legitimately by a switch, or maliciously by another party.

2.5   Routing ATM Connections

The ATM Forum's PNNI 1.0 protocol [6] is a connection signaling and routing protocol that operates over switch-to-switch links. The signaling functions provided by PNNI are a subset of the UNI 4.0 protocol, which was summarized briefly in the previous section. However, unlike UNI 4.0, which is an asymmetric protocol (i.e., a protocol that implements different procedures depending on whether the device is an end system or a switch), PNNI signaling is a symmetric protocol because each switch implements the same procedures. In addition, PNNI provides other procedures such as designated transit lists and crankback (described briefly in this section), which do not exist in UNI 4.0.

The primary feature provided by PNNI is its routing protocol. PNNI is a *link state* routing protocol, based on the Open Shortest Path First (OSPF) protocol [13], and routes connections according to the network's topology state and the QoS that the network and links can support at the time the connection is routed. This state information is tracked by the individual switches in the network and is advertised to the other switches via topology state packets.

However, the process of advertising topology state to other switches (or PNNI nodes) can result in extremely large topology databases in the switches and unacceptable network overhead due to topology advertisements as the number of nodes in the network grows very large. Therefore, to allow the network to scale, PNNI organizes nodes into *peer groups*, as shown in Figure 2.8.

When nodes are arranged in peer groups, those nodes that share the same network prefix up to a specified level (e.g., 104 bits, or 13 bytes) are members of the same peer group. In the example in Figure 2.8, nodes (switches) with addresses A.1, A.2, and A.3 form a peer group A because they share the same network prefix. One of the peer group members is designated the peer group leader (PGL), as indicated by the shaded node. The PGL is selected either through management configuration or through an automatic peer group leader election protocol. Once selected, the PGL is responsible for summarizing topology information for its peer group, and representing the peer group as a logical group node to other peer groups. For example, if node A.3 is the leader of peer group A, it advertises the LGN with prefix A to neighboring peer groups. The internal structure of peer group A is not advertised. By summarizing peer group information as an LGN, PNNI can scale to very large networks.

PNNI virtual circuit routing works as follows: When an end system that is attached to switch A.1 wishes to establish a connection to another end system that is attached to switch B.2, it issues a SETUP message with a destination address of B.2.y. When A.1 receives the request, it routes the request to

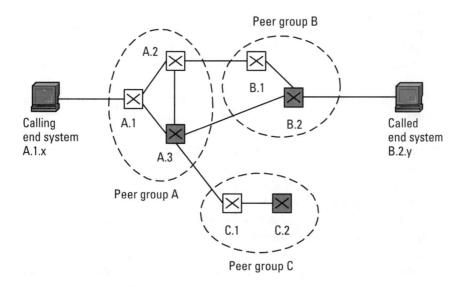

Figure 2.8 Example of peer group organization.

node A.2 because, from the topology advertisements that it received, it knows that A.2 is connected to network B, making it closer to the destination. When A.2 receives the SETUP, it does not know the internal structure of peer group B, but it knows that it is connected to LGN B. Therefore, it forwards the request to LGN B, and the request is received by switch B.1. Since B.1 knows the detailed topology of its peer group, it routes the request to the final switch B.2, which routes the SETUP to the called end system.

In PNNI node aggregation, a peer group of nodes is aggregated into an LGN, which facilitates the scalability of PNNI. In addition, links can also be aggregated. Therefore, as shown in Figure 2.8, the link connecting nodes A.2 and B.1 can be aggregated with the link connecting nodes A.3 and B.2. This aggregated link connects LGNs A and B. As with node aggregation, link aggregation reduces the amount of external reachability information that must be stored in the individual nodes.

The routing procedure described above is rather straightforward— Routing within the peer group over inside links is based on detailed topology state information advertised within the peer group. The decision to route over an uplink connecting a switch to another peer group is based on summarized topology information advertised by peer group leaders. Topology, however, is only one consideration when performing PNNI routing; one other feature provided by PNNI is routing based on network QoS.

When PNNI routes a connection request, it considers the current topology and resource availability, determines the route, and encodes the route in a designated transit list (DTL), which acts as a source-route specification for the virtual circuit. However, the information that was used to construct the DTL may be stale. For example, a new set of connections may have been established across a link connecting two peer groups, but the updated link information has not yet been sent to all nodes in the adjacent peer groups. In this case, a DTL that specifies this link may cause the new connection to be blocked. For this reason, PNNI provides a *crankback* mechanism that automatically reroutes the connection and updates the DTL to allow the connection to proceed along a new path.

To function correctly, PNNI requires all nodes to advertise correct information regarding the network topology and link state. This information must be correct because all nodes in the peer group store this information in their topology and link state databases, and use this information to construct routes and DTLs. If this information is corrupted (e.g., through malicious introduction of PNNI topology state elements), then the ability of all nodes in the peer group to construct correct DTLs is impaired, which prevents the peer group from correctly routing the connections. Furthermore, if a malicious node assumes the role of peer group leader, it can advertise false information to other peer groups and impair their ability to route connections [14]. Security mechanisms for PNNI signaling and routing are described in Chapter 10.

2.6 Multipoint Connections

As described in Section 2.2, ATM supports Pt-Pt and Pt-Mpt virtual circuits. Pt-Mpt VCs follow a tree-like structure. That is, they originate at a single root, are branched by switches that are located as close to the destinations as possible, and terminate at multiple leaves (destinations). Like Pt-Pt VCs, Pt-Mpt VCs can be configured manually as Pt-Mpt PVCs or via signaling as Pt-Mpt SVCs. The signaling flows for a root-initiated Pt-Mpt VC are shown in Figure 2.9.

When a Pt-Mpt connection is started, the first leaf is added using standard signaling for Pt-Pt connections (shown here as an abbreviated two-way SETUP-CONNECT exchange). However, when a new leaf is added to the connection, the root issues an ADD PARTY message to the network. This message contains the address of the new leaf in the called party IE, and uses the same call reference value that was used to establish the connection to the first leaf. Since the call reference is reused, the switch that receives the ADD PARTY message knows which connection is to be branched, if required.

The switches propagate the ADD PARTY message to other switches in the network, which branch the connection, if necessary. At the destination, the last switch converts the ADD PARTY message to a SETUP message, and sends the SETUP to the called party (leaf). At this point, the leaf sends the CONNECT message to its switch, and the network propagates it as an ADD PARTY ACKNOWLEDGE back to the root.

The root-initiated Pt-Mpt procedure described above is specified in UNI 3.1. In addition, UNI 4.0 specifies procedures that allow the leaves to request that they be added to the Pt-Mpt connection. This procedure is called leaf-initiated join (LIJ).

When a leaf wishes to be added to a Pt-Mpt connection, it issues a LEAF SETUP REQUEST message to the network. This request contains the address of the root and an identifier that distinguishes the desired Pt-Mpt connection from all others that are originated by the root. When the network receives the request, it finds the Pt-Mpt connection and processes it as follows:

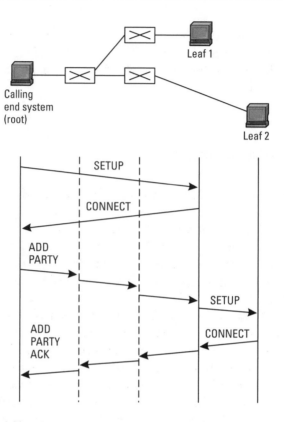

Figure 2.9 Root-initiated signaling for Pt-Mpt connections.

- *No existing Pt-Mpt connection:* The request is propagated to the root, which adds the leaf as the first leaf in a Pt-Mpt connection (as described earlier).

- *"Root LIJ" with existing Pt-Mpt connection:* In this scenario, the LEAF SETUP REQUEST is again propagated to the root, and the root adds the leaf using the ADD PARTY message, as described earlier.

- *"Network LIJ" with existing Pt-Mpt connection:* In this case, the network processes the request on its own, with no involvement by the root.

The selection of root LIJ or network LIJ is a configuration issue. Network LIJ is preferred if the multipoint connection state is highly dynamic, with leaves frequently joining and leaving Pt-Mpt connections. If the root was involved in adding each leaf in this case, it could become overwhelmed with requests, severely limiting the scalability of the system.

On the other hand, security considerations may require root involvement. Access control lists (ACLs) can reside on the root, and allow the root to restrict access to those leaves whose addresses are in the allowed set of recipients. In addition, root involvement in leaf setup allows the stronger authentication and key exchange mechanisms provided by the ATM Security 1.1 Specification [9] to be used. Key exchange is particularly important, as the destination needs to be provided with the traffic decryption key by the traffic source. While it is possible to allow switches to provide this key during a network LIJ, distributing this key to a set of switches defeats the purpose of shared secret key encryption.

2.7 Operations and Management

OAM allows devices in an ATM network to communicate layer-specific performance, alarm, diagnostic, and other information with each other. For SONET/ATM networks, OAM functions occur at two layers: the physical layer (SONET) and at the ATM layer. OAM flows at the SONET layer include the F1, F2, and F3 flows, which carry OAM information at the SONET section, line, and path levels, respectively. These OAM flows are carried in the various overhead bytes contained in the SONET frame.

In addition, ATM networks support the transport of OAM information at the ATM layer. The ATM OAM flows are the F4 flow for OAM at the virtual path level, and the F5 flow for OAM at the virtual channel level. For each OAM flow type, two subtypes are specified: end-to-end OAM flows and segment OAM flows. The applicability of F4 and F5 end-to-end and segment flows is shown in Figure 2.10 (where the end-to-end virtual channel connection (VCC) is tunneled through a virtual path connection (VPC)).

ATM OAM flows are carried via special OAM cells. These cells are carried in the VPC or VCC that they represent. In order to distinguish F4 OAM cells from other cell traffic in the VPC, the F4 OAM cells use reserved VCI values, with VCI = 3 for segment OAM cells, and VCI = 4 for end-to-end OAM cells. To distinguish F5 OAM cells from other cells on the same VCC, special PTI values are assigned, with PTI = 4 for segment OAM cells, and PTI = 5 for end-to-end F5 OAM cells.

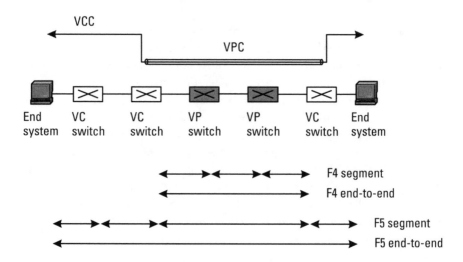

Figure 2.10 ATM OAM flows.

All ATM OAM cells contain fields that denote the OAM cell type (e.g., fault management, performance management, and system management). In addition, a function type is defined within each OAM cell type. A sample of some of the OAM function types that are currently defined is shown in Table 2.2.

End-to-end F4 or F5 OAM cells are handled by intermediate virtual path switches or virtual circuit switches as ordinary ATM cells. Therefore, the position of the end-to-end OAM cell relative to other cell traffic on the

Table 2.2
Subset of OAM Function Types

OAM Cell Type	Function Type
Fault management	Alarm indication signaling (AIS)
	Remote defect indicator (RDI)
	Loopback
Performance management	Forward monitoring
	Backward monitoring
System management	Security, non-real-time
	Security, real-time

VPC or VCC is maintained, as ATM guarantees in-order cell delivery for cells on the same connection. As described in Chapter 8, this is a desirable property for ATM cell encryption because OAM cells can be used to carry cryptographic state information, which requires cell sequence integrity between the OAM cells and the encrypted user data cells.

Although OAM cells are carefully scoped, as shown in Figure 2.10, nothing prevents a device from inserting end-to-end OAM cells from a location other than an end system. In addition, the authenticity of OAM cells is not protected. Therefore, nothing short of physical protection of the network prevents a malicious party from inserting somewhere in the path of a VPC or VCC and injecting false OAM cells into the connection (which could cause, for example, a receiving device to believe that an alarm exists, or to go into loopback mode). Of course, if an attacker gained this kind of access, he could also do many other damaging things (including complete traffic denial of service and connection teardown).

2.8 ATM Traffic Management

ATM traffic management is the mechanism that allows a network to understand the service requirements of the circuits it carries and support those requirements while, at the same time, maximizing the utilization of its links. Traffic management functions, which are specified in UNI 3.1 [8] and TM 4.0 [15], include the following:

- Call admission control (CAC);
- Usage parameter control (UPC);
- Traffic shaping;
- Flow control for ABR connections.

Call admission control is the decision made by the network at connection setup time that determines whether it will accept the connection request. This decision is based on the current conditions of the network and switches, and on the QoS requirements for the connection, as specified by the end system. The current conditions of the network are reported by the PNNI link-state routing protocol, which was described earlier in Section 2.5. The current state of the switch has a bearing on the switch's ability to accept the call and is determined via unspecified mechanisms. The switch's current state in this case is typically determined by parameters such as the existing reservations made during VPC provisioning, QoS requirements of existing connections, cell loss statistics, and congestion status.

The QoS requirements of the requested virtual circuit are specified by network management for PVCs or by special QoS information elements contained in the SVC setup request. One of the IEs contains the traffic parameters that the end system will use when sending ATM cells to the network. These parameters are:

- *Sustained cell rate (SCR):* The average rate at which the source sends ATM cells to the network, measured in cells per second;

- *Peak cell rate (PCR):* The maximum rate at which the source sends ATM cells to the network (as defined by the generic cell rate algorithm, which is specified in [15]), measured in cells per second;

- *Maximum burst size (MBS):* The maximum number of cells that are sent at the PCR;

- *Minimum cell rate (MCR):* The minimum useable cell rate that the source will accept, measured in cells per second—This parameter is used by the ABR service category, described below.

Another information element contains the QoS parameters for the virtual circuit. If the circuit is accepted, then the network agrees to abide by this traffic contract. These parameters are:

- *Maximum cell transfer delay (CTD):* The maximum end-to-end delay for the virtual circuit;

- *Cell delay variation (CDV):* The maximum variation in cell transfer delays, (i.e., the difference between maximum CTD and minimum CTD);

- *Cell loss ratio (CLR):* The ratio of lost cells to all cells transmitted into the network by the source.

The QoS contract between the end system and the network is an agreement by the network that it will provide the negotiated QoS, and an agreement by the end system to conform to its traffic parameters. To ensure that the end system is not violating its end of the contract, the network performs UPC, which is also known as *policing.* If a source violates its contract (which may risk the QoS afforded to other virtual circuits), then the network may respond according to its policies. Two possible responses include dropping offending cells, and marking them (using the cell loss priority bit in the header) as eligible for discard by switches further downstream if conditions warrant. An example of this process is shown in Figure 2.11.

A less drastic way of ensuring compliance to the source's traffic parameters is to employ traffic shaping. Traffic shaping, which may be implemented by the network or by the source (or both), uses a suitable scheduling algorithm (e.g., a leaky bucket algorithm) to smooth out bursts in the source's cell traffic. This allows the network to better multiplex the cell traffic with other cell traffic, thereby preserving the QoS of other circuits. However, this process adds CTD to the shaped traffic, and depending on the algorithm used, may result in cell loss.

Most often a source does not care about the QoS provided by a virtual circuit, and best effort delivery is adequate. In this case, the network will likely provide an unspecified bit rate (UBR) service. For this service category, the source is allowed to transmit at any rate it chooses, and if the network is congested or otherwise cannot handle the cell traffic, it discards the cells. Because this class of service is best effort, like IP, it requires higher-layer mechanisms for error control.

If neither extreme (guaranteed QoS or UBR) is acceptable, a circuit might use the ABR service category. ABR allows switches to make unallo-

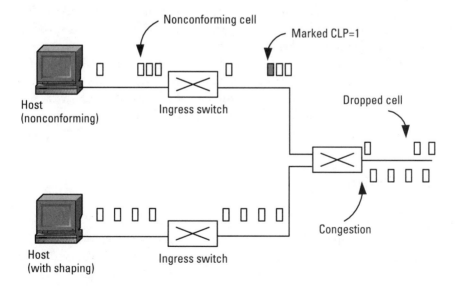

Figure 2.11 ATM cell policing and marking.

cated bandwidth available to cell traffic that does not require real-time delivery, but requires cell loss control should the network become congested. The cell loss control feature is provided by a flow control mechanism that is enabled by the use of rate management (RM) cells. RM cells allow switches to communicate available bandwidth information and congestion notifications to other switches and end systems. The end systems use the information contained in RM cells to adjust their transmission rates, thereby relieving the network of ABR traffic load when the network becomes congested.

As with OAM cells, RM cells are not authenticated in any way—They are assumed to be originated by ATM switches and contain valid rate and congestion information. Furthermore, any switch that receives RM cells may modify them to indicate congestion or reduce the rate information contained in the RM cells. This implies a chain of trust in the processing of RM cells. Therefore, a malicious party that has access to these cells can artificially throttle down the endpoints of an ABR connection. (However, as described in the previous section, if a malicious party has this kind of access, he can likely do worse damage.)

In addition, ATM QoS does not have a standard method for supporting QoS policy, which allows a network to verify that a calling party is authorized to request a certain QoS for a connection (although such features may be implemented on a proprietary, vendor-specific basis). However, if such a mechanism existed, it would likely need to be supplemented with a strong authentication mechanism to prevent an end system from spoofing the QoS privileges of another end system.

That said, ATM QoS does provide features that are very well suited for security. For example, as a matter of policy, all critical circuits in an ATM network can be configured as QoS enabled, which provides them with protection should a network link become saturated with other traffic.

2.9   ATM Services

To support higher-layer protocols (particularly IP), various ATM specifications exist that describe how to encapsulate higher-layer protocols into ATM AAL packets and provide additional services for address resolution. These services were evolved as the need for early functionality (i.e., basic IP transport and the need for adapting *legacy* LAN technologies to ATM) shifted to a need for performance. The following sections describe some of these services.

2.9.1 Classical IP over ATM

One approach for providing IP services over ATM is the classical IP over ATM (CLIP) approach specified in RFC 2225 [16]. CLIP is considered "classical" because it maintains the concept of *subnets* of IP hosts and routers that may directly communicate with each other, and communications with devices on other subnets must be performed through one or more routers.

With technologies such as Ethernet and fiber distributed data interface (FDDI), the subnetting of a network is straightforward—each Ethernet segment or FDDI ring forms the *segment*. With ATM, however, a segment is not so easily identified; in fact, a single ATM network can support multiple segments which are called logical IP subnets (LISs). In CLIP, each LIS is defined by an Address Resolution Protocol (ARP) server, which resolves IP addresses to ATM addresses for each node in the LIS.

With other technologies (such as Ethernet or FDDI), ARP is a distributed service—The requesting host sends a broadcast containing the IP address of the intended target, and the host with the IP address responds with the hardware address of its network interface. ATM, however, does not have a similar broadcast mechanism. Rather, when a host boots up, it contacts an ARP server and provides it with the host's IP address/ATM address mapping. After the host registers with the ARP server, other hosts can resolve its IP address to its ATM address by querying the ARP server, allowing the other host to connect and send it IP traffic, as shown in Figure 2.12.

In addition to this ARP mechanism, RFC 2225 also specifies a mechanism for encapsulating IP packets into an ATM AAL 5 packet. By default, this method uses the logical link control (LLC) encapsulation method defined in RFC 1483 [17]. This encapsulation method uses the IEEE 802.2 frame format, which supports the transfer of IP and other higher-layer protocol packets over a single ATM connection.

Because RFC 2225 preserves the classical IP approach via LISs, it does not allow direct connections between hosts on the same ATM network, but rather between those residing on different LISs. If such hosts send packets to each other, they must communicate through a *one-armed router* that has an ATM interface with two IP addresses, each belonging to each LIS. This presents an unnecessary bottleneck, which is addressed by the multiprotocol over ATM (MPOA) approach, described in Section 2.9.3.

The security issues associated with CLIP are the same as those associated with ARP in general. That is, a malicious node M can misrepresent itself to an ARP server as another node A when it registers, which causes connection requests meant for node A to be sent to node M instead. Of course, as

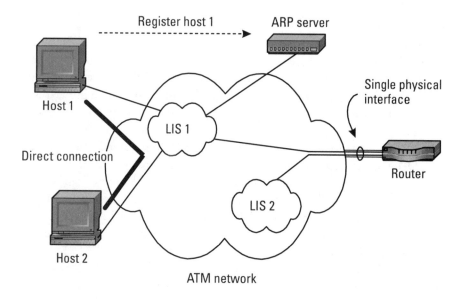

Figure 2.12 Classical IP over ATM network.

with ARP in general, if both nodes are active at the same time, then the ARP server will detect the duplication. However, if this is considered a credible threat, then the ARP server can be configured with static IP and ATM address bindings.

Another security issue with CLIP is that it relies on a single server. Unlike ARP on other networks, where the ARP response mechanism is distributed among all hosts on the subnet, a host making an ATM ARP query is dependent on the availability of the ATM ARP server and the correctness of its tables. Furthermore, the ATM ARP server is a central collection of addressing information for its LIS, making it an attractive target for network mapping and denial of service attacks. Therefore, the ATM ARP server must be carefully protected from equipment failure and unauthorized management access.

2.9.2 LANE

The problem with CLIP is that it only provides a mechanism for implementing IP over ATM. Other protocols such as IPX and NETBIOS cannot be implemented using CLIP. Back in the early days of ATM, users needed a graceful way of moving these legacy networks and protocols to an ATM infrastructure. For this reason, the ATM Forum developed LANE.

The LANE mechanism emulates LAN functions such as broadcasting and media addressing (e.g., Ethernet and Token Ring) via the following servers:

- *LAN emulation configuration server (LECS):* This server, which serves multiple emulated subnets, configures a LAN emulation client (LEC) and allows the LEC to join a subnet by providing it with the ATM address of the subnet's LAN emulation server.

- *LAN emulation server (LES):* Each subnet has an LES, which maintains a table that maps media addresses to ATM addresses. The LES stores these mappings for each node when it registers, and provides these mappings to other nodes on the emulated LAN when queried.

- *Broadcast and unknown server (BUS):* Each subnet also has one BUS, which takes broadcast packets sent by a node and distributes them to all nodes in the subnet.

- As shown in Figure 2.13, when an LEC wishes to join an emulated LAN (ELAN), it contacts the LECS (at a well-known address, a well-known virtual circuit, or an ATM address provided by ILMI) to obtain the address of the LES. Once this address is obtained, the

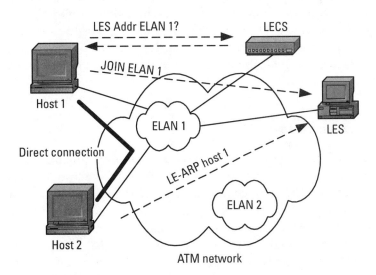

Figure 2.13 LANE components.

LEC contacts the LES and registers its media and ATM addresses with it.

If an LEC has data that it wishes to send to a particular media address, it sends a LAN emulation ARP (LE-ARP) request to the LES, which replies with the ATM address. Armed with the ATM address of the destination, the LEC establishes a connection to the destination and begins sending data.

Although LANE succeeds in its goal of emulating legacy LANs and allowing multiple protocols to use its ELANs, it does have a couple of problems. As with CLIP, the problem with IP over LANE is the fact that the LECs are grouped in subnets, and if two LECs on different ELANs in the same ATM network wish to send packets to each other, they must do so through a router. Another problem with LANE is that the LES and the BUS do not scale well, and can become overloaded as their ELAN membership grows.

As with CLIP, the servers in LANE represent both a security risk and a security opportunity. The risks with these servers are the centralization of functions and network configuration data. In addition, these servers are dependent on information (specifically, the media-to-ATM address bindings) provided by the LECs, which may be less trustworthy.

LANE also has a security advantage in that it allows access control at the time an LEC registers with the LECS. If the LEC is not authorized to join an ELAN, then it is not provided with the address of the LES, and cannot obtain media-to-ATM address bindings or send broadcasts to an ELAN via its BUS. Of course, this security feature is not strong, and can be defeated by a malicious end system that spoofs an authorized end system's ATM and media address.

2.9.3   Multiprotocol over ATM

As described in the previous sections, CLIP and LANE group their hosts in subnets, and hosts that are connected to the same ATM network, but located on different subnets, must communicate through routers. Although today's routers are very fast, the bottleneck presented by the routers and the latencies associated with the additional network transits are unnecessary. Therefore, the ATM Forum undertook the development of the multiprotocol over ATM (MPOA) specification, which allows ATM hosts on different subnets to establish direct connections with each other. The principal components of an MPOA network are shown in Figure 2.14.

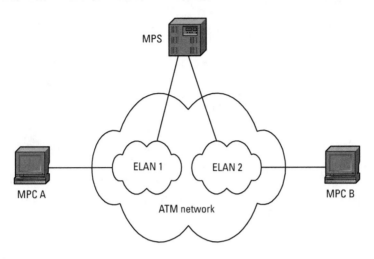

Figure 2.14 MPOA components.

With MPOA, hosts and routers are still arranged in logical IP subnets using the LANE protocol suite described earlier. Therefore, all hosts on an ELAN communicate with each other using the LECS, LES, and BUS to implement the various LANE functions. Since LANE is agnostic of higher-layer protocols (such as IP, NETBIOS, and IPX), it allows MPOA to support multiple protocols.

Data transfers using MPOA work as follows: When an MPOA client (MPC A) wishes to send data to MPC B on another ELAN, it sends it through an MPOA server (MPS), which forwards the packet as if the MPS were a standard router. However, if the session between MPC A and MPC B is of sufficient duration, then the MPS informs MPC A of MPC B's ATM address. At this point, MPC A establishes a direct ATM connection to MPC B, which is used for remainder of the session.

In this simple example, the MPS is connected to both ELANs, and therefore, knows the ATM addresses of each MPC directly. In general, however, this is not the case, and the MPS must discover the destination MPC's address. This discovery is performed using the Next Hop Resolution Protocol (NHRP), which is specified in [18]. This protocol allows MPSs to query each other to obtain the needed ATM addresses to allow an MPC to establish a direct connection.

Since MPOA uses LANE for the implementation of subnet services, the security issues described for LANE also apply for MPOA. In addition, since MPOA uses NHRP for resolving ATM addresses, the NHRP flows between MPSs must also be protected to prevent malicious introduction or modification of NHRP messages.

2.10 Summary

ATM is an extensive set of protocol specifications that support the dynamic establishment of QoS-enabled virtual circuits that quickly switch ATM cells between endpoints. To adapt higher-layer protocols and applications to ATM connection-oriented approach, supporting services such as LANE and MPOA are also specified. This chapter provided a very brief description of these protocols in order to familiarize the reader with basic ATM concepts. In addition, this chapter introduced some security issues with these protocols, setting the stage for more thorough treatment in the remaining chapters.

References

[1] de Prycker, M., *Asynchronous Transfer Mode: Solution for Broadband ISDN*, New York: Ellis Horwood Ltd., 1993.

[2] Pandya, A., and E. Sen, *ATM Technology for Broadband Telecommunications Networks*, Boca Raton, FL: CRC Press, 1999.

[3] Kwok, T., *ATM—The New Paradigm for Internet, Intranet, and Residential Broadband Services and Applications*, Englewood Cliffs, NJ: Prentice Hall, 1997.

[4] Händel, R., M. Huber, and S. Schröder, *ATM Networks—Concepts, Protocols, Applications*, Reading, MA: Addison-Wesley, 1998.

[5] ITU-T, "B-ISDN DSS2 User-Network Interface (UNI) Layer 3 Specification for Basic Call/Connection Control," Recommendation Q.2931, February 1995.

[6] The ATM Forum, "Private Network-Network Interface Specification, Version 1.0," af-pnni-0055.000, March 1996.

[7] Tesink, K., "Definitions for Managed Objects for ATM Management," Internet Engineering Task Force RFC 2515, February 1999.

[8] The ATM Forum, "User-Network Interface (UNI) Specification, Version 3.1," af-uni-0010.002, September 1994.

[9] The ATM Forum, "ATM Security Specification Version 1.1," af-sec-0100.002, March 2001.

[10] The ATM Forum, "ATM Name System, Version 2.0," af-dans-0152.000, July 2000.

[11] The ATM Forum, "Integrated Local Management Interface (ILMI) Version 4.0," af-ilmi-0065.000, September, 1996.

[12] The ATM Forum, "User-Network Interface (UNI) Signalling Specification, Version 4.0," af-sig-0061.000, July, 1996.

[13] Moy, J., "OSPF Version 2," Internet Engineering Task Force RFC 2328, April, 1998.

[14] Smith, R., D. W. Hill, and N. P. Robinson, "ATM Peer Group Leader Attack and Mitigation," *Proceedings IEEE MILCOM '99*, pp. 729–733, 1999.

[15] The ATM Forum, "Traffic Management Specification, Version 4.0," af-tm-0056.000, April, 1996.

[16] Laubach, M., and J. Halpern, "Classical IP and ARP over ATM," Internet Engineering Task Force RFC 2225, April 1998.

[17] Heinanen, J., "Multiprotocol Encapsulation over ATM Adaptation Layer 5," Internet Engineering Task Force RFC 1483, July 1993.

[18] Luciani, J., et al., "NBMA Next Hop Resolution Protocol (NHRP)," Internet Engineering Task Force RFC 2332, April 1998.

Part II:
Using ATM Security

3

ATM Security Using Traditional ATM Features

Depending on the result of an analysis of security risks for an ATM network and the available budget for protection mechanisms, security precautions provided by careful configuration of ATM network elements may be adequate. Assuming that the ATM infrastructure (switches and servers) are configured to prevent unauthorized management access, manual configuration of network connection policies via PVCs and PVPs provides reasonable isolation of flows between hosts or private networks. When switched virtual connections are required within a private network, ATM address filtering mechanisms (similar to address filtering found in IP firewalls) can be employed. This mechanism allows or rejects connections based on the addresses of the called or calling parties (which, of course, may be spoofed by a malicious party, as described later) and is commonly found in many of today's ATM switches as a means for enforcing connection policies. Finally, ATM services such as LANE can also be configured to restrict access to a need-to-know (NTK) group that connects to a common emulated LAN.

Of course, using these methods of access control to enforce connection policies in an ATM network implies adequate management access controls to the ATM infrastructure devices. Fortunately, today's products support many methods of securing management access. These methods range from simple static passwords to one-time passwords to strong Kerberos authentication with encryption [1]. Additional standards for securing management access to ATM infrastructure elements are also under consideration [2].

This chapter describes how to use features commonly found on today's ATM infrastructure devices (especially switches) to effect network connection policies and simple access control and for securing management access. In addition, this chapter also describes when these mechanisms should be used and when stronger mechanisms (such as those described in Chapter 4 and later) are required.

3.1 Implementing ATM Connection Policies

Common mechanisms provided by most ATM switches for implementing ATM connection policies are listed in Table 3.1.

As shown in the table, each mechanism has a number of properties that determine how it should be used for connection policy enforcement in an ATM network. One property of each mechanism is its *granularity* of policy enforcement. This property determines whether the mechanism can be used to enforce connection policies between individual hosts, or between ATM subnetworks.

Figure 3.1 illustrates two more properties of connection filtering: policy implementation and required switch configuration. Most policy implementation mechanisms operate in a distributed fashion, where a number of devices need to be configured correctly to provide the required connection

Table 3.1
Common Mechanisms for Implementing Connection Policies

Mechanism	Properties			
	Granularity	SVC Support	Policy Implementation	Switches Involved
PVCs	Hosts	No	Distributed	All
PVPs	Networks	Yes, within PVP tunnels	Distributed	Network border and VP switches
NSAP filters	Hosts or networks	Yes	Distributed	Network edge or border
LANE	Hosts	Yes	Centralized	None (only LANE servers)

policy. This is true for the PVC-based mechanism and the network service access point (NSAP) address filter mechanism, as shown in Figure 3.1. LANE, however, implements connection policy via access control lists located in a central server.

Figure 3.1 also shows that each mechanism differs in the amount of ATM switch configuration required. Configuration may be limited to edge switches in the case of NSAP address filters, or it can be performed in all switches in a network when using PVCs.

The following sections describe each of these connection policy enforcement mechanisms in more detail.

3.1.1   Access Control via Circuit Provisioning

As described in Chapter 2, ATM connections can be configured manually as PVCs and PVPs. PVCs and PVPs are established by configuring the switching tables in each ATM switch along the circuit or path to specify how cells are switched from input to output port, and how identifiers in the cell headers are translated. If a network only uses PVCs, then network management authorization and effort is required to establish a new connection.

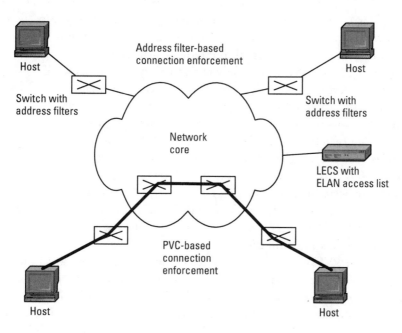

Figure 3.1 Connection policy configuration scenarios.

Because management authorization is required, ATM PVCs and PVPs can provide an effective means of enforcing ATM connection policies and separating flows between NTK groups. However, careful network design and control is required to ensure that only those end systems that are authorized to process data within a common NTK group are interconnected. Otherwise, an end system or a switch may bridge two or more groups, and leak data between them. In addition, PVCs and PVPs do not provide strong confidentiality protection from eavesdroppers or network administration personnel. Finally, the management effort required to establish PVCs in large networks makes this method costly to manage.

This section describes the use of PVCs to restrict flows between hosts within a site's ATM network and describes the use of PVPs to restrict connections between networks, possibly interconnected via a public ATM service provider.

3.1.1.1 PVCs

As shown in Figure 3.2, PVCs can be used to restrict ATM connections between hosts according to a connection policy.

In this example, the network administrator configures the switch tables in the ATM network to construct two PVC meshes connecting hosts in each group (as defined by the group membership matrix). The groups in this matrix may correspond to NTK groups or access control compartments. If an individual host is not trusted to internally maintain isolation of compartmented data, then that host is only connected to other hosts within a single group. However, if a host (e.g., host C) is trusted to maintain this separation (e.g., through careful host configuration and permission management), then it may be allowed to connect to other hosts in multiple groups.

Note that the use of PVCs to maintain NTK group separation also implies that the switches themselves are trusted to maintain separation of PVCs. This trust may be established via testing of the switch hardware to determine occurrence of switching errors, logging of ATM error statistics in hosts and switches (e.g., invalid virtual path and virtual channel information in the ATM cell headers), and careful maintenance of management access rights and access authentication.

When PVC-based separations are implemented, the network must be configured so that the nodes in one group cannot establish back door SVCs to nodes in another group. One way to implement this protection is to configure the switches with ATM NSAP address filters, which are described in Section 3.1.2.1. Another way to implement this protection is to disable signaling on the network side of the UNIs, which disables a host's ability to

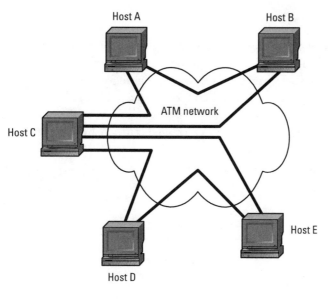

	Group 1	Group 2
Host A	✔	
Host B	✔	
Host C	✔	✔
Host D		✔
Host E		✔

Group membership matrix

Figure 3.2 PVC-enforced connection policy.

signal SVCs to other hosts. To provide even more protection, the ILMI protocol may also be disabled to prevent the network from learning the addresses of the hosts that are attached to it, providing further prevention from unauthorized SVCs.

Of course, by disabling signaling on each host's physical connection to the network, the inconvenience to the host's users is increased substantially, as management must now be consulted when a new ATM connection is needed, even to another host within the NTK group. This, in turn, places an additional burden on the network management, which must respond to user requests and must manage PVCs (a task that does not scale well, as described in Chapter 2).

3.1.1.2   PVPs

Whereas PVCs are useful for maintaining access restrictions between *hosts* within an ATM network, PVPs can be used to maintain access restrictions between *networks*. An example is shown in Figure 3.3.

In this example, each site is connected to a public ATM network with a PVP mesh connecting their border switches according to the group membership matrix. This matrix may be determined centrally by some authority that

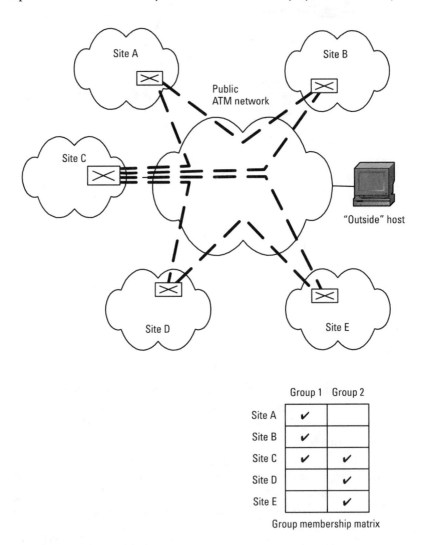

	Group 1	Group 2
Site A	✔	
Site B	✔	
Site C	✔	✔
Site D		✔
Site E		✔

Group membership matrix

Figure 3.3 PVP-enforced intersite connection policy.

has control over all the sites, or in an ad hoc fashion (with coordination with the public network provider) by subgroups that determine a need to interconnect.

To prevent nongroup members (e.g., the outside host in Figure 3.3) from using the public network's SVC services to connect to a group member's site, each group member must disable SVC signaling on all virtual paths except those that terminate the PVP tunnels in the mesh.

With signaling enabled on the authorized PVP tunnels, hosts within each group member's network can use SVC signaling to establish connections to hosts on other group members' networks. This improves the scalability of connection management. However, care must be taken at sites that belong to multiple groups (e.g., site C) to prevent the site's border switch from allowing connections to bridge two VP tunnels. To prevent this from happening, the border switch must be configured with address filters that reject connection attempts from one VP tunnel to another.

However, while PVPs may be a good practice for restricting SVC connections to those within a group of sites, they do nothing to protect the confidentiality of data flowing between group sites. If this traffic flows over an untrusted public network, there are no guarantees that the links and switches are protected from eavesdroppers, or that the PVPs were configured correctly between sites. Therefore, if confidentiality is required, or if stronger mechanisms are needed to prevent connections from nongroup members, then encryption and strong (cryptographic) authentication are required. These mechanisms are described in the following chapters.

3.1.2 Access Control for Signaled ATM Circuits

In the previous sections, access control implementations using PVCs and PVPs are described. Recall that PVC-based access controls are best for small networks where interhost connection policies are to be applied. The use of PVCs for enforcing connection policies, however, does not scale well and requires management configuration of all switches that process each virtual circuit, including those switches in the core of the network. Furthermore, PVC-based policy enforcement does not permit the establishment of new connections without administrative involvement (which may be good or bad, depending on the site's level of paranoia).

This section describes two additional mechanisms that permit the enforcement of connection policies between hosts. These mechanisms, which are commonly found on today's ATM switches, allow hosts that are authorized to connect to do so using SVCs. The first mechanism, NSAP address filtering, is a distributed mechanism that functions independently of the service that maps higher-layer protocols to ATM (and is therefore protocol- and application-transparent). The second mechanism is a centralized mechanism for providing access control, but it is specific to the ATM LANE service.

3.1.2.1   Address Filtering

Address filtering allows connection policies to be applied to SVCs during connection establishment. As shown in Figure 3.4, filter specifications can be applied on ATM switch ports to allow or reject connections between specified ATM addresses.

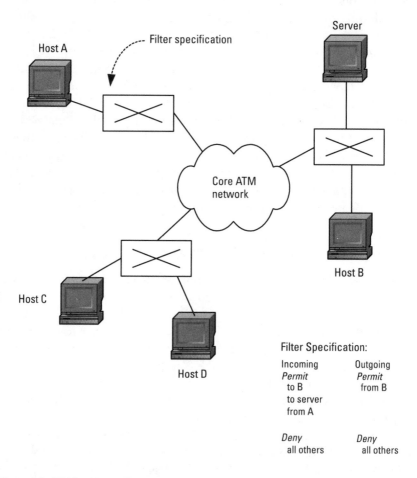

Filter Specification:

Incoming	Outgoing
Permit	*Permit*
to B	from B
to server	
from A	
Deny	*Deny*
all others	all others

Figure 3.4 NSAP address filtering.

The connection policy for the example in Figure 3.4 specifies that A and B are allowed to initiate connections to each other. A, however, is not allowed to connect to C or D. Finally, an asymmetric connection policy is specified between A and the server. That is, A is allowed to initiate a connection to the server, but the server is not allowed to initiate a connection to A. The filter specification in the figure pertains to the ATM switch port that is connected to A, and it reflects this connection policy. (The structure of the filter specification in this example is similar to the way filters are specified in many commercially available switches.)

NSAP filtering can be used to enforce connection policies between ATM subnetworks and peer groups as well as between hosts. This is accomplished through the use of address masks in the NSAP filter specification. Mask values of 104 bits (13 bytes) or less correspond to the NSAP prefixes and are used to enforce connection policies at the ATM subnetwork level. Therefore, filter aggregation is provided by matching filter specifications to the address prefixes in the calling or called party information elements in the SETUP message.

Address filters are implemented in a distributed fashion. Since filter processing adds to the connection setup latency in switches, filters (particularly those that implement host-level access controls) are best placed at the edges to minimize the number of filters in each switch. However, filters that implement access controls based on network prefixes may also be implemented on switches on the border between ATM networks. Because filters are distributed to edge and border switches, care must be taken to ensure that the switches' filter specifications are consistent with the overall connection policy (note that this need for configuration consistency may also be considered a security risk). That is, changes to individual switch filter specifications must be compared to the overall policy, and changes to the overall policy must be propagated to the switches' filter specifications. The management complexity of NSAP filters depends on the variability of connection policies and the design of the network (e.g., complexity is reduced if hosts in a common NTK group are assigned the same network prefix). However, since NSAP filter specifications need only be configured in edge or border switches, the management complexity of address filters is less than that for PVCs.

The drawback to address filtering (particularly address filtering based on calling party addresses) is that it is vulnerable to address spoofing attacks. If a malicious calling party M knows the address of an authorized host A, then M can spoof A's address to allow its connection to another host to pass through any address filters that may exist in the network. If this threat is a concern, then two possible steps can be taken (in the absence of strong authentication, which is described in later chapters). The first approach is to use PVCs, as described earlier. The second approach is to configure the edge switches to reject connection requests with calling party identifiers that do not correspond to the address of the connected host (as determined by the ILMI protocol when the host physically connects to the switch). An example of the latter approach is shown in Figure 3.4, where host A's switch port is configured to check that A's address is contained in the calling party information element in the SETUP message and that this address matches the address determined by ILMI. If they do not match, then the connection request fails. Note that this protection must be applied to *all* UNI ports, and requires one to exercise care in configuring the ingress NSAP filter to ensure that the filter specification matches the address of the attached host.

3.1.2.2   LANE Access Control Lists

Recall from Chapter 2 that if a LAN emulation client (LEC) wishes to join an ELAN, then it first contacts a LECS to obtain the address of the LES for that ELAN. This procedure provides an opportunity for the LECS to make an access control decision—if the address of the LEC is one of an authorized LEC, the LEC is allowed to join the ELAN and it is provided with the address of the ELAN's LES. This procedure is shown in the join request protocol exchange from host A in Figure 3.5.

Therefore, with LANE-based access control, hosts within a common NTK group are assigned to a common ELAN, with the access control list maintained by the LECS. If an unauthorized LEC wishes to join an ELAN (e.g., host C in Figure 3.5), then the LECS does not provide it with the address of the LES, and the host does not join the ELAN.

What if the LEC somehow knows the address of the LES for a particular ELAN that it is not authorized to join? To address this possibility, some manufacturers' LESs can be configured to consult the LECS before allowing the LEC to join. In this way, ELAN membership policies can still be maintained in a central location without allowing a rogue LEC to bypass them. This example is shown in Figure 3.5, where host C attempts to contact the LES directly to join the ELAN.

The advantage of using LANE to enforce policy is the fact that the policy information is stored in a central location (the LECS), which simplifies policy management. However, the policy that is maintained by the LECS is ELAN membership policy, not connection policy. That is, with only the LANE-based approach, one must assume that all members of the same ELAN are allowed to connect to each other (that is, they belong to the same

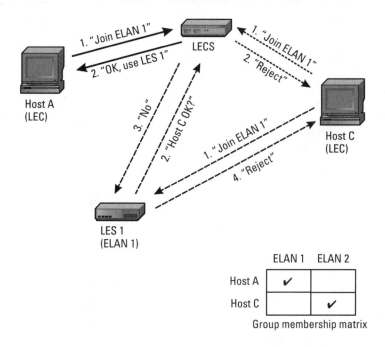

Group membership matrix

	ELAN 1	ELAN 2
Host A	✔	
Host C		✔

Figure 3.5 LANE access controls.

NTK group). If different (e.g., more restrictive) policies are required, then this method can be augmented with NSAP address filters. Also, since security policy enforcement with LANE uses the NSAP address reported by the LEC to determine ELAN membership, this method is also susceptible to spoofing and may require other mechanisms (e.g., PVCs or NSAP filtering at the network attachment point) to mitigate this threat.

3.2 Network Configuration Security

The mechanisms described in the previous sections for implementing network connection policies require network infrastructure devices (i.e., ATM switches and the LANE servers) to be properly configured according to the site's security policy. Therefore, the mechanisms used to change infrastructure configuration must be suitably secured. This includes the major components for switch configuration management, as shown in Figure 3.6.

The first step in maintaining configuration control is to secure physical access to the switch, its configuration data, and the audit logs. If the switch is

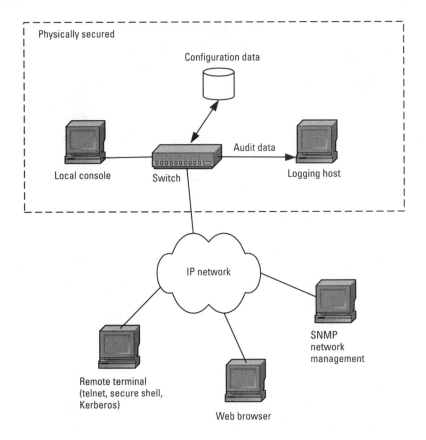

Figure 3.6 Switch configuration management components.

not physically secured, then an unauthorized person with physical access can cause the switch (through a number of steps, depending on the particular switch) to grant him permission to modify configuration data. This is also true if the configuration data is not physically secured. Finally, if the audit logging facility is not physically secured (either collocated with the switch, or at some other location), then it can be booted to provide unauthorized root access, or powered-down or disconnected to cause it to miss event information related to switch configuration changes.

The next step in configuration security is creating management accounts on the switch, which typically provide varying levels of management privileges. When creating these accounts and assigning them to users who are authorized management access, one is advised to adhere to the *principle of least privilege*; that is, each operator should only be assigned enough rights to do his job. This prevents an operator from intentionally or inadvertently changing configuration when he is not authorized. When creating accounts, one should also adhere to proper procedures for generating, storing, and protecting the confidentiality of passwords, and change the default passwords and SNMP community strings on the switch when it is installed.

A logging facility should also be configured as part of the switch management system. This facility allows for storage and later analysis of management accesses and actions (including configuration changes), which is useful for uncovering the source of a problem or deterring malicious activity. To be effective, this facility must be carefully protected to ensure that the logs are not modified to "cover tracks" resulting from unauthorized behavior. This includes adequate physical as well as remote access protection.

All switches allow management access to occur on a local console port (via a terminal connected to a serial port) or using remote access protocols across an IP network. If remote access is allowed, then extra steps are required to ensure proper access control and authentication of users. Many switches permit the configuration of IP access lists, which allow a switch to restrict remote access to only those hosts whose IP addresses are allowed. If this capability exists, then it should be used to act as a first line of defense to deter and prevent unauthorized login attempts from remote locations. However, IP addresses of authorized hosts can be spoofed, so IP access lists must be supplemented with good passwords or other authentication methods.

Remote management access can occur using many methods, including remote terminal sessions, configuration access using Web browsers (with an HTTP server running on the switch), and SNMP network management stations. In all these cases, authentication of the user who desires management access is required in order to determine proper management authorizations. The set of authentication methods provided by the switch depends on the manufacturer, but it typically includes the following:

- *Static plaintext passwords:* These are used for remote terminal access (e.g., telnet) and access using a Web browser. These passwords must be chosen carefully, and static passwords that are passed across the IP network without encryption are susceptible to replay attacks that capture such passwords for later (unauthorized) use.

- *One-time plaintext passwords:* These passwords (e.g., SecurID and s/key) are also used for remote terminal or HTTP access, but change with each login attempt to thwart password capture and replay attacks.

- *Static encrypted passwords:* These passwords (e.g., Kerberos, secure shell, and Secure Sockets Layer) are static passwords that are encrypted along with other remote terminal or HTTP traffic using a shared secret key. This secures not only the password, but also subsequent management traffic, which protects the session from eavesdropping (which leads to password replay attacks) or session takeover attacks.

- *Public key authentication:* This authentication method (e.g., Secure Sockets Layer, Transport Layer Security, and secure shell) is based on cryptographic authentication protocols using a private key held by the authenticating agent to prove his identity to the switch. These methods often provide session encryption as well.

From the above list, it is evident that many options exist for securing management access to a switch. To help the industry converge to a set of common methods, the ATM Forum is currently developing a specification [2] that will facilitate interoperability and best practices securing such access.

3.3 Summary

This chapter described various mechanisms for enforcing connection policies in an ATM network using mechanisms that are found in most ATM switches and LANE servers. The mechanisms described in this chapter are PVCs, PVPs, NSAP address filters, and access control lists in LECSs. The selection of mechanisms to apply in an ATM network depends on the outcome of a security threat analysis, as described in Chapter 1. If stronger mechanisms are required, then cryptographic mechanisms, such as those provided by the ATM Security 1.1 Specification [3], may be required.

The amount of configuration required to implement connection policies as described in this chapter vary with the mechanism. For example, PVCs require all switches between two endpoints to be configured with switching information, whereas NSAP address filtering only requires configuration in border or edge switches. However, the security afforded by these mechanisms also varies. PVCs implement "authentication by management" and rely on the consent by network management in order to authorize a new connection. Other mechanisms that use address-based authentication (e.g., NSAP address filtering and LANE) also require management authorization, but may be vulnerable to address spoofing attacks, requiring careful protections if such spoofing is considered a threat.

Since all of these mechanisms are based on careful configuration of switches and servers, management access to these devices must be carefully controlled. Rights to view or modify switch configurations must be carefully assigned according to the principle of least privilege, and access to management accounts (especially remote access) must be authenticated in a manner that is commensurate with the threat of attack.

References

[1]   Kohl, J., and C. Neuman, "The Kerberos Network Authentication Service (V5)," Internet Engineering Task Force RFC 1510, September 1993.

[2]   The ATM Forum, "Methods for Securely Managing ATM Network Elements—Implementation Agreement Version 1.0 (draft)," BTD-SEC-MPS-00.04, April 2001

[3]   The ATM Forum, "ATM Security Specification Version 1.1," af-sec-0100.002, March 2001.

4

ATM Security Using the ATM Forum Security 1.1 Mechanisms

Recall from Chapter 1 that a security design must consider the assets that require protection, the threats to those assets, and appropriate threat mitigation measures (security mechanisms). As described in Chapter 3, some amount of security can be provided by standard ATM functions such as PVCs and NSAP filters. Certain threats, however, cannot be addressed by these mechanisms, particularly those from determined attackers and those on data traversing public networks (which are maintained by untrusted operators and provide services to untold numbers of potential attackers). For example, while PVCs can be used to protect a virtual circuit from being tapped via a multipoint join request from another end system, they cannot be used to protect the confidentiality of the data that traverses a public network (e.g., where untrusted network operators may tap the circuit). In this case, encryption is required to provide confidentiality between two sites that possess a shared secret key.

Security mechanisms beyond those provided by the "standard" ATM functions can be provided by application-level security such as Secure Sockets Layer [1] and S/MIME [2]. Host-based, application-level security has the advantage in that it provides true end-to-end security, which requires no trust in the network elements to properly handle data on an unsecured segment. Application-level security, however, increases complexity associated with security management. For example, users must acquire passwords or security tokens and protect them properly, the public-key infrastructure must be scalable to provide one or more keys per user, and users must be responsible for using security according to site policy. Furthermore, the number of application-level security products that must be evaluated for trust (either through extensive testing or line-by-line review of source code) is staggering, leading to insufficient evaluation and occasional security weaknesses in applications that can be exploited. Finally, application-level security can be slow, as the same processor that runs the application may also be the processor that implements security algorithm processing.

Security at the ATM level addresses some of these issues by embedding security processing in the network. ATM-level security provides transparent security for all protocols and applications (e.g., IP, e-mail, and native ATM video) over the protected ATM segment. Furthermore, by providing encryption at the enterprise network border, confidentiality can be provided as a service for enterprise users, and the complexities of security configuration and policy management can be relegated to those personnel who are skilled in such matters. Finally, devices that provide security can be optimized for their particular functions and perform them very quickly and efficiently. The cell-switched property of ATM facilitates fast encryption of fixed-length cells in hardware, allowing encryption of ATM cell streams at rates above 1 Gbps [3]. In addition, the connection-oriented nature of ATM allows initial security functions such as authentication and key exchange to occur in the connection establishment signaling protocol without additional end-to-end protocol flows (which increases the latency incurred while establishing a security association).

This chapter describes the security measures provided by the ATM Forum Security Specification Version 1.1 (which are stronger than the protection mechanisms described in Chapter 3) and how these measures are deployed in ATM networks. This chapter starts by describing the Security 1.1 model, including such key elements as the security agent and security message transport mechanisms. Next, the Security 1.1 services are described, including the initial security services that are provided during the establishment of a security association, and the remaining security services that are provided during the duration of the virtual circuit. Configuration considerations for the Security 1.1 security services are also described.

4.1 Security 1.1 Model

ATM security is structured according to the ATM reference model, which specifies three planes: the user plane, control plane, and management plane (as described in Chapter 2). The scope of Security 1.1 focuses primarily on the protection of user plane traffic; however, limited control plane security is also provided to address important threats to the correct operation of ATM networks. Management plane security is not specifically defined in Security 1.1 but can be provided via the Security 1.1 user plane security services.

Security services are provided by security agents (SAs). When SAs are paired to provide a security service (e.g., encryption), this pairing is called a security association. (Note: in this book, "SA" refers to security agent, not to security association.) Security associations exist for each security service that is applied to a user plane or control plane virtual circuit, and they define the particulars of the security services, including algorithms, algorithm parameters, keys, and sensitivity labels.

One peculiarity with the ATM Security Specification is that it does not define a default security association. That is, default algorithms for services such as encryption, authentication, and integrity checking are not specified. This decision was made early in the specification's development when the working group struggled to identify the defaults. The obvious disadvantage of this decision is that two implementations might not share a common set of algorithms, which results in failed negotiation during the establishment of a security association. However, considerations such as export laws, royalties, and rapid advances in brute-force key searching techniques complicated the selection of defaults. Therefore, no defaults were selected, and implementations must rely on negotiation or administrative configuration to select algorithms or algorithm profile groups (which are used to specify collections of algorithms that commonly occur together) for the security association.

The SA is the key component to the ATM security model. It is responsible for developing security associations with other SAs to implement the security services that are to be applied to the user plane or control plane virtual circuit. An SA is composed of several elements that perform specific functions during the establishment and lifetime of the security association. Furthermore, SAs can be located anywhere in an ATM network, including end systems and ATM switches. Therefore, multiple security associations may exist on a user plane or control plane virtual circuit. For this reason, SAs are specified to support nested topologies. Finally, SAs may provide proxy security, that is, security services at the request of an end system that cannot perform those services itself.

SAs located in end-systems provide end-to-end security between ATM-attached hosts, which is required if the network is untrusted. SAs located in switches provide bulk security services for end systems on its protected network, but the security association only spans part of the virtual circuit (it is assumed that the other part crosses a network that is trusted, for example, through physical access restrictions).

Security associations can be configured manually or automatically. Automatic configuration of security association is performed using the Security Message Exchange (SME) protocol. This protocol can be transported within signaling at SVC setup time, or within the user plane virtual circuit during SVC setup time or after the PVC has been configured (but before user traffic is allowed to pass).

4.1.1   Security Agent

The security agent is responsible for negotiating and providing Security 1.1 services. Security is provided at two distinct phases during a security association: During the establishment of a security association and during the life of the virtual circuit. Security services that are provided during the establishment of the security association are performed within the context of the SME protocol, described further in Section 4.2.1. With SME-based security services, one SA is designated the *responder*, and the other is designated the *initiator*. As their names imply, the initiator SA is responsible for starting an SME protocol exchange, while the responder SA waits for the first SME message from the initiator. The initiator/responder role of the SA is determined in two ways: automatically through observation of SVC signaling (see Sections 4.1.2.1 and 4.1.2.2), or via management for PVCs (see Section 4.1.2.2).

An SA is composed of four elements, which together implement the security services at both phases of the security association along with configuration and security association maintenance functions. These four elements and their relationships are shown in Figure 4.1.

The four elements of an SA and their interactions with other elements are as follows:

- *SA$_{service}$:* This element implements the security service that is applied to a virtual circuit during its lifetime (i.e., user plane confidentiality, user plane integrity, and control plane authentication/integrity). This element is configured by the SA$_{policy}$ and SA$_{SME}$ elements, and works closely with the SA$_{misc}$ element to maintain cryptographic state information.

- *SA$_{misc}$:* This element performs miscellaneous functions such as maintenance of the security association on the virtual circuit during data transfer. The Security 1.1 services provided by the SA$_{misc}$ element are session key update and cryptographic synchronization. This element

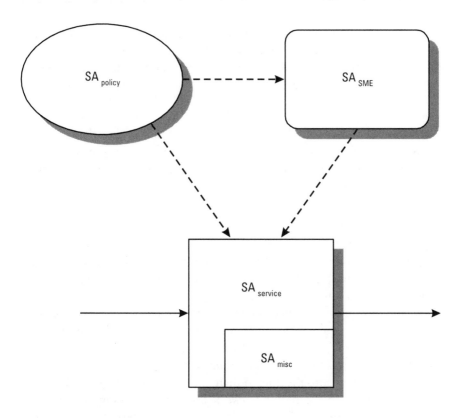

Figure 4.1 Relationship between SA elements.

works closely with the SA$_{service}$ element to obtain and transfer correct state information.

- *SA$_{SME}$:* This element implements security services during security association establishment (i.e., authentication, key exchange, certificate exchange, negotiation, and access control). This element is configured with policy information by the SA$_{policy}$ element, and it configures the SA$_{service}$ element with the results of SME negotiation (e.g., keys and algorithm parameters).

- *SA$_{policy}$:* This element determines the security services, algorithms, and algorithm parameters (e.g., key length) that the SA implements on a virtual circuit during security association establishment and during the virtual circuit lifetime. Other security-related configurations are also contained in this element, including access control lists and rekey intervals. Furthermore, this element defines the sets of services, algorithms, and algorithm parameters it requires when it processes incoming security association requests from other SAs. This element provides its policy information to the SA_{SME}, $SA_{service}$, and SA_{misc} elements.

The ATM Security 1.1 Specification does not define the interfaces between these elements, nor does it specify how these elements are implemented. Rather, these elements comprise a conceptual model for the internal structure of an SA.

4.1.1.1 Nested Security Agents

A pair of peer SAs provides each security service for an ATM virtual connection (which is either a virtual channel connection or a virtual path connection). However, multiple independent SA pairs may be active on a VC. This situation may arise when multiple security services are required simultaneously (e.g., integrity and encryption), or when the policies of two sites or transit networks require different security services to be applied to different portions of a VC. When multiple SA pairs are active on the same portion of a VC, the SA pairs must be arranged in a *nested* configuration.

For example, consider the configuration shown in Figure 4.2. Here, two sites connect to the public network through encrypting SAs, and the sites' policies require all ATM VCs that originate and terminate within the sites to be encrypted. Furthermore, site B's policy requires all signaled VCs to machines in the engineering department to be strongly authenticated by the department's ATM firewall. Therefore, when an end system at site A wishes to signal a connection to a host in site B's engineering department, the VC is encrypted over the public network and strongly authenticated between the host and the department firewall. For this connection, the encryption security association is nested within the authentication security association, and both services are provided independently.

In general, nested security associations are an example of the *security topology* for a VCC or VPP. The ATM Security 1.1 Specification requires the security topology to have no overlapping security associations. If multiple security associations are present, then they must either be disjoint (no overlap whatsoever) or contained in one another (completely overlapping). Security associations that partially overlap are not allowed (see Chapter 5). Furthermore, Security 1.1 restricts the maximum level of nesting to 16 levels for the integrity and encryption services, or 256 levels for services provided by the SME protocol (e.g., authentication and label-based access control). These

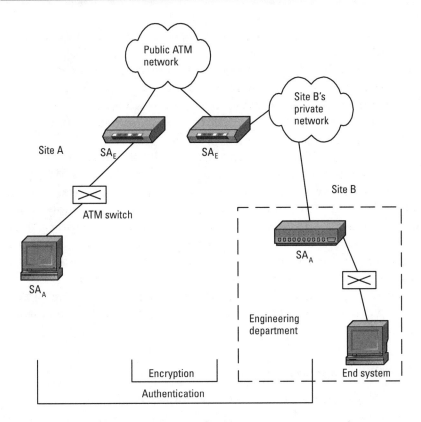

Figure 4.2   Example SA nesting scenario.

restrictions are not excessive. In practice, the number of nested encryption and integrity services will rarely exceed three—one level for end-to-end integrity, a second level for workgroup-to-workgroup encryption, and a third level for site-to-site encryption.

4.1.1.2   Endpoint Requests for Security

In the example in Figure 4.2, SA_E at site A can be configured to encrypt all traffic between site A and site B. This kind of blanket protection, however, removes flexibility from site A's end systems to choose whether their traffic is encrypted (which is not necessarily a bad thing). If this kind of flexibility is desired, one solution is to provide ATM cell encryption in all hosts in site A's network. However, Security 1.1 also allows the use of proxy security agents. This option allows an SA located somewhere in the network to provide security services on behalf of an end system, at the end system's request.

When an end system wishes to request proxy security services for a switched virtual connection, it indicates this request and specifies which services it wants in the SETUP message for the virtual circuit. When the proxy SA receives the request, it establishes a security association with the remote SA using the SME protocol and sends a confirmation back to the requesting end system. At this point, the SA performs $SA_{service}$ processing (i.e., encryption) on the ATM virtual circuit, if requested.

One caveat with the proxy architecture is that the proxy SA assumes the identity and authentication keys of the hosts for which it provides proxy security. Therefore, when a remote end system establishes a security association with a proxied end system, it thinks it is establishing a security association with the end system, when, in fact, it is associated with the proxy. In this case, the remote end system trusts that the proxy with which it is associated can accurately "vouch" for its hosts. Therefore, the portion of the network between the end system and the proxy SA must be secured via some other means (e.g., physical access protections) to prevent malicious end systems from spoofing authorized end systems and using the proxy SA to misrepresent them.

4.1.2 Security Message Transport

SAs exchange security protocol messages with each other when establishing security associations. Three methods are provided by Security 1.1 to transfer security messages: signaling-based transport, in-band transport, and signaling-based with in-band fallback. At least one of these mechanisms must be supported by compliant implementations, although there is no default method. Typically, the selection of a transport method is performed at configuration time, depending on considerations such as network support for security-augmented signaling messages. However, if the network's ability to carry security messages is not known, then the security association setup can be attempted in signaling, with fallback to the in-band method if necessary. Each of these mechanisms is described below, along with other considerations that affect the selection of a particular transport method.

4.1.2.1 Signaling-Based

When peer SAs establish a security association, signaling messages can be used to carry security-related information. This method is shown in Figure 4.3.

In this example, an end system, which is part of a *private network*, requests a switched virtual connection to another end system at a remote site,

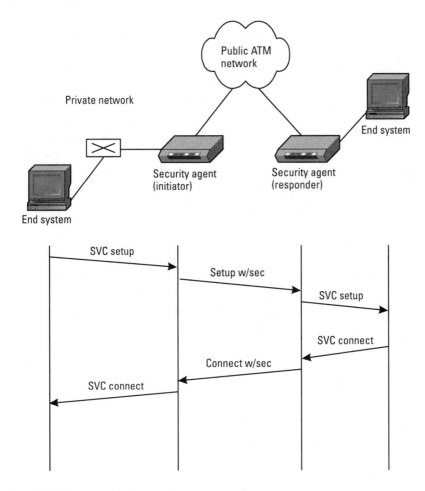

Figure 4.3 Signaling-based security message exchange.

which is connected to the same *public ATM network*. Both sites' connections to the public network pass through SAs, which implement security services such as encryption and authentication. The initiating end system sends a virtual circuit SETUP message to its private network, which is forwarded to the local SA. At this point, the SA identifies itself as the initiator (because the signaling message came in from the interface that is attached to the private network), and it augments the SVC SETUP message with an information element (IE) that contains security-related information for the remote SA. Next, the augmented SETUP message is sent to the public network, which processes the connection request.

At the remote end, the SA receives the SETUP message and identifies itself as the responder (because the signaling message came in from the interface that is attached to the public network). The SA performs responder processing on the security information contained in the IE, and if everything is acceptable, it sends the SETUP request to the destination host. If the destination host wishes to accept the connection, it sends a CONNECT message back to the network. At the responder SA, this message is augmented with another IE containing security information, and it sends the CONNECT message to the public network. At the initiator SA, the security information in the CONNECT message is processed according to the initiator procedures, and if everything is acceptable, it sends the CONNECT message to the initiating host.

When SAs are nested, the security services information element (SSIE) is extended to contain security information for each nesting level. As the signaling message passes through each SA, the SA performs its security processing, updates the SSIE, and forwards the signaling message. This preserves the two-way nature of signaling and the security message exchange, allowing security processing to be completed more quickly than with the in-band approach described in the next section.

4.1.2.2 Within User Plane Virtual Circuit

Alternatively, security association setup traffic can be carried in the user plane virtual circuit, as shown in Figure 4.4.

For SVCs using the in-band approach, the VC is signaled as before, but the messages are not augmented with security information. Rather, the SAs note their initiator/responder status as they process the SETUP message. When the CONNECT message traverses the network, it is held at the initiator, and the two SAs perform the SME protocol in the user virtual circuit that now connects them. Once this protocol completes successfully, the initiator allows the CONNECT message to proceed to the end system, and the two end systems are connected by the new (secured) virtual circuit.

The in-band protocol also supports security for PVCs. In this case, one SA is designated (via management) as the initiator and the other the responder. The responder is instructed to wait a period of time for a security message exchange request from the initiator, and the initiator is instructed to start the protocol. Before the protocol starts, and while the protocol is in progress, the initiator and responder block user traffic from passing. Once the protocol completes successfully, the SAs allow user data to pass over the secured segment.

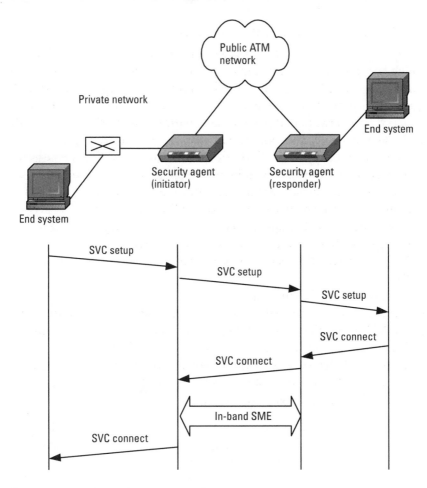

Figure 4.4 In-band security message exchange.

When SAs are nested, and the in-band protocol is used to secure SVCs, each pair of SAs performs SME when the CONNECT message reaches each initiator. When establishing each security association, the initiator must hold the CONNECT message, perform the in-band protocol with its responder (three end-to-end message flows), and release the CONNECT message toward the calling end system or to the next initiator. This multiplies the number of end-to-end message flows, which increases the amount of time required to bring up all nested security associations when compared to the signaling-based messaging mechanism described in the previous section.

4.1.2.3 Trade-Offs and Interoperability Considerations

Why are there two protocols for security message exchange? While signaling-based security message exchange is more efficient, it is not possible to perform signaling-based SME in networks that do not support the SSIE. In general, it is difficult to assume that every switch in a public network (or in a private transit network that one does not control) will support transfer of the SSIE. Unless one knows for certain that all switches that process SVC SETUP requests support the SSIE, the in-band approach should be selected. Note that if two private networks that support SSIE processing are connected across a public network using a VPC tunnel (as shown in Figure 4.8), then the two private networks are logically adjacent, and the public network does not process SVC requests between these networks. In this case, the signaling-based SSIE transport method may be selected.

Other trade-offs associated with each protocol are summarized in Table 4.1.

As shown in the table, the in-band method of security message transport is the only method that can be used with PVCs (because they are not established by signaling). In addition, the in-band protocol supports mutual authentication using the challenge-response protocol (described in Section 4.2.2.1), which removes the requirement for synchronization of the SAs' clocks. Finally, because the in-band protocol provides three end-to-end message flows, it supports negotiation of security associations.

Table 4.1
Security Message Transport Trade-Offs

	Signaling-Based	In-Band
Security Message Exchange protocol	Two-way	Three-way
Provides authentication at VC setup (ATM firewalls)	Yes	No
Efficient setup of nested security associations	Yes	No
Requires support at intermediate switches	Yes	No
Authentication requires clock synchronization	Yes	No
PVC support	No	Yes
Negotiation support	No	Yes

4.1.2.4 Signaling-Based with In-Band Fallback

If the network's ability to support SSIE transport is not known, then the in-band method may be selected by default. Alternatively, SAs may be configured to attempt SA negotiation first in signaling, and if that fails, they can try again using the in-band method. The decision to revert to in-band transport can be made by the network by dropping the SSIE, or by the responding SA by setting a flag in the SSIE.

In some cases, attempting security message transport in signaling with fallback to the in-band approach combines the advantages of both methods. For example, if the network supports SSIE transport, then authentication can accompany signaling, and negotiation of encryption algorithms can be performed during the in-band phase.

4.2 Security 1.1 Services

The ATM Security 1.1 services fall into two broad categories: those security services that are provided initially during the establishment of a security association and those that are provided during the lifetime of the virtual circuit.

Initial security services are provided in the context of the SME protocol. This protocol uses one of the security message transport mechanisms described in Section 4.1.2 to provide the following user plane security services:

- *Security declaration and negotiation:* Establishes common services and parameters for the security association;

- *Initial authentication:* Allows two SAs to prove their identities to each other;

- *Access control:* Associates a data sensitivity or release restriction label to the VC;

- *Key exchange:* Allows two SAs to agree upon shared keys for encryption or integrity services;

- *Certificate exchange:* Allows two SAs to pass their public key certificates to each other, in support of the initial authentication and key exchange functions.

In addition, Security 1.1 provides user plane security services that are used to protect data exchanged during the lifetime of the virtual connection. These services are:

- *Data origin authentication:* Allows the receiving SA to verify that the data was not modified after it left the sending SA;

- *Confidentiality:* Protects data from unauthorized disclosure.

Security 1.1 also provides control plane security; however, the control plane security portion of the specification is limited to data origin authentication/integrity on a hop-by-hop basis using preplaced keys. Nevertheless, since signaling uses ATM VC for message transfer, user plane security mechanisms such as encryption may be used to provide additional security for control plane messages.

The confidentiality and data origin authentication services use master keys (i.e., key encryption keys) and initial session keys (i.e., traffic encryption keys) that are exchanged during the establishment of the security association. For bidirectional VCs, separate session keys are used in each direction and a single master key is shared between both SAs. This master key is used to encrypt new session keys when they need to be changed. This session key update process is performed independently in both directions, and at a rate determined by site policy.

4.2.1 Security Message Exchange

The SME protocol is the fundamental mechanism of Security 1.1. In fact, because it is responsible for establishing security associations, implementations that claim compliance to the Security 1.1 Specification must implement some form of SME. The procedure for establishing a security association involves two processes: identifying the desired SA that is to respond to a security association request and declaring or negotiating the desired security services, algorithms, and parameters to or with the peer SA.

Two variants of the SME protocol are defined in the Security 1.1 Specification: the *two-way* and *three-way* SME protocols. The choice of SME variation is determined by the transport mechanism that is selected (see Section 4.1.2). If SME services are to be provided within SVC signaling, then the two-way protocol is used, as signaling itself only provides two end-to-end message flows. However, if SME services are provided in the user plane VC (before user data is transferred), then the three-way protocol is used. The trade-offs associated with using either of these protocols are described in Section 4.1.2.3.

Additional technical details regarding the SME protocol, addressing, and declaration/negotiation are provided in Chapter 5.

4.2.1.1 Security Agent Addressing

In the SME FLOW-1 message, the initiating SA must identify the SA with which it would like to establish a security association. Two addressing mechanisms are provided for this purpose. The first addressing mechanism, *explicit addressing*, uses a globally unique identifier for the targeted responding SA. The second mechanism, *implicit addressing* (the Security 1.1 Specification uses the term "non-explicit addressing") identifies a responding SA by the network in which it resides and its location within the network. Both methods assume that the ATM network topology is designed such that the VC will be routed to the explicitly addressed or implicitly addressed SA.

Explicit Addressing

Explicit SA addresses are globally unique identifiers that must be known a priori by the initiating SA. These addresses can be configured into the initiator or be provided by a directory service (which is outside the scope of the Security 1.1 Specification). These identifiers take one of two formats: an ATM end system address (AESA) or an X.509 distinguished name.

The AESA (also known as the NSAP address) is the most straightforward addressing mechanism, as the SA (as an ATM entity) will likely be assigned an ATM address already. The advantage of using the SA's AESA is that it is an inherently unique identifier that does not need to be managed separately. This uniqueness is guaranteed by the fact that the ATM address contains a network prefix and a globally unique end system identifier (as described in Chapter 2). Furthermore, the use of the network prefix in the SA identifier allows the future possibility of SVC routing based on the identifiers of the SAs that must operate on the VC (as described in Chapter 11). The disadvantage of coupling the SA ID to its AESA is that the SA's network prefix, and hence its SA ID, may change if the SA is relocated.

Another approach to explicit addressing is to use the SA's X.509 distinguished name (which is uniquely assigned by the owning organization and derived from the organization's distinguished name) as the SA ID. As with the AESA, the SA is likely to be assigned an X.509 distinguished name. This is particularly true if the SA has been provided with a public key certificate. The advantage of using an SA's X.509 distinguished name is that the SA ID is not as likely to change if it is moved to another location in the network.

However, the X.509 is another identifier that must be assigned to the SA, and it is managed separately from the SA's ATM address.

Implicit Addressing

The problem with explicit addressing is that it requires the initiator to know the AESA or X.509 distinguished name of the responder. One way around this is to use a directory service to resolve a called party's address to an SA identifier. However, this method becomes difficult if more than one SA fronts an end system (e.g., nested SAs).

Implicit addressing allows an initiator to specify a responder according to the network in which the responder is located, and its location within that network. When taken together, these two attributes (the *region* and *role*, respectively) are called the *scope* of the responding SA. The possible region and roles are shown in Figure 4.5.

The region portion of the SA scope defines the network in which the responder resides, relative to the initiator's network. Therefore, from the figure, SA_6 is considered "remote" if SA_1 is the initiator. This determination is made by comparing the network prefix of the calling and called party addresses against the network prefix for the SA. If the SA prefix matches the calling party's prefix, then the SA is "local." If the SA prefix matches the called party's prefix, then the SA is "remote." If the SA prefix does not match either the calling or called party prefixes, then the SA is "transit." Since the length of the network prefix is variable, the prefix length that the SA must use in this comparison is a configurable parameter.

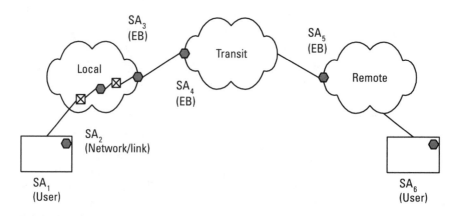

Figure 4.5 Region and role positions for SAs.

Although the region portion of the scope is determined automatically, the role portion must be configured in the SA when it is installed. The role of the SA is configured according to its function, which in turn is usually determined by its placement in the local, remote, or transit network. An SA is configured as a "user" SA if it resides in an end system (e.g., a host or an IP router), or acts as a proxy for an end system (see Section 4.1.1.2). If the SA resides on the physical link between two organizations' networks (e.g., between an enterprise and its ATM service provider, or ASP), then it is configured as an "enterprise border" SA. Finally, if the SA resides between two ATM switches in the same network (e.g., a workgroup encryptor), then it is configured as a "network/link" SA.

Table 4.2 shows the scope assignments for the SAs shown in Figure 4.5.

The initiator uses implicit addressing (the scope field) to identify its intended responder when it does not know the responder's explicit identifier. The initiator specifies a responder by setting the appropriate region bits (local, remote, and/or transit) and role bits (user, enterprise border, and/or network/link). More than 1 bit may be set in the region and role fields if the initiator allows SAs in different regions and roles to respond. For example, if

Table 4.2
Scope Assignments for Security Agents in Figure 4.5

Security Agent	Scope		Function
	Region	Role	
SA_1	Local	User	Security services for local end system
SA_2	Local	Network/link	Security services for workgroup at local site
SA_3	Local	Enterprise border	Security services for local site
SA_4	Transit	Enterprise border	ASP-provided security services and/or security services for ASP
SA_5	Remote	Enterprise border	Security services for remote site
SA_6	Remote	User	Security services for remote end system

SA₁ wants an encrypted virtual connection to the remote end system's SA (SA$_6$) or its enterprise border SA (SA$_5$), then it specifies "remote" for the region, and it specifies "user" and "EB" for the role. If the initiator does not care about the region and/or role of the responder, then it codes the appropriate fields to 0.

An SA reacts to an implicit specification by performing a region test and a role test, and if both tests return true, then the SA is the responder. The SA performs the region test by comparing its network prefix to the prefixes in the calling and called party IEs using a configured prefix length, as described earlier. The location of the SA as determined by this procedure is compared with the location specified in the region field, and if there is a match, then the region test returns true. The SA performs the role test by comparing its configured role against the role specification provided by the initiator, and if there is a match, then the role test returns true. If the initiator coded the region and/or role field to 0, then that test automatically returns true without further processing.

4.2.1.2 Declaration and Negotiation of Security Attributes

The SME protocol allows the parameters of a security association to be declared or negotiated by the participating SAs. These parameters are the security services, algorithms (or transforms), and algorithm parameters. Without declaration or negotiation, SAs would need to be manually configured with these attributes, and these attributes must match those used by all SAs with which it must communicate. This would quickly become unmanageable for large networks!

Declaration allows an initiator to define which services, algorithms, and parameters are to be used in the security association. During SME, the responder looks at the initiator's declaration, and if it finds the declaration acceptable, it accepts the security association. Otherwise, it rejects the security association (and the call, if the security association is being established for a switched virtual connection). Although declaration is essentially a "take it or leave it" process, it improves the security management problem described earlier because it does not require the responder to know the initiator's security attributes a priori—It simply takes the attributes provided by the initiator.

Negotiation improves upon the all-or-nothing approach of declaration by allowing the initiator to propose a list of security attributes (e.g., DES and triple DES encryption) to the responder rather than a single specification of security attributes. The responder must then select from this list the attributes according to its local policy (e.g., triple DES) for the security association. Negotiation significantly improves the chances for successful establishment of security associations because it provides more choices for the responder. Negotiation also simplifies the management and configuration of SAs because SAs only need to know their capabilities and the policy by which they will accept security attributes and security associations.

Policy configuration plays an important role in accepting declared or negotiated security associations. The policy configurations for SAs are implementation-specific but can include the following:

- Peer SA identifier;
- Calling/called party addresses;
- Security services declared or proposed;
- Algorithms declared or proposed;
- Parameters declared or proposed (e.g., key lengths);
- Sensitivity labels.

The definition of an SA policy is based on the site's up-front security analysis as described in Chapter 1, which takes into account the assets to be protected, the potential threats, and the goals of the organization.

The use of declaration or negotiation is determined by the type of SME protocol to be used. If the two-way SME protocol is used, then declaration must be used to select security attributes. However, if three-way SME is used, then security attributes can be negotiated. Negotiation is not supported in the two-way SME protocol because the services, algorithms, and parameters must be known in order to generate authentication signatures and key exchange information in the first SME flow.

4.2.2 User Plane Security Services

User plane security services are those services that are provided for VCs that typically carry traffic between ATM end systems. These services are applied at different times in the life of the VC. Initial authentication and access control services are provided during the establishment of a security association, and allow the participating SAs to determine if the connection should be allowed under policy. The data origin authentication and confidentiality services, on the other hand, protect user plane traffic between two SAs after the security association has been established.

4.2.2.1　Initial Authentication

Initial authentication is the security service that allows an SA to prove its identity to another SA. Initial authentication is important because it is a basic security service upon which other security services rely. Access control often relies on strong authentication to prevent a malicious party from spoofing a legitimate party's identity to gain access. Similarly, authentication is required to establish an encrypted VC and exchange keys. Otherwise, a malicious party (e.g., a man in the middle) could spoof another SA and obtain keys to encrypted data.

Authentication can be unilateral (where one SA proves its identity to another) or mutual (where both SAs prove their identities to each other). The "proof of identity" is actually a proof that the SA possesses a secret key that only it knows, or that it shares with the SA to which it is authenticating. This secret is used in the computation of a digital signature over a set of authentication tokens. When asymmetric (public key) signature algorithms such as RSA [4] and DSA [5] are used, the digital signature is generated using the signer's private key and validated using the signer's public key. When symmetric (secret key) digital signature algorithms (or more precisely, message authentication codes) such as HMAC SHA-1 [6] and DES/CBC MAC [7] are used, the digital signature is generated and validated using the same secret key that is shared between the two parties.

The authentication procedure is implemented within the SME protocol and can be used with the two-way and the three-way variants. Each of these protocols uses information fields (tokens) to ensure that the authentication protocol flows are unique and that they occur in sequence.

In the three-way protocol, authentication is achieved by the exchange of challenges and responses in three flows. When mutual authentication is performed, the initiator provides a random number challenge in the first flow for the responder. The responder signs the initiator's challenge for its response, and provides another challenge of its own in the second flow. Upon receiving this flow, the initiator checks the response, signs the responder's challenge, and sends its signed response in the third flow, which is checked by the responder. Once unilateral authentication is performed, then one party provides the challenge and the other party provides the response. By using a challenge/response protocol, each flow is guaranteed to be unique and in sequence.

In the two-way SME protocol, authentication is achieved through the use of timestamps and challenge/response tokens in two flows between the SAs. When mutual authentication is performed, the initiator provides a challenge for the responder along with a timestamp and a digital signature of the timestamp in the first flow. The responder checks the timestamp to ensure that it is unique and that its value is within a synchronization window W of the time it was received. If so, the responder signs the challenge and sends its response in the second flow. Upon receiving this flow, the initiator checks the challenge and signature for correctness. If unilateral authentication is performed, then the initiator signs the timestamp, or the responder signs the challenge.

Authentication using the two-way SME protocol uses timestamps and challenge/response tokens to provide uniqueness and sequencing of authentication flows. In addition, the timestamp verifies the freshness of the first flow from the initiator. That is, it guarantees that the message was not generated outside a time window W. This protocol, however, requires that the SAs to be synchronized within the window W and that they use a common coordinated time (Greenwich mean time is specified in Security 1.1). Therefore, in situations where synchronization is a problem, authentication using the three-way SME protocol is preferred. However, if authentication must accompany ATM VC signaling (e.g., an ATM firewall), then the two-way protocol must be used, and measures must be taken to ensure synchronization between the two SAs (e.g., using the Network Time Protocol [8]).

Additional technical details regarding the initial authentication service are provided in Chapter 6.

4.2.2.2 Access Control

Access control is the service that restricts the establishment of virtual connections and/or security associations according to the sensitivity or release restrictions associated with the data that is to be transferred on the VC. The VC requestor specifies the data sensitivity or release restriction using a special security label according to the FIPS-188 format [9].

Security label information allows an SA to determine if a VC with the indicated sensitivity can be accepted. Sensitivity labels have two components: a hierarchical component (e.g., public, proprietary, and strategic) and a compartment (e.g., technical data, human resources, etc.) that is associated with each hierarchical level, as shown in Figure 4.6. An SA accepts a labeled connection if the hierarchical level of the data falls in the range allowed by the SA, and the compartment specification for the VC is a subset of the set of compartments allowed by the SA.

For example, consider an SA that is configured (and trusted) to accept connections with a compartment specification of "technical data" and "marketing," and hierarchical level between "public" and "proprietary," inclusive.

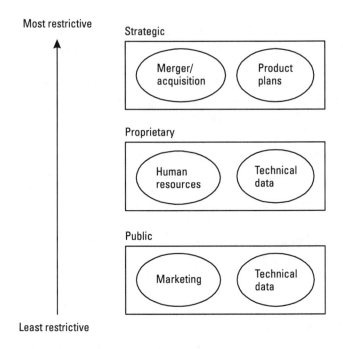

Figure 4.6 Example of information sensitivity labels.

In this case, the SA would accept connections that specify "public marketing," "public technical data," and "proprietary technical data." However, this SA would not accept connections that specify "proprietary human resources" nor any "strategic" information.

SAs that provide label-based access control must be configured with the types of labeled security associations that it will accept and the sensitivity of the information on the private network to which it is connected. For example, if an SA is connected to a "proprietary, human resources" network, then it must label all outgoing connection requests from this network as such, and it must only accept incoming connections with labels that have hierarchical and compartment components that include "proprietary, human resources."

Additional details regarding the access control service are provided in Chapter 9.

4.2.2.3 Data Origin Authentication (Integrity)

Data origin authentication (also known as "data integrity" in the Security 1.1 Specification) is the security service that allows a data recipient to verify that the data has been generated by a host with which it shares a secret key, and that the data has not been modified in transit. Data origin authentication complements initial authentication in that it protects an initially authenticated connection from connection takeover by a third party after the connection has been established.

The integrity service is provided through the use of message authentication codes, which are computed across an AAL 3/4 or AAL 5 service data unit (SDU), appended to the SDU, and transmitted on the user plane virtual circuit. At the receiving end, the MAC is calculated over the SDU and compared to the MAC that accompanied it. If the MACs match, then the SDU is accepted.

These MACs use secret keys that are shared by the message source and destination. These keys are exchanged manually, or by using the initial key exchange service, and they can be periodically updated using the session key update mechanism (see Section 4.2.2.5). By using keyed MACs, protection from malicious modification attacks is provided.

The Security 1.1 Specification provides two forms of integrity protection: one with replay/reordering protection and one without. Replay/reordering protection works by appending a sequence number to the AAL SDU before calculating the MAC over the combination of the SDU data and sequence number. On the receiving side, the SA checks the MAC to verify that the SDU/sequence number combination was not modified, and it checks the sequence number to verify that it is greater than the sequence number of the previously received SDU. (Note that the sequence number check does not necessarily detect dropped SDUs. Detection of dropped SDUs is a function of the higher-layer protocol.) If the MAC and sequence number checks both pass, then the SDU is accepted.

Why not use replay/reordering protection all the time? In most cases, this mode should be selected. However, the sequence number used by replay/reordering protection adds some overhead to the message (in addition to the MAC), which may be unacceptable in low bandwidth situations or for VCs with tight traffic contracts. In addition, sequence numbers on replay-protected VCs may be unnecessary when the AAL traffic already contains higher-layer mechanisms for handling duplicated/reordered traffic (e.g., TCP). Finally, replay protection adds cost to implementations due to the extra memory required to hold the additional per-VC state required by sequence numbers.

When configuring SA policy regarding integrity protections, the administrator must select which algorithm will be used to generate the MAC, and whether replay/reordering protection is used. Replay protection may require consideration of the higher-layer protocol or application that will use the integrity-protected virtual circuit. In addition, the frequency at which integrity keys are to be changed must also be configured.

The data origin authentication/integrity service is described in more detail in Chapter 7.

4.2.2.4 Confidentiality

As with the integrity service, the confidentiality service is performed directly on the user data after SME. However, this service operates on ATM cells rather than AAL SDUs. Specifically, the ATM cell payloads are encrypted, but not the headers (otherwise, intermediate switches, which may not be trusted, would have to decrypt the cell to figure out how it should be switched). By encrypting ATM cells rather than AAL SDUs, the encryption device can be placed anywhere in the ATM network (e.g., at the enterprise border) to bulk-encrypt traffic for a large number of users.

Confidentiality is provided using symmetric (secret key) encryption algorithms and secret keys that are shared between the peer SAs. Although asymmetric (public key) encryption algorithms could also be used for this service, they are not specified in Security 1.1 because they are much slower than the symmetric encryption algorithms. The encrypting SAs that provide the confidentiality service use the initial key exchange protocol described in Section 4.2.2.5 to determine two keys: the initial traffic encryption key and the key encryption key, which is used to periodically rekey the encryptors, as described in Section 4.2.2.5.

As with the integrity service, the confidentiality service is performed on a per-VC basis. This allows different keys to be applied to separate VCs. This concept, known as *key agility*, is shown in Figure 4.7.

In this example, the virtual circuit from A to B is encrypted by $SA_{E,1}$ using key K_1; and the VC from C to D is encrypted by $SA_{E,1}$ using key K_2. When a cell arrives at $SA_{E,1}$, $SA_{E,1}$ uses the VPI/VCI in the cell header to look up the proper key and other encryption context information for the VC (e.g., the previous ciphertext block if CBC mode is used) before encrypting the cell payload. Although key agility requires the encryptor to maintain additional state per VC (which adds cost), the alternative would be to use one key at $SA_{E,1}$ for all VCs and share that key with all SAs that it might connect with it. This would open the possibility for D to snoop traffic from A to B that is intended to be confidential.

The confidentiality service can selectively apply encryption to VCCs or VPCs. VPC encryption is particularly useful for creating a virtual private ATM network between multiple sites using a VPC mesh, as shown in Figure 4.8. In this example, each site's switch terminates a VPC tunnel to two other

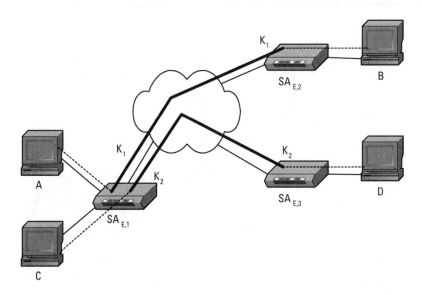

Figure 4.7 Key-agile ATM encryption.

sites in the virtual private ATM network, and each direction is encrypted with a separate key.

As stated before, the confidentiality service encrypts cell payloads on the user VCC or VPC. However, not all cell payloads for a given VCC/VPC are encrypted. OAM cells, for example, may be bypassed through the encryptor to allow switches in the open network to send OAM information (e.g., alarm indications) to other switches that process the VC, including those in the protected networks. Likewise, rate management cells, which carry congestion and flow control information, may also be bypassed.

Encryptors are not only configured with an encryption algorithm, but also with an encryption mode of operation. The three modes of operation that are allowed by the Security 1.1 Specification are the electronic codebook (ECB), cipher block chaining (CBC), and the counter mode. Each mode of operation (which is described in more detail in Chapter 8) has its trade-offs, which are summarized in Table 4.3.

Additional details regarding ATM encryption are found in Chapter 8.

4.2.2.5 Support Services for Key Management

All of the user plane security services can be configured manually; however, this would not be very useful, manageable, or scalable. For example, as the number of ATM encryptors increases, the number of keys that must be

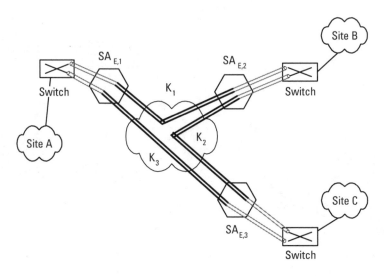

Figure 4.8 Encryption of VPC mesh.

distributed increases on the order of n^2, so that in a fully connected network of 20 encryptors, a total of $20 \times 19 = 380$ unidirectional keys must be loaded. Therefore, supporting protocols are required to facilitate automated establishment and maintenance of security associations.

First, initial key exchange and rekeying mechanisms are required to establish and maintain secret keys for the integrity and confidentiality services. The initial key exchange mechanism defined in Security 1.1 exchanges two keys during SME: a master key (key encryption key) and an initial session key (traffic encryption or authentication key). Security 1.1 also provides a session key update mechanism for periodically changing keys, which increases the level of security on the encrypted VC.

Table 4.3
Trade-Offs with Encryption Modes

Mode	Property		
	Self-Synchronizing	Scalable	Dictionary Lookup Protection
ECB	Yes	Yes	No
CBC	Yes	No	Yes
Counter mode	No	Yes	Yes

To allow SME authentication using public key algorithms, both parties must have access to each other's public keys. To prevent a malicious party from misrepresenting his public key as the public key of an authorized party, public keys are typically distributed in certificates that are signed by a trusted authority.

Initial Key Exchange

Initial key exchange is performed in the context of SME. This process determines two key values: a master key and an initial session key. The initial session key is used for traffic encryption or MAC generation, and the master key is used with the session key update service for encryption of subsequent session keys.

The details for exchanging keys vary according to the algorithms that are used. However, in all point-to-point VCs, the master key is a shared bidirectional key that is determined by contributions by both SAs, and the initial session keys are unidirectional keys selected at random by both SAs. For Pt-Mpt VCs, when leaves are added to the VC, the leaf SA is provided with the master key and initial session key and does not contribute to the development of either key.

Session Key Update

Session key update (SKU) is the service that allows confidentiality or integrity session keys to be changed while the service is being provided. This increases the strength of the service because it reduces the amount of ciphertext or the number of MACs produced under a given session key. This reduces the probability of a successful brute-force attack.

For bidirectional virtual connections, SKU is performed independently in each direction. Each SKU is performed in two phases: a session key exchange (SKE) phase, followed by a session key changeover (SKC). The SKE phase is responsible for encrypting the new session key with the master key that was exchanged during initial key exchange (described earlier). The new (encrypted) session key is transmitted to the peer SA, where it is decrypted and stored for later activation. This key is not activated immediately because the delay in decrypting this key may cause subsequent cells to be decrypted with the wrong session key. Rather, it is held for the session key changeover phase.

After sufficient time has passed, the upstream SA notifies the downstream SA in the SKC phase that it intends to encrypt the next ATM cell with the new key from the SKE phase. Upon receiving this notification, the downstream SA immediately loads the new key and uses it for decrypting future data on the VC.

Two aspects of SKU must be configured by the administrator: the selection of time-based versus volume-based update and the selection of the update interval. Time-based update implies that the SKU interval is based on the elapsed time from the previous update (or the beginning of the security association). Alternatively, a volume-based update policy can also be selected; in which case, SKU is triggered after a certain amount of data has been processed. Separate policies may be selected for each direction in a bidirectional VC. In both cases, the refresh interval (in terms of time or amount of data) must be determined. Smaller intervals provide more security, but result in more overhead due to increased SKU frequency.

Certificate Infrastructure

When public key algorithms are used for authentication and key exchange, each SA must obtain the other SA's public key. This key may be locally stored, provided by the peer SA, or obtained from a public key directory server. In any case, the binding between the SA's name and its public key must not be compromised. Otherwise, a malicious SA could develop its own public/private key pair and provide a false public key/name binding to impersonate another SA.

This concern is addressed through the use of public key certificates. These certificates contain the identifier and public key of the SA, and are signed by a certificate authority (CA) that can vouch for the public key/name binding. If both SAs trust the same CA, then all is well. Otherwise, as shown in Figure 4.9, SAs must obtain certificates for the CAs, and repeat until a common *root* CA (or a common pair of CAs that trust each other) is reached. That is, they must traverse the certification hierarchy to a common point of trust. The collection of certificates is called a certificate chain.

In this example, SA_2 obtains the certificates of $CA_{1,0}$, $CA_{1,1}$, and SA_1. Since it has the public key of the root CA, it uses this key to validate $CA_{1,0}$'s certificate. Using $CA_{1,0}$'s public key, it can validate $CA_{1,1}$'s certificate. Finally, using $CA_{1,1}$'s public key, it can validate SA_1's certificate, and hence, its public key.

As stated earlier, certificates and certificate chains can be provided via configuration, certificate exchange, or directory services. The Security 1.1 Specification allows certificates and certificate chains to be exchanged during SME. However, if SME is performed in signaling, certificate exchange is limited to X.509 Version 1.0 certificates only, and the length of the certificate chain is severely limited. These restrictions, however, do not apply for in-band SME.

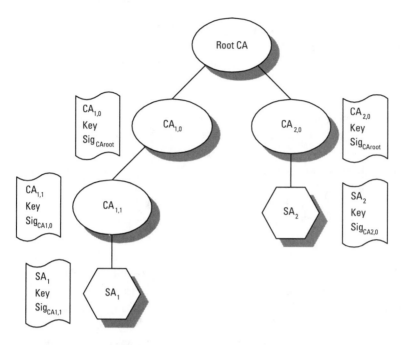

Figure 4.9 Certification hierarchy.

When SAs support public key certificates, they must be configured to exchange certificates and, depending on the SME transport method, the certificate chains. SAs may be configured with the public key certificates of all its CAs up to and including the root CA, or they may be configured with the address of a directory server, for vendor implementations that allow SAs to look up certificates from a directory server.

4.2.3   Control Plane Security Services

ATM uses its control plane protocols (e.g., UNI and PNNI signaling) to establish SVCs and perform other network control functions. Since these signaling protocols affect the state of ATM network elements, the introduction of malicious signaling entities could impair network availability. The Security 1.1 Specification addresses this issue by providing a control plane authentication/integrity service, which allows a switch that receives control plane messages to authenticate the source of the message.

One may also determine a need to maintain confidentiality of control plane messages. Although ATM Security 1.1 does not explicitly provide such a service, it can be provided through the use of the user plane confidentiality service on the control plane VC.

4.2.3.1 Control Plane Authentication

Control plane authentication allows a switch to verify that the contents of a received signaling message were generated by a (presumably trusted) switch or endpoint with which it shares a secret key, and that the contents were not modified in transit. This service uses the user plane integrity mechanism described in Section 4.2.2.3. Specifically, the control plane authentication mechanism uses the data integrity service with replay/reordering protection to calculate the message authentication code over the signaling AAL message.

The Security 1.1 control plane authentication mechanism works on a hop-by-hop basis. That is, signaling messages are integrity-protected between two logically adjacent devices (e.g., switches that signal each other over a physical link or a virtual path connection). End-to-end control plane authentication is not provided in this version of the specification because intermediate switches may modify some of the information elements within the signaling messages, thereby corrupting the digital signature. Future versions may provide end-to-end protection of signaling messages by authenticating certain invariant fields contained in the signaling message.

Control plane authentication is configured manually. Therefore, all of the standard security association attributes (i.e., algorithms, algorithm parameters, and keys) must be manually configured in the switches before using control plane authentication. Automatic SKU, however, using pre-placed master keys, can still be used with the control plane authentication service. The requirement for manual configuration will change in future addenda to Security 1.1, as described in Chapter 10.

4.2.3.2 Implementing Control Plane Confidentiality via User Plane Security Services

Control plane authentication addresses some of the more serious threats to the ATM control plane (i.e., threats of malicious injection or modification of signaling messages into an ATM network). Other security considerations, however, may also require that these messages be encrypted. For example, traffic flow security requirements may dictate that the source and destination addresses, along with traffic contract information, be suppressed from the view of someone who may be examining signaling traffic.

Although Security 1.1 does not provide explicit mechanisms for encrypting control plane traffic, the user plane confidentiality mechanisms may be used for this purpose. That is, since control plane traffic is transferred over VCCs and VPCs, standard VCC and VPC encryption techniques can be applied to control plane virtual circuits. For example, standard UNI signaling over a link on VPI = 0, VCI = 5 can be encrypted using VCC encryption modules on each signaling entity. Likewise, VPC encryption can be used to encrypt signaling and user data traffic over a VPC tunnel as shown in Figure 4.8.

As with the control plane authentication mechanism, control plane confidentiality is performed on a hop-by-hop basis between logically adjacent ATM signaling entities. Also, the use of SME for encrypted control plane connections is limited to in-band SME only (since signaling-based SME would not work if the signaling channel is not up yet). Naturally, a manually configured preplaced security association containing algorithm and key information may also be established.

4.3 Summary

This chapter describes how to implement ATM security protections using the mechanisms provided by the ATM Forum's ATM Security Specification Version 1.1. The key component of the Security 1.1 model is the security agent, which is responsible for negotiating and implementing security services. The model also provides three methods of transporting security messages and allows a security administrator to select a transport method based on the required security functions and the ability of the network to transfer security messages within SVC signaling.

This chapter also describes the security services provided by the Security 1.1 Specification, including the initial security services performed during security association establishment and the security services performed during data transfer. Configuration considerations such as SA addressing and policy configurations are described along with configuration guidelines for specific security services.

References

[1]   Freier, A. O., P. Karlton, and P. C. Kocher, "The SSL Protocol Version 3.0," available at http://www.netscape.com/eng/ssl3/, November 1996.

[2]   Ramsdell, B., "S/MIME Version 3 Message Specification," Internet Engineering Task Force RFC 2633, June 1999.

[3]   Pierson, L.G., et al., "Context-Agile Encryption for High Speed Communication Networks," *ACM Computer Communication Review*, Vol. 29, No. 1, 1999, pp. 35–49.

[4]   Kaliski, B., and J. Staddon, "PKCS #1: RSA Cryptography Specifications Version 2.0," Internet Engineering Task Force RFC 2437, October 1998.

[5]   U.S. Department of Commerce National Institute of Standards and Technology, "Digital Signature Standard," Federal Information Processing Standards Publication 186-1, December 1998.

[6]   Krawczyk, H., M. Bellare, and R. Canetti, "HMAC: Keyed-Hashing for Message Authentication," Internet Engineering Task Force RFC 2104, February 1997.

[7]   International Standards Organization, "Information Technology—Security Techniques—Data Integrity Mechanism Using a Cryptographic Check Function Employing a Block Cipher Algorithm," ISO/IEC 9797, 1994.

[8]   Mills, D. L., "Network Time Protocol (Version 3) Specification, Implementation, and Analysis," Internet Engineering Task Force RFC 1305, March 1992.

[9]   U.S. Department of Commerce National Institute of Standards and Technology, "Standard Security Label for Information Transfer," Federal Information Processing Standards Publication 188, September 1994.

Part III:
Implementing ATM Security

5

SME Protocol

SME is the fundamental mechanism of the ATM Security Specification Version 1.1 [1] that must be implemented in compliant security agents. SME allows security agents to establish a security association and to carry out security functions that are performed at the beginning of a security association. The security functions that are performed by SME include authentication, key exchange, certificate exchange, access control, and negotiation of security services, algorithms, and parameters.

The SME protocol uses the SSIE to transfer information required by these security functions. The SSIE contains one or more security association sections (SASs), which are used to carry security information for each security association. Within each SAS, type-length-value (TLV)-encoded fields contain specific information for each of the services provided by SME.

The structure of the SSIE (using SASs and TLVs within each SAS) provides an extremely flexible foundation for negotiation of security associations and identification of peer security agents. Services can be selectively specified to varying levels of detail, and a variety of security topologies are supported, including nested security associations, and proxy security services. Nested security associations allow simultaneous application of security services between different pairs of security agents. Proxy security associations are those requested by end systems that do not implement ATM security services but would like to have them provided by the network.

SME is also flexible in its transport method and the number of flows required. SME messages can be carried within ATM signaling flows (i.e., control plane) or in-band within the user virtual connection (switched or permanent). SME uses two or three flows to complete the protocol, depending on the security requirements, site policies, and other network design considerations. Finally, SME can be applied to PVCs or SVCs, in point-to-point or point-to-multipoint connections.

Label-based access control is also performed within SME, but since it is a unidirectional protocol (as described in Chapter 9), it is logically separate from the two-way and three-way SME protocols.

5.1   SME Fundamentals

The fundamental design of SME is based on ISO/IEC 9594-8 [2], which describes authentication using public-key algorithms, and ISO/IEC 11770-2 [3], which describes authentication using secret-key algorithms. These protocols use information fields (tokens) that convey additional information such as authentication parameters, certificates, keys, etc. Two SME protocols are defined in Security 1.1: *two-way SME* and *three-way SME*. Each of these protocols has advantages and disadvantages. For this reason, both protocols are specified, providing maximum flexibility.

5.1.1   Two-Way Message Exchange

The two-way message exchange protocol is specified in Security 1.1 to allow SME to occur simultaneously with virtual circuit signaling, which uses two end-to-end message flows to establish switched virtual connections.

The two-way SME protocol, shown in Figure 5.1, works as follows:

1. The initiator sends a FLOW-1 message containing the following information:

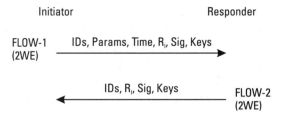

Figure 5.1 Two-way security message exchange protocol.

- *IDs:* Unique identifiers for both the initiator and responder that are assigned by the site that is responsible for the SA (required);
- *Params:* A specification of the security services and options for the requested security association (required);
- *Time, R_I, and Sig:* A timestamp for the flow (GMT), a random number challenge for the responder, and a signature (optional, used with the authentication service);
- *Keys:* Encrypted keying information (optional, used with the key exchange service).

2. The responder checks the information in the FLOW-1 message. If the message is acceptable, it sends a FLOW-2 message to the initiator that contains the following information:

- *IDs:* Identifiers for both the initiator and responder (required);
- *R_I and Sig:* The random number challenge sent in FLOW-1 along with a digital signature (optional, used with the authentication service);
- *Keys:* Encrypted keying information (optional, used with the key exchange service).

3. The initiator checks the information in the FLOW-2 message. If the message is acceptable, it accepts the connection. Otherwise, it rejects the call (see Section 5.3.1).

The advantage of the two-way SME protocol is that it occurs simultaneously with virtual circuit establishment. That is, the signaling message for the switched connection contains security information for authentication and/or access control. This allows a site to enforce access policies at a border security agent to restrict access to those who are allowed to signal into the network and connect to internal resources.

The two-way protocol is also used to add leaves to a Pt-Mpt connection. SME for multipoint connections is described in Section 5.3.3.

One disadvantage of the two-way protocol is that it requires the two participating security agents to maintain a certain degree of clock synchronization. This requirement derives from the fact that the two-way SME protocol uses timestamps and sequence numbers to guarantee that no two flows are exactly alike (otherwise, a malicious party can capture the flow and replay it to impersonate a legitimate party). The receiver must verify the received timestamp is unique; therefore, it must save the last timestamp it received from the sender. However, saving these timestamps indefinitely places unnecessary storage requirements on the receivers. Therefore, a timeout value W is specified to allow a receiver to age-out its last received timestamps. If a security agent receives a message from another SA for which it does not have a recent timestamp value in memory, then the timestamp in the received message must be within W seconds of the receiver's current time. Again, this prevents other parties from replaying messages that are more than W seconds old. This process implies that the sender and receiver's clocks must be synchronized within W seconds of each other. Larger values of W imply larger storage requirements and looser synchronization requirements, whereas smaller values imply the opposite. The authentication process within the two-way SME protocol is described in detail in Chapter 6.

The two-way protocol does not support negotiation. However, security parameters for a connection may be declared by the initiator and either accepted or rejected by the responder. If rejected, then the responder will reject the connection.

Another drawback of the two-way protocol is that it places additional processing burden on the signaling channel. Security information elements (described later) can be quite large, and since signaling exchanges are not typically included in billing of a VCC, they represent *unbillable bandwidth* for the service provider.

5.1.2 Three-Way Message Exchange

The three-way protocol is provided to remove some of the drawbacks of the two-way protocol. In theory, if ATM signaling provided three or more end-to-end flows, then this protocol could operate in the context of UNI, PNNI, and AINI signaling flows. However, in the current signaling specifications, this is not the case. Therefore, the three-way SME protocol operates in the established user virtual circuit.

The three-way SME protocol, shown in Figure 5.2, works as follows:

1. The initiator sends a FLOW-1 message containing the following information:

   - *IDs:* The initiator's identifier (required), and the responder's identifier (optional);

   - *R_I:* A random number challenge for the responder (required, in case responder wants to perform authentication);

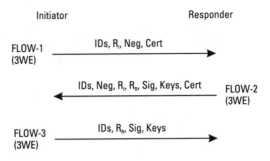

Figure 5.2 Three-way SME protocol.

- *Neg:* A specification of the requested security services and options for the requested security association (required, for negotiation);
- *Cert:* Certificate information (optional, used with certificate exchange service).

2. The responder checks the information in the FLOW-1 message. If the message is acceptable, it sends a FLOW-2 message to the initiator that contains the following information:

- *IDs:* Identifiers for both the initiator and responder (required);
- *Neg:* A specification of the selected security services and options for the security association (required, for negotiation);
- *R_I, R_R, and Sig:* The random number challenge sent in FLOW-1, another random number challenge for the initiator, and a digital signature (optional, used with the authentication service);
- *Keys:* Encrypted keying information (optional, used with the key exchange service);
- *Cert:* Certificate information (optional, used with certificate exchange service).

3. The initiator checks the information in the FLOW-2 message. If the message is acceptable, it sends a FLOW-3 message to the responder that contains the following information:

- *IDs:* Identifiers for both the initiator and responder (required);
- *R_R and Sig:* The random number challenge sent in FLOW-2 and a digital signature (optional, used with the authentication service);
- *Keys:* Encrypted keying information (optional, used with the key exchange service).

4. The responder checks the information in the FLOW-3 message. If the message is acceptable, it accepts the connection. Otherwise, it rejects the call (see Section 5.3.2).

The three-way SME protocol uses the in-band protocol for message transport. The in-band protocol, described in detail in Section 5.3.2, performs SME message transfer in the user plane virtual circuit (after the connection is established and billing has started), allowing SME to occur in networks that do not support transfer of the SSIE in signaling messages.

Because the three-way SME protocol provides three end-to-end message flows, the two participating security agents can use a challenge-response protocol to guarantee flow uniqueness (and protect against replay attacks). The challenge-response protocol uses random numbers (or nonces) to achieve uniqueness of flows. The authentication process within the three-way SME protocol is described in detail in Chapter 6.

The three-way SME protocol also allows two security agents to negotiate parameters for the security association. The initiating security agent specifies the supported security services (e.g., encryption, key exchange, etc.) along with the algorithms and parameters for each supported security service. The responding security agent picks the services, algorithms, and parameters that are to be applied to the security association and communicates these choices back to the initiating SA. If the initiator provides a rich set of supported services, algorithms, and parameters, then this negotiation process increases the likelihood of successful establishment of a secure circuit. The negotiation process is described in more detail in Section 5.2.3.1.

One disadvantage of the three-way protocol is that it requires a user plane virtual circuit between the security agents. Thus, it consumes connection resources before the security agent can determine if a virtual circuit is authorized. However, this reduces the burden on the signaling channel, as security information elements in the signaling messages are small (in fact, they are not always required).

5.1.3 Endpoint Requests for Security Services

In the previous SME protocol scenarios, security associations are established explicitly between two security agents. In these scenarios, if an end system requires security services, it must implement a security agent internally or be part of a network that is afforded uniform security services by a network security agent. However, implementing security agents in end systems can become expensive for large networks, and blanket protection of all hosts in a network removes flexibility and policy decisions from individual hosts.

For these reasons, a mechanism exists that allows an endpoint to request at SVC setup which security services are to be performed on its behalf by a *proxy security agent*. This allows, for example, an endpoint to be provided with encryption services on selected virtual circuits without encryption implemented in the endpoint.

To perform a request for security service, the endpoint is required to implement part of the SME protocol. In addition, the endpoint must be aware of security service availability in the network, and the network must route the virtual circuit through the desired SA.

The proxy request option is only performed within signaling—The use of in-band SME to request proxy security services is prohibited. Therefore, to support endpoint requests for security, the network elements between the end system and the proxy security agent must carry the SSIE. Detailed security agent procedures for requesting and granting proxy security services are described in Section 5.3.5.

5.2 SME Details

The previous descriptions of the SME protocol variations provide the reader with an overview for the services it provides. However, it is the protocol's flexibility in addressing security agents and performing security negotiation that makes it truly unique. The structure of the SSIE and its component SASs provides this flexibility. The following sections describe the SSIE format and the services provided by the SME protocol in more detail.

5.2.1 SSIE

The SSIE consists of a standard 4-byte information element header, followed by a variable number of SASs, as shown in Figure 5.3.

There are two types of SSIE SASs: the SME SAS and the label-based access control SAS. If the SAS type field indicates that the SAS contains SME data, then the SAS will include security service data (SSD), which contains the following information:

- Security agent identifiers (distinguished names);
- Security service specification parameters;

Security Services Information Element Header

SAS1
    Type
    Length
    Version, transport, flow ID, discard
    Scope
    Relative ID
    Target security agent ID
    Security service data

SAS2
    Type
    Length
    Version, transport, flow ID, discard
    Scope
    Relative ID
    Target security agent ID
    Security service data

SASn
    Type
    Length
    Version, transport, flow ID, discard
    Scope
    Relative ID
    Target security agent ID
    Security service data

Figure 5.3 SSIE format.

- Security algorithm specification parameters;
- Confidential parameters;
- Authentication parameters.

If the SAS type indicates label-based access control, then the SSD will contain labels that designate to the sensitivity of the corresponding user plane data, as described in Chapter 9.

5.2.1.1 General SSIE Principles

TLV encoding is used throughout the SSIE and its constituent SASs. This type of encoding allows variable-length fields that can be reordered or omitted, which is required since many of the SSIE fields are optional.

Many SAS TLVs allow the use of user-defined codepoints (algorithm identifier codes) to designate algorithms that are not included in the standard list of algorithms in Security 1.1. In all TLVs where user-defined codepoints are allowed, the user-defined codepoints are indicated with a 1 in the most significant bit. If a user-defined algorithm is specified, then the organizationally unique identifier (OUI) of the organization or company that defined the algorithm must accompany the user-defined codepoint. The OUI is a 3-byte number assigned by the Institute for Electrical and Electronics Engineers (IEEE), which is unique for each equipment manufacturer. Because the OUI is unique for each manufacturer, it avoids collisions between identical user-defined IDs assigned by different organizations.

Some codepoints are sequential codepoints and some are bitmaps. Bitmaps are used when fields can take on multiple values simultaneously (e.g., when specifying the set of services provided by a security agent).

5.2.1.2 Standard SAS Fields

SAS Type. This field indicates whether the SAS contains SME protocol information or label-based access control information.

SAS Length. The SAS length field defines the length (in octets) of the remainder of the SAS (excluding the SAS type and SAS length fields).

Version. This field denotes the version number of the security specification for which this SAS conforms.

Although Security 1.1 security agents do not directly interoperate with Security 1.0 security agents, a mixture of security agents may be present on a virtual circuit, as long as each initiator/responder pair implements the same version. In addition, dual-mode security agents that can operate at either version may be implemented. However, there are nesting implications when mixing version 1.0 and 1.1 implementations. These implications are described in Section 5.2.2.3.

Transport Indicator. The transport indicator specifies whether signaling-based or in-band SME should be used. This is actually a negotiable parameter, and security agents can modify the transport indicator from signaling-based (which may not be supported, depending on the network's support for SSIEs) to in-band, which is always supported by the network. Rules for modifying this field are provided in Section 5.3.4.

Flow Indicator. The flow indicator's primary purpose is to identify which flow in the SME protocol is contained in this SAS, thereby affecting how the receiving security agent should process it. This field is coded as 0 for FLOW-1, 1 for FLOW-2, and 2 for FLOW-3 (if applicable).

Its secondary purpose is to indicate to the receiving security agent which scoping fields should be used for SAS addressing. For FLOW-1, the scope field (described below) is used for security agent addressing. For FLOW-2 and FLOW-3, the relative ID field is used instead.

Discard Indicator. The discard indicator instructs the receiving security agent to discard or forward the SAS after it is processed. Since access control decisions based on flow sensitivity labels can be made at more than one point in the virtual circuit, the label-based access control service allows this bit to be coded as 0 to instruct security agents to forward the SAS after processing. All other Security 1.1 services code this bit as 1 to indicate that the SAS should be discarded.

Scope. The SAS scope field is used by the initiator to specify an intended responder for the SME protocol. The procedure for addressing responding security agents is described in detail in Section 5.2.2.

Relative ID. Once the SME FLOW-1 is completed, both security agents know that they are involved in the establishment of the security association. At this point, use of the scope field to specify security agents in FLOW-2 and FLOW-3 adds unnecessary complexity. Instead, a small identifier (the relative ID) is used to allow security agents to discern SME flows belonging to multiple security associations and to other security agents. The RID works by identifying the nesting level for the security association, as described in Section 5.2.2.3.

Target Security Agent Identifier. The target security agent identifier (TSAID) is used in a FLOW-1 message to explicitly target a responding security agent. The TSAID is a copy of the responder distinguished name identifier (in the SSD), if present. Otherwise, a security agent distinguished name is created and placed in the TSAID location.

Security agents that receive explicitly addressed SASs compare the TSAID to their distinguished name, which is assigned when the security agent is configured. If the ID matches its distinguished name, then the security agent processes the FLOW-1 message, otherwise, the SAS is passed.

5.2.1.3   Security Service Data

The security service data section provides information required by the SME protocol for negotiation of security services and for implementation of specific security services such as authentication and key exchange. In addition, the SSD section is used for transporting access control labels.

Security Agent Identifiers.   These parameters are used by the authentication and key exchange services for identifying the security agents that are involved in the protocol. The SA identifiers must be globally unique distinguished names, such as X.509 distinguished names [4] or AESAs [5].

If explicit security agent addressing is used, and there is a responder distinguished name identifier in the SSD, then this identifier is replicated and used as the TSAID.

Security Service Specification.   The security service specification section is used by both the two-way and the three-way SME protocols. In the two-way protocol, the security service specification section is used to *specify* the services, algorithms, and parameters that are to be used in the security association. In the three-way protocol, it is used to *negotiate* services, algorithms, and parameters.

The procedures for negotiation are described further in Section 5.2.3.1.

Confidential Parameters.   The confidential parameters section contains fields for exchanging keying information when a security association is established. The confidential data field within the confidential parameters section contains the master keys and initial session keys for the virtual circuit. These keys are initially in plaintext form when they are coded in the confidential data field, and are subsequently encrypted before the SAS is sent.

The key exchange procedures are described further in Section 5.2.3.3.

Authentication Parameters.   The authentication parameters section contains the initial authentication tokens for the two-way and three-way SME protocols. Two digital signature fields are also provided in this section: one for the digital signature of the SME tokens and one for a digital signature of the entire SAS (which is used to protect the SAS from modification).

The initial authentication service, and the use of the authentication parameters section, is described in detail in Chapter 6.

5.2.2   Security Agent Addressing

Security agents work in pairs, and this pairing is determined by an addressing mechanism that allows the initiating security agent to specify the intended responding SA. Two addressing methods are provided by the Security 1.1 Specification: explicit addressing and implicit addressing. Explicit addressing is used when the initiator knows the address of the intended responder. Implicit addressing allows the initiator to specify the desired responder based on the responder's location in the network and/or the role that it performs.

Both addressing methods are supported by the SAS scope field. This field is comprised of two subfields that specify the region and role of the target security agent, as shown in Figure 5.4. The region subfield designates the network in which the targeted SA resides and also designates which addressing method (explicit or implicit) is used in the SME protocol. The role subfield designates the SA's placement within the specified region when implicit addressing is used.

Once a responder is identified, a relative identifier (RID) is used to reference the initiator and responder in future SME flows. The RID allows security agents to be arranged in a variety of nested topologies.

5.2.2.1   Explicit Security Agent Addressing

If the *explicit* flag in the region subfield (in Figure 5.4) is set, then the targeted responding SA is specified in the TSAID. As described earlier, the TSAID is a copy of the responder distinguished name identifier (described in

Bit position	8	7	6	5	4-1
Region	Explicit	Local	Remote	Transit	rsvd
Role	User	Enterprise border	Network/link	rsvd	rsvd

Figure 5.4 Scope subfields.

Section 7.1.2 of Security 1.1) if it is present elsewhere in the SAS. Otherwise, a security agent distinguished name (described in Section 7.1.3) is created and placed in the TSAID location.

The TSAID (as well as the SA distinguished names) can be an X.509 distinguished name or an AESA. X.509 distinguished names are useful when X.509 certificates are used and if SAs are to be referenced based on their location in the organizational hierarchy, as implied by X.509 certificates (e.g., if the ATM address of the responding SA is not known). However, X.509-based addressing requires SAs to be allocated separate identifiers. When AESAs are used, SAs will not (usually) require separate addresses, as they are already likely to be configured with an AESA. However, knowledge of the responding SA's AESA is required when using AESA-explicit addressing. Furthermore, the responding SA's address may change if it is connected to another switch. (Note, however, that this type of addressing provides the option in the future for allowing PNNI routing to route a call through a specified SA, as described in Chapter 11.)

5.2.2.2 Implicit Security Agent Addressing

If the explicit flag in Figure 5.4 is cleared, then the targeted SA is implicitly specified and the region and role bitmaps are used to specify the targeted SA. The region bitmap specifies the following security agent locations:

- *Local:* The targeted responding SA is located in the same network peer group as the calling party (identified in the UNI calling party information element);

- *Remote:* The targeted responding SA is located in the same network peer group as the called party (identified in the UNI called party information element);

- *Transit:* The targeted responding SA is located in a network peer group other than the calling and called party peer groups.

A responding SA may be further specified according to its role. The role bitmap specifies the following security agent types:

- *User:* The security agent performs security functions on behalf of an end system;

- *Enterprise border:* The security agent provides security services for an enterprise;
- *Network or link:* The security agent provides services within an enterprise or service provider, but not for an end user.

When a security agent receives an implicitly addressed SA, it accepts the SAS if both the region and the role tests are true. The region test is true if the SA's region (as determined by address comparisons) matches any of the bits in the region bitmap or if the region bitmap is coded with all 0s (indicating "don't care"). Likewise, the role test is true if the SA's configured role matches any of the bits in the role bitmap, or if the role bitmap is coded with all 0s.

5.2.2.3 Relative Identifier and Nested Security Associations

The scope field is used in FLOW-1 to designate a desired responder. In subsequent flows, however, the RID is used to denote the SA that is to receive the flow. The RID, shown in Figure 5.5, is composed of the security association ID (SAID) and SAS number. The SAID is allocated such that it indicates the level of nesting, with SAID = 0 indicating the outermost level of nesting, and incrementing by one for each step inward. The limit of the number of nested levels in an end-to-end connection is 256.

Security Association Identifier. This field specifies the nesting level for the security association.

SAS Number. This field allows a security agent to specify the order in which SASs with the same SAID values are processed by its peer.

The initiator allocates these values during FLOW-1 as follows:

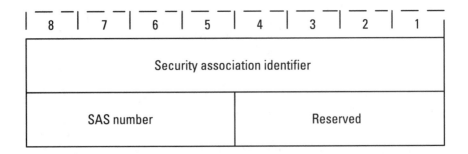

Figure 5.5 Relative ID format.

- The SAID values in all of the received SSIE SASs are examined, the largest value is noted, and the new SAID is this value plus one. The initiator remembers this value for subsequent flows.

- For each security service that the initiator wishes to perform in this security association, SAS numbers are allocated such that the SASs are processed by the responder in decreasing order of SASNs.

In the example in Figure 5.6, there are three levels of nesting. The end-to-end integrity service is conducted using SASs with SAID = 0 and SASN = 0. When the FLOW-1 SSIE with the level 0 SAS reaches the authentication SA (SA_A), the SA constructs a new SAS with SAID = 1 and SASN = 0 and appends it to the SSIE. When this SSIE reaches the SA that performs encryption and authentication ($SA_{E,A}$), the SA constructs two new SASs with SAID = 2 and SASN = 0 and 1 for the encryption and authentication services, respectively. This allows the authentication SAS to be processed first when it is received by the responding SA, followed by the encryption SAS. Once these SASs are constructed, they are appended to the SSIE and transmitted by $SA_{E,A}$.

The receiving SA uses these values as follows:

- In FLOW-1, the receiving SA selects all SASs with the largest SAID value and performs responder processing on the SASs that match its scope (using either the explicit or nonexplicit addressing

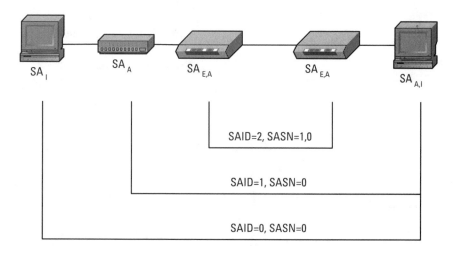

Figure 5.6 Example of SA nesting.

techniques). If no SASs with matching scope exist, then the receiving SA passes the SASs without modification. If some SASs match and some do not, then a nesting violation has occurred, which results in a processing error. Otherwise, the receiving SA processes the SASs, remembers the SAID values for use in subsequent flows, and proceeds with SASs that have the next lowest SAID value.

- In all other flows, the receiving security agents process SASs as they are received in descending order of the SAID and SASN.

The allowed nesting scenarios are shown in Figure 5.7. These nesting arrangements are called *concentric* because inner nesting arrangements are completely contained by the outer arrangements.

A nesting scenario that is not allowed is shown in Figure 5.8. In this nesting scenario, the innermost security association is not completely contained by the outermost security association. For some security services, this results in erroneous operation. For example, when encryption is applied in each of these security associations (i.e., super-encryption), traffic that is encrypted with K0 and then K1 is decrypted with K0 and then K1, which leads to improper decryption.

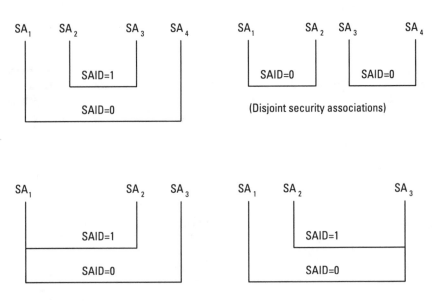

Figure 5.7 Allowed nesting scenarios.

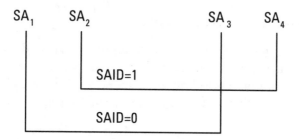

Figure 5.8 Disallowed nesting scenario.

If this scenario is attempted, then the security agent SA_3 receives an SAS with SAID = 0 and matching scope. However, another SAS with SAID = 1 exists that does not match the scope of SA_3. Therefore, SA_3 detects this condition as an error using the procedure described above.

If there is a mixture of Security 1.0 and 1.1 SAs on a virtual circuit, then nesting must be arranged such that the versions of the peer security agents match. Three allowed nesting scenarios for mixed 1.0/1.1 security support are shown in Figure 5.9. In the upper two examples, both pairs of SAs implement the same security version. In the lower example, a dual-mode SA participates in two security associations with different security versions.

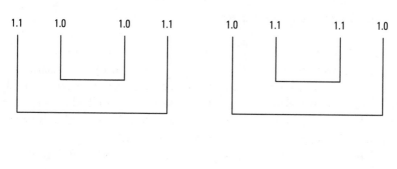

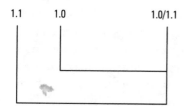

Figure 5.9 Example of mixed 1.0/1.1 security configurations.

5.2.3 Security Association Establishment

SME supports the establishment of security associations between nested pairs of security agents. Establishment of a security association involves the agreement of security algorithms and parameters that are to be used, and may also involve authentication and exchange of encryption or data integrity keys.

5.2.3.1 Security Parameters Negotiation

The three-way SME protocol provides negotiation of security services and algorithms. This negotiation process works as follows:

1. The initiator proposes one or more services, and for each service, proposes one or more algorithms (listed in preference order) with associated parameters. The initiator also indicates which services it supports, in case the responder requires them. This information is included in FLOW-1.

2. The responder examines the proposed services and selects which ones it wants to use. For each selected service, the responder selects from the list of algorithms and parameters the first one that it supports. The selected service and corresponding algorithm/parameters are communicated to the initiator in FLOW-2.

3. The initiator uses the selected algorithms.

Negotiation information is communicated using the security services specification section, described in Section 7.2 of Security 1.1. Security services are negotiated using the security service option section, whereas the algorithms and parameters for each of these services are specified in the security service algorithm section. (The security service declaration section is not used in the negotiation protocol. Its use is described later.)

When the initiator wishes to propose a service in FLOW-1, it identifies the service in the security service options section and indicates whether the service is required, or whether it will be supported if selected by the responder. (However, for the integrity service, things are more complicated because two modes are specified: integrity *with* replay protection and integrity *without* replay protection. In this case, the initiator may require either mode, may support either or both modes, or require that one of the modes be implemented; that is, it does not care which mode is selected.) The security service options may be listed in any order. Services that are *not* supported may also be listed or omitted.

For each service that it requests, the initiator includes a corresponding security service algorithm description section. Algorithms may be specified individually or in *profile groups*. Profile groups allow convenient specification of groups of algorithms that naturally occur together (e.g., DSA and SHA-1 for authentication). Both individual algorithms and profile groups may be user-defined. However, to avoid collisions between user-defined codepoints, the OUI for the organization that defined the codepoint is included in each security service algorithm description. Both the individual algorithms and the profile groups are listed in order of preference. For each service, however, either the individual algorithms or the profile groups may be listed, but not both.

When the responder receives the security service options, it looks at the services that the initiator requires or supports and decides if the service is required or not supported for the security association. It also selects the algorithm and parameters from the list presented by the initiator, and communicates its selection back to the initiator in the FLOW-2 message using the security service options and the security service algorithm description section. If the responder requires a service or algorithm that is not listed by the initiator, it assumes that it is not supported and may decide to reject the call.

The responder uses the selected algorithms to perform security functions within SME FLOW-2 (e.g., authentication and key exchange) and thereafter (e.g., encryption and integrity). Likewise, when the initiator receives FLOW-2, it uses the selected algorithms in FLOW-3 and thereafter.

Security Service Declaration

As mentioned before, the security service declaration is not used for negotiation. Its purpose is to compactly indicate to a peer or proxy security agent which security services it supports, requests, or provides. In both situations, the security service declaration is only used in signaling. Therefore, it cannot be used for negotiation.

In the peer-to-peer case, the security service declaration allows security agents to determine if a full SME protocol exchange is worth the effort. The declaration octet group is used by the initiator in FLOW-1 to indicate which services it does or does not support. The responder does the same in FLOW-2, and it may or may not consider the initiator's declaration. Both parties use this information to determine if the three-way SME protocol should be performed in-band.

The use of the security service declaration in the proxy security agent scenario is described in Section 5.3.5.

Implicit Negotiation for Two-Way SME

Negotiation of services and algorithms is only allowed in the three-way SME protocol. However, the security service options and security service algorithm description sections may be used by the initiator to indicate to the responder which services, algorithms, and parameters it intends to use in the security association. If the responder finds the choice unacceptable, it may choose to reject the call.

5.2.3.2 Authentication

SME allows SAs to mutually authenticate each other, or an initiating SA to unilaterally authenticate to a responding SA. Authentication is provided within SME because it is often a required security service that must accompany other initial security functions such as access control or key exchange. Initial authentication is also considered independent security service, and for this reason, it is discussed separately in Chapter 6.

5.2.3.3 Key Exchange

Keys are required for the confidentiality and integrity services to encrypt and/or sign data. These keys can be preplaced via management; however, this approach does not scale well as the number of SAs increases. A better way to manage confidentiality and integrity keys is to exchange them as the security association is being established.

The ATM key exchange service is provided as part of the two-way and three-way SME protocols. Two shared keys are exchanged in this process: a single master key (MK) and two initial session keys (ISKs), one for each direction. The ISK, along with all other session keys, is used directly by the security service to encrypt or generate message authentication codes. The MK, on the other hand, is used as a key-encryption key, allowing session keys to be changed periodically.

The key exchange process requires the SAs to be configured with or to develop an initial key exchange key (IKEK), which is used to encrypt the MK and ISK. One of three IKEKs is used in the key exchange process, depending on the key exchange algorithm that is used. For symmetric key exchange algorithms, the IKEK is a shared, preplaced key that is configured in each SA. For asymmetric (public key) key exchange algorithms, the IKEK is the public key of the receiving peer SA. When using a key development algorithm (i.e., Diffie-Hellman or Elliptic Curve Key Agreement Scheme), the IKEK is determined from the key that is developed under the algorithm.

When performing key exchange, both parties must agree to a common MK, and this is used in both directions in a bidirectional virtual circuit. For the symmetric and asymmetric algorithms (other than key development algorithms), the initiator and responder each contribute 128 bits to the MK and place their contributions in the confidential parameters octet group (Section 7.3.1 of Security 1.1), which is encrypted with the IKEK. In the two-way SME protocol, the initiator places its contribution in FLOW-1, and the responder places its contribution in FLOW-2. In the three-way SME protocol, the responder places its contribution in FLOW-2, and the initiator places its contribution in FLOW-3. The shared MK is determined by concatenating the two contributions, with the initiator's contribution in the most significant position, and the responder's in the least significant position. Since each contribution is a maximum of 128 bits, the maximum size of the MK is constrained to 256 bits in Security 1.1.

For symmetric and asymmetric algorithms (other than key development algorithms), ISKs are exchanged along with the master keys. The ISKs are determined at random by each SA, and are unique for each direction in the virtual circuit. The ISKs are placed in the confidential parameters octet group, and encrypted along with the MKs using the IKEK and the appropriate algorithm.

With a key development algorithm such as Diffie-Hellman, the IKEK and MK are identical and are determined from the result of the shared key development process. In FLOW-1, the initiator's public contribution to the shared key is placed in the key exchange octet group of the security service Algorithm Description section (Section 7.2.3.5 of Security 1.1). When the responder receives FLOW-1, it calculates its contribution to the shared key and determines the shared key that is developed by the algorithm. At this point, it can also determine the IKEK and MK by taking the lowest 256 bits from the result of the key development algorithm. Next, the responder sends its contribution to the initiator in FLOW-2, and the initiator determines the result of the key development algorithm, the IKEK, and the MK using the same procedure. Note that when using key development algorithms, the master key is determined through public parameters that are exchanged in the security service algorithm description section of the SSIE SAS. Therefore, the master key octet group in the confidential parameters section is not used in this process.

The ISK exchange process is slightly different when using a key development algorithm. As in the other cases, the initiator and responder determine separate ISKs at random, place them in the confidential parameters section, encrypt them, and send them to their peer. However, since the key development algorithm does not provide encryption, the Zmask algorithm, described in [1] and based on [6], must be used for encrypting the confidential parameters. The IKEK (which is also the MK in this case) is used for encrypting the ISKs with the Zmask algorithm. Since the Diffie-Hellman IKEK is determined in the key exchange process (as opposed to configured, as with the other key exchange algorithms), two flows are required to allow the initiator to have the necessary key to encrypt and send its ISK. Therefore, key exchange using Diffie-Hellman and any other key development algorithm can only be used in the three-way SME protocol.

In Pt-Mpt connections, all security agents in the connection receive the same MK and ISK. When connecting to the first leaf in the multipoint connection, the Pt-Pt procedures described above are used to establish the first MK and ISK. However, when additional leaves are added to the multipoint connection, the initiating SA informs the responder of the keys that it should use by placing the existing MK and ISK in the confidential parameters section, and encrypts it using the specified algorithm and the IKEK. The responder takes these values and uses them as is (i.e., the responder does not contribute to the MK). For symmetric and asymmetric (non-Diffie-Hellman) key exchange algorithms, the IKEK is the shared secret key or the receiver's public key and is determined beforehand via configuration or other means (e.g., certificate lookup). With key development algorithms such as Diffie-Hellman, the Zmask algorithm is used to encrypt the MK and ISK, using an IKEK that is configured via management, or determined from some prior key exchange.

5.2.3.4 Secret Key Storage Considerations

The public-key, secret-key, and Diffie-Hellman key exchange protocols described in the Security Specification 1.1 are secure and are widely used in other security standards. When security implementations are successfully attacked, however, the breach often occurs not in the protocol, but in the way that keys are stored in the device. When building an implementation, careful consideration must be given to the way keys are accessed and stored, and to whether a plaintext key is available to other processes via lookup in memory, disk files, or in swap space.

5.3 SME Message Transport

Information for each flow in both the two-way and three-way SME protocols is contained in the SSIE. For the two-way SME protocol, described in Section 5.1.1, SSIEs are contained in signaling messages. For the three-way SME protocol, described in Section 5.1.2, SSIEs are contained in special messages that are signaled within the user plane VC.

The following sections describe the SSIE, two-way signaling-based SME, and three-way in-band SME in more detail.

5.3.1 UNI 4.0 Point-to-Point Signaling

When the SSIE is transported in signaling messages, the security association can be established at the same time as the switched virtual connection. This approach is advantageous in that it reduces the amount of time required to establish a security association, and it allows ATM firewall devices to strongly authenticate and allow or disallow virtual circuits from *outside* devices.

The FLOW-1 and FLOW-2 messages for the two-way SME protocol can be transported in SVC signaling messages, as shown in Figure 5.10. These flows can occur during signaling of point-to-point connections as well as point-to-multipoint connections. As with the other transport methods,

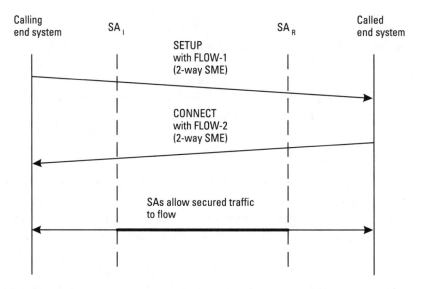

Figure 5.10 Signaling-based protocol for SVCs.

the SSIE is used for transferring SME protocol information in signaling. However, unlike the in-band method described later, the signaling-based method limits the length of the SSIE to 512 bytes in order to bound the amount of security information transported in signaling.

To support signaling-based SME, modifications are required to the signaling implementations of devices that are expected to encounter SSIEs in signaling messages (i.e., devices that either implement SAs, or are located between SAs that implement signaling-based SME). These modifications are described in the signaling addenda [7] and [8].

For Pt-Pt connections, the FLOW-1 message (contained in an appropriate SSIE SAS) is added to the SVC SETUP message on the UNI, PNNI, and AINI interfaces. Likewise, the FLOW-2 SME message is contained in the CONNECT message.

As described in the UNI, PNNI, and AINI signaling addenda, the SA is the first entity to process incoming raw signaling messages (as received from the signaling ATM adaptation layer, or SAAL) and the last entity to process outgoing raw signaling messages. These procedures are specified for two reasons: to allow an SA to filter only correct (from a security perspective) signaling messages to reach the call/connection management entity, and to allow future SAs to apply control plane security (e.g., authentication or confidentiality) to the outgoing signaling message.

Specific signaling-based SME procedures are described for four cases: initiating SA processing of call initiation messages, responding SA processing of call initiation messages, responding security agent processing of call completion messages, and initiating SA processing of call completion messages. These cases, along with in-bound and out-bound procedures that are common to both SAs, are summarized as follows.

Call Setup Procedures

In-Bound Processing. If an SA receives a call setup message containing an SSIE (e.g., a security agent residing in a switch), it takes all SASs with the highest SAID. If the scope fields match this SA's TSAID or region/role, then the receiving SA checks if it is to be a proxy SA using the procedures described in Security 1.1, Section 5.1.4.5. If the SAS is not an endpoint proxy security request, then the security agent follows the responder security agent call setup procedures for that security association. Otherwise, it follows the initiator SA call setup procedures.

Initiator. Before the outgoing signaling message is transmitted, the initiating SA either builds a new SSIE SAS for a new security association or modifies the existing SAS in the case where it is processing a request for security services by proxy. As part of this process, the SA must allocate a new SAID for the new SAS. This is accomplished by examining all SSIE SASs, taking the highest SAID in the RID fields, adding 1, and checking for overflow.

Multiple SSIE SASs may be inserted for a given security association. If the processing order of these SASs is significant, then SAS numbers are assigned in decreasing order, that is, so that the SASs with the highest SAS numbers are processed first, etc.

Conceivably, an SA implementation can support both Version 1.1 and Version 1.0 SAs (although the Version 1.1 SA is preferred). Without knowing the capability of the responding SA, the initiating SA should use Version 1.1 messages and procedures.

If the initiating SA does not care which SA is to respond, then it should use nonexplicit addressing, coding each of the region and role bits as 0. Otherwise, it should use explicit or nonexplicit addressing, as described earlier in Section 5.2.2.

Finally, the flow indicators are coded as 0.

As the SETUP message leaves the security agent, the SSIE is built with the new SASs and the SASs that are forwarded, and the message is sent to the next hop.

Responder. Upon receipt of a connection setup request, the responder takes all SASs with the highest SAID as described above to identify all SASs that it is to process. Next, it checks the scope fields and version numbers to determine disallowed nesting of SAs (as described previously in Section 5.2.2.3). For each SAS that it processes, it examines the security service specification sections to determine if a match exists between the requested services/algorithms and those supported by the responding SA. Those that match are processed further. Those that do not match are forwarded unmodified once security processing completes.

If the responder cannot find an SSIE SAS that it requires, the responder may decide to clear the call or include an SSIE indicating its desire to perform in-band SME, based on site policy. This is covered in more detail in Section 5.3.3.

For those scoped SASs that match the indicated services and algorithms, the responding SA processes each one in descending order according to the RID field (i.e., SAID and SAS number). Each SAS is processed to completion before starting the next one. During processing, the SA stores the RID values for use in sending the FLOW-2 message during call completion. Once the SAS is processed, the security agent looks at the SAS's discard indicator to determine whether the SAS should be forwarded in the SETUP message or held until later.

Out-Bound Processing. After the signaling protocol processes the SETUP message, the security agent packages the SSIE with the added SASs or the SASs that either did not match scope, did not contain matching algorithms, or had their discard bits coded as 0. The completed SSIE is appended to the SETUP message, and the message is sent.

Call Completion Procedures

In-Bound Processing. When an SA receives a call completion (e.g., CONNECT) message, it already knows whether it is functioning as an initiator or responder and has stored the relevant SAID values.

Responder. When the responder receives the CONNECT message, it double-checks the SAID fields of each of its held SASs against the SASs contained in the SSIE. If no SSIE exists, then the SAIDs of the held SASs should be zero. Otherwise, the SAIDs should be one greater than the largest SAID in the SSIE. If these checks end in failure (perhaps due to a problem in the security agent topology), then the call is rejected as a "security protocol processing failure."

Otherwise, it builds one or more SASs according to the SME protocol, inserts the SAID value(s) stored earlier, sets the flow indicator to 1, and appends the SASs to the SSIE. The SSIE and the rest of the signaling message are sent to signaling.

Initiator. When the initiator receives the CONNECT message with an SSIE, it obtains all SASs that contain SAID fields that the initiator allocated in FLOW-1. If there is no SSIE or if the SSIE contains a partial set of expected SASs with matching SAID, then the initiator determines whether the call is in error or if it wishes to accept the call. If the SSIE contains no SASs with matching SAID, then an error has occurred and the call is cleared.

Why the distinction? If there is no SSIE, then the initiator decides if it accepts a connection with no security. If there is an SSIE with a less-than-expected set of SASs matching the SAID, then the initiator must decide if it wants a security association below what it initially wanted. However, if the initiator receives an SSIE with no SASs with matching SAID, then somehow its responder did not handle the CONNECT message properly, which is an error.

At this point, the initiator may need to invoke an in-band SME protocol with its responder. The initiator makes this determination based on the transport indicator in the received SAS (see Section 5.3.4).

If the initiator is a proxy security agent, then it must build an SAS that will acknowledge to the requesting endpoint which security services are provided by the security association (as described in Section 5.3.5).

Out-Bound Processing. After the signaling protocol processes the CONNECT message, the SSIE is packaged with the added SASs or the SASs that either did not match the security agent's SAID or had their discard bits coded as 0. The completed SSIE is appended to the CONNECT message, and the message is sent.

5.3.2 In-Band

The in-band protocol allows SME messages to be passed in the user plane virtual connection after it has been established between a pair of security agents. In Security 1.1, this protocol applies to switched as well as permanent Pt-Pt, bidirectional connections. (In Security 1.1, the in-band protocol is not used to secure Pt-Mpt connections and simplex connections because no bandwidth is allocated in the responder-to-initiator direction.) The in-band protocol uses AAL 5 for message transport, with a special message format that uses the same SSIEs as the signaling-based protocol. The messages are transferred using a special protocol that provides reliable, in-order delivery of each SME flow.

The in-band method of SME transport allows SME to occur if conditions do not allow it in signaling. Such conditions include the following:

- *If three-way SME is required:* As described earlier, signaling can only support the two-way SME protocol because signaling only provides two end-to-end flows. If additional flows are required, then the in-band protocol must be used.

- *If the switches between security agents are not expected to support SSIE transport in signaling:* If the SSIE cannot be transported in signaling, then it must be transported in-band. In-band transport can occur alone or as a fallback to a failed attempt to perform SME in signaling.

- *If PVCs are used:* Since PVCs are not signaled, security negotiation and key exchange can only occur in-band.

- *If signaling-based SME is disabled due to site policies:* Site policies may preclude signaled virtual circuits or not allow signaling or SSIEs to traverse the public-private boundary.

- *If SSIEs are too large for signaling:* SSIEs are limited to 512 bytes when used with signaling. If certificate information is included in the SSIE, then it may be too large for transport in signaling. The in-band approach allows transport large SSIEs (up to 64 KB).

5.3.2.1 PVCs

The in-band protocol for PVCs is depicted in Figure 5.11.

The in-band protocol for PVCs works as follows:

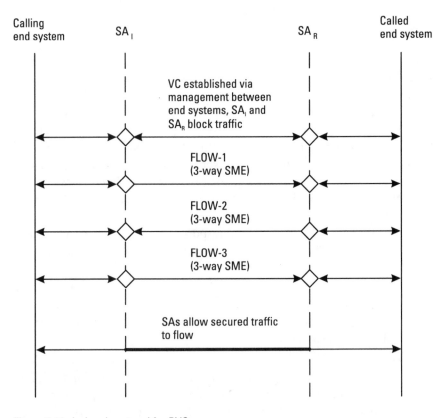

Figure 5.11 In-band protocol for PVCs.

1. The PVC is established between the two end systems, but the SAs do not yet allow traffic to flow between them. This PVC must be a Pt-Pt connection and must be configured with sufficient bandwidth to allow the in-band protocol to complete in a reasonable amount of time.

2. One SA is designated the initiator, and the other is designated the responder. The responder is instructed (via management) to wait for a period of time for the in-band protocol to complete, as configured in the P_Wait (PVC wait) parameter.

3. The initiator is instructed (again, via management) to begin the in-band SME protocol (described in Section 5.3.2.3), using the VPI and VCI of the user virtual channel connection or the VPI of the user virtual path connection and VCI = 1.

4. If the protocol completes in error, or the P_Wait timer expires, then the initiator and/or responder terminate SME processing and continue to block traffic on the VC. The error is reported to the peer SA.

5. If the protocol completes successfully, then both SAs unblock traffic on the VC and apply traffic security (e.g., encryption) if required.

The in-band protocol may be nested for both permanent and switched VCs. For permanent VCs, management must enable the innermost security agents first and proceed outward until all SA pairs have performed in-band SME.

5.3.2.2 SVCs

The in-band protocol for SVCs is depicted in Figure 5.12.

The in-band protocol for SVCs works as follows:

1. The calling end system issues a SETUP message, which is allowed to propagate through the network. The SAs check to ensure that the VC is a Pt-Pt VC with sufficient bandwidth to allow the SME protocol to complete quickly (i.e., before the signaling state machines in the end systems or switches time out). If these conditions are not met, the call is rejected.

2. The security agents determine their SME roles by noting whether the SETUP message arrives on the inside (plaintext) or outside (ciphertext) interface.

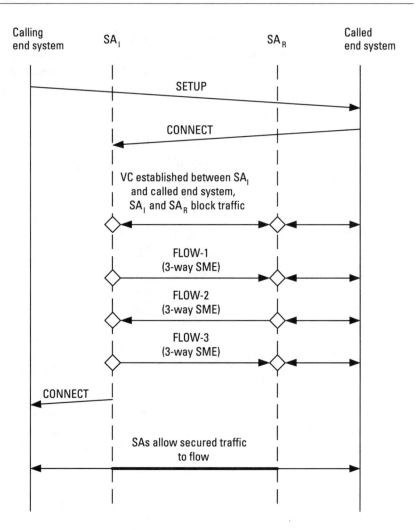

Figure 5.12 In-band protocol for SVCs.

3. The called end system issues a CONNECT message. When the message reaches SA_R, SA_R starts its in-band SME state machine, blocks traffic, and propagates the CONNECT toward the calling end system. When the CONNECT message reaches SA_I, it holds the message and continues to block traffic on the signaled VC. SA_I uses the VPI and VCI of the signaled virtual channel connection, or the VPI of the VPC and VCI = 1 to perform the in-band protocol (described in Section 5.3.2.3).

4. If the protocol completes in error, then the initiator and/or responder terminate SME processing, continue to block traffic on the signaled VC, and clear the connection.

5. If the protocol completes successfully, then the initiator forwards the CONNECT message to the calling party, and both SAs unblock traffic on the VC and apply traffic security (e.g., encryption) if required.

As in the case for PVCs, the in-band SME protocol for SVCs allows security associations to be nested, with security associations negotiated from the innermost pair outward. However, nesting increases the time for circuit establishment, which increases the risk for timeout of the connection establishment process by at least one of the switches or end systems.

5.3.2.3 In-Band Message Exchange Protocol

In the case of signaling-based transport, the signaling protocol uses the reliable delivery and framing mechanisms provided by SAAL. In addition, signaling provides a well-defined, extensible message format. With the in-band SME protocol, these mechanisms are no longer available from signaling and therefore are provided separately in the Security Specification 1.1.

The message structure for in-band SME is similar to the structure of UNI signaling messages. The in-band messages are variable length, provide message type identifiers, and carry variable-length information elements. Signaling's *cause* information element is used in the in-band protocol to transfer error codes and diagnostics. Likewise, the SSIE is used to transfer security-related information, and its format is identical to the SSIE used in signaling. However, since the message length restriction is relaxed for in-band SME, information that would make the SSIE exceed signaling's 512-byte limit (most notably certificate information) is allowed in the in-band SSIE.

There are five in-band SME messages defined in Security 1.1. Three of the messages correspond to the flows of the three-way message exchange protocol. These are the FLOW-1, FLOW-2, and FLOW-3 messages. These messages contain the SSIE, described earlier in Section 5.2.1. Another message, CONFIRM-AP, provides a fourth end-to-end flow that allows the responder to inform the initiator that it has completed the SME protocol. Finally, a FAULT message is defined to allow either SA to inform its peer that an error of some kind has occurred.

There are two state machines defined in Security 1.1 for the in-band protocol: one for the initiator and one for the responder. The detailed state machines are defined in the specification and are described briefly below:

1. The responder starts its state machine first and waits for the first flow from the initiator. The responder also starts the P_Wait timer, and if this timer expires, then an error has occurred.

2. The initiator builds an SSIE for flow 1, puts it in a FLOW-1 message, and sends it to the responder over the VCC, or VCI = 1 for a VPC. The initiator then starts the T100 timer, and waits for a FLOW-2 message. If this timer expires, it checks the FLOW-1 retry counter. If the retry maximum is reached, then an error has occurred. Otherwise, the counter is incremented, the message is resent, and the timer is restarted.

3. The responder receives the FLOW-1 message and checks it. If it is valid, it processes the SME message, builds an SSIE for flow 2, encapsulates it in a FLOW-2 message, and sends it over the VC. The responder then starts the T102 timer, and waits for a FLOW-3 message. If this timer expires, it checks the FLOW-2 retry counter. If the retry maximum is reached, then an error has occurred. Otherwise, the counter is incremented, the message is resent, and the timer is restarted.

4. The initiator receives the FLOW-2 message and checks it. If it is valid, it processes the SME message, builds an SSIE for flow 3, encapsulates it in a FLOW-3 message, and sends it over the VC. The initiator then starts the T101 timer, and waits for a CONFIRM-AP message. If this timer expires, then an error has occurred. If it receives another FLOW-2 message, it resends the FLOW-3 message.

5. The responder receives the FLOW-3 message and checks it. If it is valid, it processes the SME message, builds a CONFIRM-AP message, and sends it to the initiator. The responder activates any required traffic security on the VC and enables the VC.

6. The initiator receives the CONFIRM-AP message. It activates any required traffic security on the VC and enables the VC.

5.3.3 Pt-Mpt Connections

When establishing the first party of a point-to-multipoint SVC, SME occurs as for point-to-point connections (i.e., in signaling or in-band). When subsequent parties (leaves) are added to the Pt-Mpt connection, however, the protocol is performed within signaling. When a leaf is established, the FLOW-1 message is contained in the UNI ADD PARTY message (and the equivalent PNNI and AINI messages), arriving at the called UNI in the SETUP message. The FLOW-2 message is included in the CONNECT message at the called UNI, is transported in the equivalent PNNI and AINI messages, and arrives at the calling UNI in the ADD PARTY ACK message. This is shown in Figure 5.13. (Detailed SA procedures are the same as those described in Section 5.3.1.)

The process for adding leaves to a Pt-Mpt connection can be initiated by either the root (the calling party in the above example) or the leaf (the called party). In the root-initiated case, the protocol for adding leaves proceeds as shown in Figure 5.13.

For the leaf-initiated case, two subcases exist: leaf-initiated join with root prompting and leaf-initiated join without root involvement. In the first case, when a leaf wishes to join a Pt-Mpt connection, it notifies the root, and if the root decides to add the leaf, it adds the leaf as shown in Figure 5.13. In

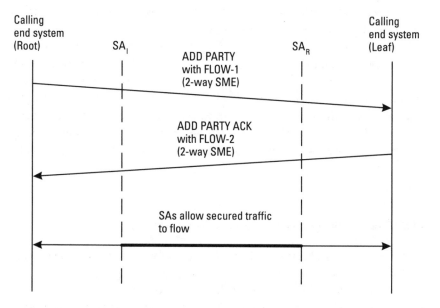

Figure 5.13 Signaling-based SME transport for Pt-Mpt SVCs.

the second case, when the leaf requests to join a Pt-Mpt connection, the network adds the leaf automatically without root involvement. However, due to the security management complexities of this scenario, leaf-initiated joins without root notification are not supported in the Security Specification 1.1. The other two methods for adding leaves (i.e., root-initiated and leaf-initiated with root prompting) are supported.

5.3.4 Signaling-Based with In-Band Fallback

The two SME transport methods defined in Security 1.1 are not mutually exclusive. In certain situations, it is possible that both the signaling-based and the in-band methods are used together, with SME attempted first in signaling, followed by the in-band method as the fallback mechanism. Specifically, an initiator SA may attempt SME in signaling, not knowing whether the downstream SA supports signaling-based SME. In this case, the initiator constructs an SAS with the transport indicator field set to "signaling," and puts the corresponding SSIE in the SETUP message. If the downstream security agent decides that it cannot continue SME in signaling, or if it knows that the network cannot support SME in signaling, then it can change the transport indicator to "in-band messaging" in the CONNECT message.

It may appear that if in-band fallback is used, then the first signaling flow is wasted. This is not necessarily true. The responding SA can use the first flow to determine if in-band negotiation is worthwhile. This decision can be made by looking at the security service declaration to determine if the initiator and the responder are incompatible. This decision can also be based on authentication information in FLOW-1 and whether the initiator is allowed to establish a security association with the responder. If these checks on the FLOW-1 (signaling-based) message pass, and the responder determines that it requires in-band negotiation, then it can modify the transport indicator.

5.3.5 Endpoint Requests for Proxy Security Services

As described earlier, Security 1.1 provides a capability that allows an end system to request security services to be provided by a proxy security agent located somewhere else in the network. The network between the end system and the proxy SA is assumed to be secured via other means (such as physical access controls), as no ATM security services are active in this path.

The proxy security services function is best described via an example (shown in Figure 5.14).

In this example, an end system requires encryption services that are provided by an encryptor located somewhere in the private network. The endpoint requests the proxy service by including an SSIE in the SETUP message (see Section 5.1.4.5 of Security 1.1), with the SME format identifier in the SME data section coded to indicate that the SME protocol type is "unspecified." This codepoint is used because the end system does not care which protocol (two-way or three-way SME) is used.

In addition, the end system includes a security service declaration (described in Section 7.2.1 of Security 1.1) to indicate that the encryption security service is requested, along with algorithm descriptions for each

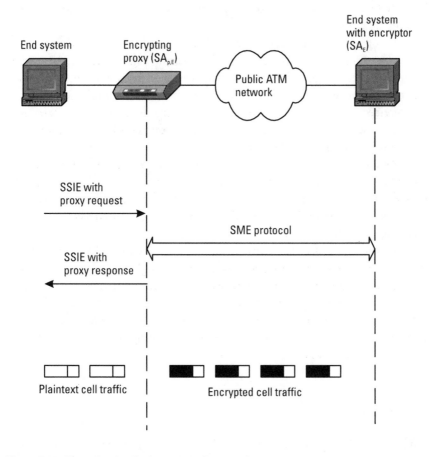

Figure 5.14 Example of endpoint request for security.

desired encryption algorithm (Section 7.2.3 of Security 1.1), listed in order of preference.

When $SA_{p,E}$ receives the SSIE, it attempts to honor the request according to its capabilities and policies. In some instances, a security agent that is capable of honoring a request for security services may choose not to provide the service because the endpoint is not authorized. In this example, assuming that the end system is authorized, $SA_{p,E}$ selects the first acceptable algorithm from the list, and attempts an SME protocol exchange to initiate the service.

The SME exchange between $SA_{p,E}$ and the remote security agent SA_E is performed using an appropriate SME protocol and transport method. When SME completes $SA_{p,E}$ confirms to the end system that it is providing the requested security service. This indication is performed by including an SSIE in the CONNECT message with the SME format identifier (ID) set to "unspecified" and using the security service declaration to indicate which services are being provided by the proxy.

It is possible that the list of provided security services is different from the list of requested security services. That is, the proxy security agent may elect to implement security services that were not requested, or not implement requested security services. Either way, if the list of implemented security services is not acceptable to the end system, then the end system may choose to clear the connection. Again, this is a decision based on the policy rules configured in the end system.

As shown in Figure 5.14, ATM cell traffic between the end system and the proxy security agent is not encrypted. Furthermore, the astute reader will notice that the protocol that implements endpoint requests for security services is also not secure. Therefore, this path must be secured via some other means (e.g., physical access controls).

In this example, the network topology constrains ATM connections such that all outgoing connections will flow through the encryptor. This is actually a fundamental assumption behind the endpoint request service, as Security 1.1 provides no mechanism for selectively routing connections so that they pass through the proper security agents. Mechanisms for automatic security service discovery and security-based routing are topics for future study (see Chapter 11).

5.4   Summary

SME is a flexible protocol for negotiating a security association and for performing initial security services such as certificate exchange, authentication, and exchange of encryption and integrity keys. SME can be performed using two flows (i.e., when quick security association establishment is required) or three flows (i.e., when negotiation and challenge-response authentication is required), depending on the security requirements for the connection. SME flows can be carried within signaling messages, or in-band within the user virtual circuit, depending on the network's ability to carry such information. SME messages may be addressed to specific security agents based on their address or based on their location and ATM security role. A variety of security topologies are also supported by SME, including nesting and proxy security services.

References

[1]　The ATM Forum, "ATM Security Specification Version 1.1," af-sec-0100.002, March 2001.

[2]　International Standards Organization, "Information Technology—Open Systems Interconnection—The Directory: Authentication Framework," ISO/IEC 9594-8, 1995.

[3]　International Standards Organization, "Information Technology—Security Techniques—Key Management—Part 2: Mechanisms Using Symmetric Techniques," ISO/IEC 11770-2, 1996.

[4]　ITU-T, "The Directory: Authentication Framework," Recommendation X.509, 1997.

[5]　The ATM Forum, "User-Network Interface (UNI) Specification, Version 3.1," af-uni-0010.002, September 1994.

[6]　Bird, R., et al., "The KryptoKnight Family of Light-Weight Protocols for Authentication and Key Distribution," *IEEE Transactions on Networking*, Vol. 3, No. 1, pp. 31–41, February 1995.

[7]　The ATM Forum, "PNNI Version 1.0 Security Signaling Addendum," af-cs-0116.000, May 1999.

[8]　The ATM Forum, "UNI Signaling 4.0 Security Addendum," af-cs-0117.000, May 1999.

6

Initial Authentication

Initial authentication is the ATM security service that allows an *ATM entity* to prove its identity to another entity when a VCC or VPC is established. The ATM entity is an ATM security agent that is implemented in an ATM device (e.g., switch, end system, or network encryption device), and ATM entities can authenticate unilaterally (where only one entity authenticates to the other) or mutually (where two entities authenticate to each other). Initial authentication is an important ATM security service for a number of reasons. The obvious reason is to protect against spoofing attacks. When ATM connection policies are enforced (e.g., through NSAP address filtering), initial authentication supports this enforcement, even in the case where malicious ATM systems attempt to spoof the calling party address of an authorized system. In addition, for virtual circuit security mechanisms such as data origin authentication (integrity) and encryption, strong initial authentication is required to ensure that keys are only exchanged with authorized equipment—protecting against man in the middle attacks.

Recall from Chapter 1 that initial authentication is the procedure by which two parties who wish to communicate prove their identities to each other during session establishment. (Data origin authentication, described in Chapter 7, authenticates the source of each message after a communications session has been established.) Initial authentication is used in many contexts: for example, when a person identifies himself to an automatic bank teller machine, when a user logs into a computer system, and when a computer requests network services through a firewall. Many types of authentication protocols may be used, including personal identification numbers (PINs), persistent passwords, one-time passwords, and cryptographic digital signatures.

Strong authentication is provided by the use of cryptographic digital signatures in conjunction with a secure authentication protocol. The digital signature is typically computed using the entity's digital signature key over the output of a cryptographic hash function, which is computed over a message that contains specific information in the form of "tokens." These tokens ensure that the authentication message has the following properties:

- *Freshness:* The digital signature must have been generated recently. This property is typically ensured by tokens that contain time-stamps, or one-time numbers (nonces).

- *Uniqueness:* Each authentication attempt must result in a unique digital signature value in order to prevent replay attacks (where one party attempts to use an authentication message sent by another party to spoof its identity). This property is ensured by tokens that change with each authentication attempt between two parties (e.g., timestamps and/or nonces, and the party identifiers), and by using private or secret digital signature keys.

- *Ordering:* The authentication message must provide the necessary tokens to allow a receiver to determine if the message has been received at the correct time in the authentication protocol. This property is afforded by timestamps and/or nonces.

Two authentication protocols are specified in the ATM Security Specification: one based on asymmetric digital signature algorithms (derived from [1]) and one based on symmetric digital signature algorithms (derived from [2]). Asymmetric digital signature algorithms are implemented using hash functions along with public-key algorithms. Since public-key algorithms are computationally intensive, a hash function is used to reduce the authentication tokens (i.e., source and destination identifiers, timestamps, and/or nonces) into a small unique value. Once the unique hash value is determined, the digital signature is calculated using the hash value and the digital signature key.

Symmetric digital signature algorithms are also supported in the ATM Security Specification. These digital signature algorithms use hash functions along with a shared secret key to calculate a MAC. The same tokens that are used in the asymmetric case are also used here to guarantee freshness, uniqueness, and ordering.

There are a number of trade-offs that must be considered when selecting a digital signature algorithm for use in ATM authentication. One area is performance: Typically, digital signatures that are generated with symmetric algorithms are computed more quickly than those generated with asymmetric algorithms. However, symmetric digital signature algorithms require both parties to share the same key. By sharing these digital signature keys between two or more entities, it is possible that any of these entities could impersonate any other entity. With asymmetric digital signatures, each entity can have a unique key, thereby ensuring that no other entity can impersonate it.

6.1 Authentication Protocols

In Chapter 5, two SME protocols are described, and each of them is compatible with the authentication techniques based on asymmetric or symmetric digital signature algorithms. These protocols are the two-way message exchange protocol and the three-way message exchange protocol. Both protocols implement unilateral and mutual authentication, and support the required digital signature attributes of freshness, ordering, and uniqueness (which, in the case of symmetric algorithms, implies uniqueness within the group members that possess the shared secret authentication key). In addition, these protocols provide a mechanism to transfer other information that must be digitally signed (e.g., keys for subsequent encryption and/or integrity services).

The two-way message exchange protocol implements authentication through the exchange of two messages: one from the initiator to the responder and the other in the opposite direction. Since this protocol uses only two messages, it can be used within ATM signaling (i.e., in the SETUP and CONNECT messages). In the first flow, the initiator includes the identifiers of the initiator and responder, along with a timestamp and a random number (nonce) that it issues as a challenge to the responder. The purpose of the timestamp in this flow is to provide a token that guarantees the uniqueness, freshness, and ordering for the flow by virtue of the fact that time monotonically increases. When the responder receives the flow, it checks the timestamp against the timestamp of the previous flow from this initiator (if one is stored), and if the new timestamp is more recent, it processes the message.

If the responder does not have a previous timestamp stored (e.g., the old one timed-out of memory, or the responder has never received a time-stamp from this initiator), then it checks the new timestamp to see if it was sent "recently" (within a user-configured time window that corresponds to the length of time the responder stores previous flows from the initiator). This implies that the responder must share the initiator's concept of time (i.e., that the two SAs are synchronized within a certain window of time and use a common, coordinated time system like GMT). If the responder receives this flow (and it has no record of an earlier flow from the initiator), then it must check that the timestamp falls within the time window, and if it fails this check, then the message is discarded.

Assuming that the first flow is correct, then the responder sends a flow back to the initiator and includes a digital signature of the source and destination tokens, along with the initiator's challenge. Note that a timestamp is not included in this flow—Since the initiator's challenge is a nonce, it is by definition a unique value, which provides protection from replay attack.

The three-way message exchange protocol provides the same services as the two-way protocol, but relaxes the requirement for time synchronization between the initiator and responder by using a challenge-response protocol. As in the two-way protocol, the initiator in the three-way protocol includes a challenge in the first flow that the responder must sign. The initiator, however, does not include a digital signature in this flow, as it expects to receive a similar challenge from the responder that it must sign. In the second flow, the responder includes a digital signature that is computed across the required tokens, and includes a challenge for the initiator. In Flow 3, the initiator signs the responder's challenge, along with the other required tokens.

Because the three-way message exchange protocol requires three messages, it cannot be performed entirely in ATM signaling. Although the use of a third signaling flow was discussed during the development of the ATM Forum Security Specification, this approach was eventually dropped as the specification reached its final stages. Therefore, the in-band message exchange protocol must be used to implement this protocol.

For both SME protocols, when a message is formatted and signed, the format of the digital signature buffer must follow the format specified in Section 7.4.5 of the Security Specification 1.1. In addition, SSIE fields that contain algorithm-specific information (e.g., digital signatures, algorithm-specific parameters, etc.) must be encoded according to the methods that are appropriate for the algorithm, as specified in Section 8.6 and Section 8.7 of Security 1.1.

6.2   Using Secret-Key MACs

As described earlier in this chapter, implementers and users may decide to use secret-key message authentication codes to implement the initial authentication service. This option has a performance advantage over the asymmetric digital signature option, but it requires that two or more parties share secret keys. These keys must be placed in the SA via management, as ATM Security provides no mechanism for automatically exchanging symmetric authentication keys.

Two types of MAC algorithms are specified in Security 1.1 for the symmetric MAC option: keyed message digests and the use of a block cipher (e.g., DES) in CBC mode. These algorithms are described further below.

6.2.1   Keyed Message Digests

Cryptographic hash functions, such as MD5 and SHA-1, are designed to provide the following properties:

- Based on the hash value, it is impossible to uniquely determine the input message;

- It is computationally infeasible to determine a different message that produces the same hash value.

Because of these properties, a message that contains a secret-key token (along with all of the other required tokens) can be hashed so that the output is a hash value that is unique to that key. Because the hash value is unique to the key, the process of hashing a key with other authentication tokens serves as an effective (and relatively fast) method for generating MACs.

The ATM Forum Security Specification defines the use of the hashed message authentication code (HMAC) algorithm [3], along with the MD5, SHA-1, and RIPEMD-160 hash functions, for generating message authentication codes. HMAC computes a message authentication code by prepending a padded shared key with the digital signature buffer (which contains all of the authentication tokens), and calculating the hash value of this buffer using the selected hash algorithm. The result is appended to the same key (which is padded differently), and the resulting buffer is hashed again. The result of this operation is the message authentication code. (See [3] for details on HMAC.)

6.2.2   Block Cipher in CBC Mode

Another method for generating a MAC is to use a block cipher (such as DES or FEAL) in cipher block chaining mode [4]. This method, shown in Figure 6.1, is advantageous in that it can be implemented with the same hardware that is used for encrypting ATM cells.

Briefly, this algorithm uses a block cipher in CBC mode to cause a modification in the protected message to be manifested in the MAC. This algorithm works as follows: A digital signature buffer is constructed and padded to a multiple of 64 bits (the block size for DES and FEAL). The block algorithm is then applied to this buffer, using the secret key K. Since CBC mode is used in this process, the first block (D_1) is encrypted, producing a ciphertext output block (O_1), which is XORed with the second block (D_2), which is encrypted next (producing O_2). This process continues until the entire buffer is encrypted, producing a final ciphertext output O_q. Finally, O_q is subjected to an *output process* by decrypting it with a second key K1, which is the bitwise complement of K, and reencrypting the result with the original key K. The final result is the MAC.

6.3   Using Public-Key Signature Algorithms

Public-key signature algorithms are the preferred authentication mechanism in ATM networks for the following reasons:

- *Nonrepudiation:* Public-key algorithms allow the authentication key (i.e., the private key) to be held by only one entity, whereas with secret-key techniques, more than one entity may hold the authentication key(s).

- *Scalability:* For any-to-any authentication, secret-key techniques suffer from the notorious "key distribution problem" as the size of the network increases. Specifically, with secret-key techniques, the key management complexity increases $O(n^2)$, where n is the number of nodes. With public-key authentication, the key management complexity increases $O(n)$.

- *Distribution of validation keys:* With public-key authentication, the authenticating entity uses its private key and validating entities use its public key. This public key can be made available to any entity that wishes to use it through mechanisms such as public-key directories or certificate exchange mechanisms.

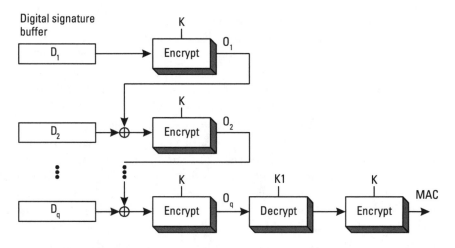

Figure 6.1 Block cipher/CBC MAC.

The ATM Security Specification describes the use of four public-key digital signature algorithms: RSA, DSA, Elliptic Curve/DSA-like, and ESIGN. As stated earlier, public-key algorithms are computationally intensive. Therefore, when public-key digital signatures are generated, they are typically generated over a hash of the message, rather than the entire message itself. The specification defines the following algorithms for use with the public-key digital signature algorithms: MD5, SHA-1, RIPEMD-160.

Each of these public-key algorithms and hash functions has unique properties that must be considered when selecting an algorithm (not all of which are technical). Some of these properties include:

- Computational complexity;
- Relative complexity of signature generation and validation (e.g., fewer computational steps required for signature validation);
- Encryption capability, as well as authentication;
- Licensing and royalty issues;
- Export/import control.

The reader is urged to consult a cryptography text such as Schneier [5] for more detail on these issues.

As with secret-key authentication, public-key authentication is performed within the context of SME. Therefore, public-key authentication can be applied to the two-way and the three-way security message exchange protocols. In addition, the processing steps described for both of these protocols are identical for both types of algorithms.

However, when public-key algorithms are used in the three-way message exchange protocol, the option of exchanging public-key certificates is allowed. Public-key certificates are a mechanism for providing the validation (public) keys to the receiver without requiring a directory server or preplacement via management. However, to protect against spoofing attacks (where a malicious entity forges a public/private key pair and claims that the public key belongs to an authorized entity), a mechanism must be used in which a trusted entity vouches for the entity/public key association. This mechanism is provided when the public-key certificate is signed by a trusted CA. If the validating entity knows the public key of the CA, then it can easily check the authenticity of the certificate. However, if it does not, it needs to obtain the CA's own certificate, which is signed by another CA that is typically at the next higher layer in the certification hierarchy. If CA's certificate checks out, then the CA's public key can be used to check the claimed public key of the authenticating entity. If the CA certificate does not check out, then the validating entity must obtain the certificate of the next CA in the certification hierarchy. This process continues until a CA certificate is found to be signed by a well-known, trusted CA.

Note that public-key certificates are allowed in the three-way message exchange protocol, but not in the two-way protocol. This is because public-key certificates can grow very large, and can exceed the 512-octet limitation for SSIEs when used in signaling. Therefore, since signaling can only support the two-way SME protocol, the two-way protocol is not allowed to carry certificates. If certificates are required for validating signatures in the two-way SME, then they must be obtained through some other means (e.g., management or a certificate server).

6.4 Example

To better understand the use of the ATM initial authentication service, consider the example illustrated in Figure 6.2.

In this example, Host$_A$ contains a security agent SA$_A$, which implements public-key authentication using the DSA digital signature algorithm with the SHA-1 hash function. The distinguished name for SA$_A$ is 0x000102030405060708090a0b0c0d0e0f00010203, which corresponds to the host's NSAP address.

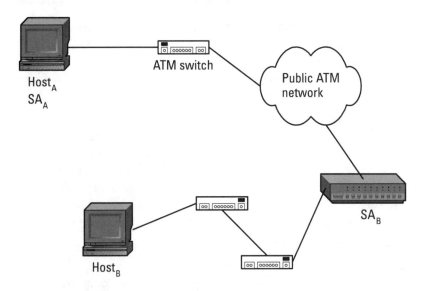

Figure 6.2 Example of an initial authentication scenario.

Host$_A$ wishes to establish a connection with Host$_B$. However, Host$_B$'s private network has an ATM firewall SA$_B$, which filters incoming connection requests to accept only those hosts that are allowed to connect and can authenticate to it. (Additionally, SA$_B$ can be configured to accept connection requests originating behind other ATM firewalls.) Like SA$_A$, SA$_B$ also uses the DSA algorithm, and it has its own private/public key pair, with its public key contained in the certificate Cert$_B$. SA$_B$'s responder distinguished name is 0x030201000f0e0d0c0b0a09080706050403020100.

6.4.1 Initiator Security Agent (Host) Processing

Since SA$_B$ is filtering signaling messages, the two-way message exchange protocol is used for initial authentication. Therefore, when Host$_A$ generates a SETUP message, SA$_A$ augments the message with an SSIE that contains FLOW1-2WE. However, before the SSIE can be appended to the message, SA$_A$ must determine the values of the various SSIE fields:

- *A: Initiator distinguished name.* This field contains the NSAP address of SA$_A$ (and Host$_A$).
- *B: Responder distinguished name.* This field contains the NSAP address of SA$_B$ (the ATM firewall).

- *SecOpt: Security options.* This field contains the security options for the initial authentication service (in this case, the DSA and SHA-1 algorithm identifiers and parameters). Note: The DSA "P" and "Q" parameters are public parameters and are included in SA$_A$'s certificate. Therefore, they are not included in the "signature algorithm details" field.

- *T$_a$: Timestamp.* This field contains the current 32-bit time value and a 32-bit sequence number. The time value is in GMT, and is encoded in the same fashion as UNIX encodes time (that is, corresponding to the number of seconds since 00:00:00 GMT on January 1, 1970). The sequence number is the number of authentication flows (including this one) that have occurred for this time value.

- *R$_a$: Random number.* This field contains a 32-bit random number, which is a challenge for SA$_B$.

- *Sig$_a$: Digital signature.* SA$_A$'s digital signature computed using its private key or secret key, which it shares with SA$_B$. Note: The digital signature is computed using the following digital signature buffer constructed using the procedures described in section 7.4.5.1.1 of the Security 1.1 Specification. For this example, the message to be signed is shown in Table 6.1.

6.4.2   Responder Security Agent (Firewall) Processing

When the responder receives FLOW1-2WE, it must perform a number of checks to ensure that the flow is authentic and that the SETUP message is allowed to proceed into the private network that it protects. These checks are:

Table 6.1
Contents of Message Signed by Initiator SA$_A$

Symbol	Description	Value (Hex)
A	Initiator distinguished name	821502000102030405060708090a0b0c0d0e0f00010203
B	Responder distinguished name	831502030201000f0e0d0c0b0a09080706050403020100
T$_a$	Time-variant timestamp	d638b21c8200000000
R$_a$	Initiator random number	d434a690d7
SecOpt	Security service specification section	889381a40102a60102

- Whether the responder distinguished name (B) is the same as SA$_B$'s distinguished name. If the distinguished names do not match, then the flow is rejected.

- Whether the received timestamp value is greater than or equal to the timestamp received from a previous flow from SA$_A$. If not, then the flow (and SETUP request) is rejected. If the received timestamp is equal to the previously received timestamp, SA$_B$ checks if the received sequence number is greater than the previously received sequence number. If not, then the flow is rejected; otherwise, the flow is accepted and the timestamp and sequence number is stored for future reference. If the received timestamp is greater than the previously-received timestamp (or if no previous timestamp has been recorded), and value falls within a window W (a configurable parameter, determined according to site policy) of SA$_B$'s current time value, then the flow is accepted, and the timestamp and sequence number are stored for future reference. Otherwise, the flow is rejected. (Note: The parameter W allows the responder to remove stored timestamp and sequence number values after W seconds, but implies that the initiator and responder clock must be synchronized within W seconds of each other. Therefore, small values of W reduce the amount of storage, but require tighter clock synchronization between initiator and responder.)

- Whether SA$_B$ supports the algorithms contained in the security specification section of the SSIE.

- Whether the digital signature is correct given the initiator's public key or shared secret key. If the signature is not correct, then the flow is rejected.

- Whether Host$_A$ (authenticated by SA$_A$) is allowed to initiate a connection into the private network protected by SA$_B$. If not, then the flow is rejected.

If all of these tests pass, then the SETUP message is propagated to the called host.

When the CONNECT message passes through SA$_B$, it is augmented with an SSIE to allow SA$_B$ to authenticate to SA$_A$. This SSIE contains the following FLOW2-2WE message fields:

- *A: Initiator distinguished name.* This field contains the NSAP address of SA_A (and $Host_A$). The encoding for this field is identical to that received in FLOW1-2WE.

- *B: Responder distinguished name.* This field contains the NSAP address of SA_B (the ATM firewall). The encoding for this field is identical to that received in FLOW1-2WE.

- *Ra: Random number.* This field contains the 32-bit random number generated by SA_A and sent to SA_B in FLOW1-2WE.

- *Sigb: Digital signature.* SA_B's digital signature computed using its private key or secret key, which it shares with SA_A. Note: The digital signature buffer is constructed using the procedures described in section 7.4.5.1.2 of the Security 1.1 Specification. For this example, the message to be signed is shown in Table 6.2.

6.4.3 Initiator Security Agent (Host) Processing

When FLOW2-2WE is received, the initiating SA must validate it before it permits completion of the connection. Therefore, SA_A performs the following checks:

- Whether the initiator distinguished name (A) is the same as SA_A's distinguished name. If the distinguished names do not match, then the flow is rejected;

- Whether the received R_a is the same as the one it sent in FLOW1-2WE. If not, then the flow is rejected;

- Whether the digital signature is correct. If the signature is not correct, then the flow is rejected;

Table 6.2
Contents of Message Signed by Responder SA_B

Symbol	Description	Value (Hex)
A	Initiator distinguished name	8215020001020304050607080090a0b0c0d 0e0f00010203
B	Responder distinguished name	831502030201000f0e0d0c0b0a09080706 050403020100
R_a	Initiator random number	d434a690d7

- Whether hosts authenticated by SA$_B$ are allowed to connect to Host$_A$. If not, then the flow is rejected.

6.5 Summary

The ATM Security 1.1 Specification provides two authentication schemes that are based on existing international standards. These authentication schemes use asymmetric (public key) and symmetric (secret key) cryptographic algorithms to digitally sign tokens that provide uniqueness, freshness, and correct sequencing of the SME authentication flows. Symmetric digital signatures are generated using keyed hash functions such as HMAC, or a block cipher in CBC mode. Asymmetric digital signatures are computed over the hashed contents of a message, using a public-key digital signature algorithm such as RSA.

ATM Security 1.1 provides flexibility in the selection of the particular authentication approach. This is due to the number of trade-offs involved in the various approaches. For example, authentication using the two-way SME protocol requires security agents to have synchronized clocks, but allows firewalls to restrict incoming switched virtual circuits to those remote devices that are authorized and can strongly authenticate in signaling. Likewise, the selection of authentication algorithms presents trade-offs. Public-key algorithms have more scalable key management properties but are typically slower than secret-key algorithms.

References

[1] International Standards Organization, "Information Technology—Open Systems Interconnection—The Directory: Authentication Framework," ISO/IEC 9594-8, 1995.

[2] International Standards Organization, "Information Technology—Security Techniques—Key Management—Part 2: Mechanisms Using Symmetric Techniques," ISO/IEC 11770-2, 1996.

[3] Krawczyk, H., M. Bellare, and R. Canetti, "HMAC: Keyed-Hashing for Message Authentication," Internet Engineering Task Force RFC 2104, February 1997.

[4] International Standards Organization, "Information Technology—Security Techniques—Data Integrity Mechanism Using a Cryptographic Check Function Employing a Block Cipher Algorithm," ISO/IEC 9797, 1994.

[5] Schneier, B., *Applied Cryptography*, Second Edition, New York: John Wiley and Sons, 1996.

7

Data Origin Authentication

ATM data origin authentication, or data integrity, is the security service that allows a recipient to verify that the data came from a source with which it shares a secret key, and that the data has not been modified in transit. There are two varieties of integrity protection that are provided in the ATM Security Specification 1.1: data integrity with replay/reordering protection and data integrity without such protection. By performing data origin authentication immediately after two parties perform initial authentication, the virtual circuit is protected from malicious modification attacks and from attacks that could result in the "hijacking" of a virtual circuit by a malicious third party.

As with the data confidentiality (encryption) service, the integrity service is a security service that becomes operational once the virtual circuit is established; therefore, it must be very fast. The integrity service requires a shared secret key to operate, and the operational parameters of the integrity service (such as algorithm selection and shared master and session keys) can be either negotiated automatically using the SME protocol or configured via management.

When the integrity and confidentiality services are used together, the integrity service is applied to the plaintext (i.e., before encryption and after decryption). Although it may be tempting to rely solely on encryption to secure a virtual circuit, encryption alone does not necessarily provide a data origin authentication service. This is true for two reasons. First, encryption does not (by itself) provide a message integrity check. If data is encrypted with the wrong key, or if the ciphertext was modified in transit, then the decryption process would improperly decrypt the received data. However, without some other message integrity check, the decryptor would not know if the result was properly decrypted or not—Another mechanism is required to determine if the random gibberish should be discarded. Secondly, if encryption is used with a self-synchronizing mode of operation (such as CBC mode), and the ciphertext was modified, then the decryption process would recover synchronization and proceed. (Integrity-checking modes of operation are possible, but none of the Security 1.1 ATM encryption modes implement this feature.)

Unlike encryption, the ATM integrity service operates at the ATM adaptation layer (AAL). Specifically, in the ATM Security Specification Version 1.1, the integrity service is specified for AAL 3/4 and AAL 5; AAL 1 and AAL 2 are not currently supported. Since only VCCs may be terminated by an AAL, the integrity service is not specified for VPCs. Furthermore, since AAL entities typically reside in ATM end systems, integrity is provided on an end-to-end basis instead of via a "bump in the fiber" integrity device.

The following sections describe the ATM integrity service in more detail and describe the algorithms that are specified in the Security Specification for implementation of this service.

7.1   Implementation Overview

As stated earlier, data origin authentication is provided only for AAL 3/4 and AAL 5 service data units. This mechanism works by appending a keyed MAC (described in Section 7.3) to the AAL SDU.

Recall from Chapter 6 that a keyed message authentication code works in two ways. The first method, the keyed hash function, builds a string that contains the shared secret key and the message to be signed and generates a hash value using this string. Alternately, a block cipher in CBC mode can be used. The latter method uses a block encryption algorithm with a shared secret key, processes the message in CBC mode, and performs an output processing function on the last block to determine the MAC.

As with the data confidentiality (encryption) service, the integrity service requires shared secret keys. Either the master key (which remains constant during the life of the virtual circuit) or the initial session key may be negotiated using the SME protocol (either in-band or via signaling). Alternately, these keys may be configured via management. Like encryption keys, integrity keys may be changed periodically using the session key update protocol described in Chapter 8. However, because the integrity service operates on AAL SDUs, when SKC is performed, it is performed on an AAL boundary rather than at an arbitrary cell boundary.

7.2 Implementation Details

The Security Specification 1.1 describes two forms of data origin authentication: with replay/reordering protection and without. When replay/reordering protection is provided, a receiving device verifies that an AAL SDU was not modified or replicated in transit and that it was not reordered relative to other AAL SDUs on the virtual circuit.

If replay/reordering protection at the AAL level is required, then a 48-bit sequence number (which is sufficiently large for high-bandwidth circuits, as described later) is used to indicate ordering to the receiver. This sequence number is set to zero at the beginning of the virtual circuit and is incremented for each AAL SDU that is sent. When the SDU is generated, the sender appends the sequence number to the SDU, and calculates the MAC using the secret key it shares with the receiver, as shown in Figure 7.1.

When the SDU arrives at the receiver, the receiver validates the MAC and checks the AAL SDU sequence number. The receiver performs two checks on the sequence number to provide antireplay/reordering assurance: It checks that the newly received sequence number is greater than the sequence number for the previous AAL SDU and that the sequence number did not wrap past zero. (Note that by only checking that the sequence number is greater than the previous sequence number, this mechanism does not attempt to detect and handle lost SDUs. This is the responsibility of the higher-layer protocol.) Although the sequence number is incremented at the sender for each AAL SDU, discard mechanisms in the ATM network may result in entire SDUs being discarded before reaching the receiver. If either the MAC validation or the sequence number check fails, then the SDU is discarded and error-handling procedures should be performed. If both of these checks succeed, then the receiver stores the current sequence number for use when checking future AAL SDUs.

It is important that the sequence number not wrap during the lifetime of the virtual circuit. If it did wrap, then the receiver must discard it because the receiver cannot determine if the sequence number has wrapped or if the AAL SDU was duplicated. For high-speed ATM links (e.g., OC-192, which is approximately 10 Gbps), this number could wrap quickly, effectively

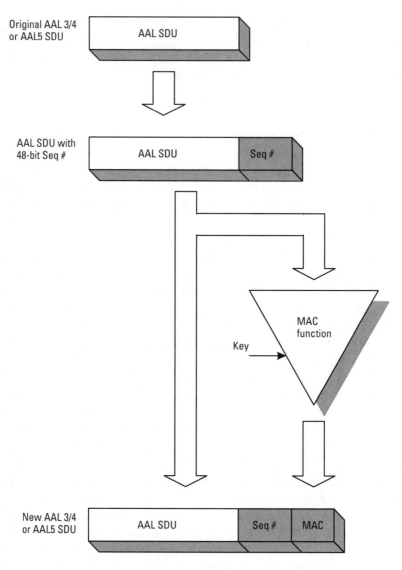

Figure 7.1 AAL integrity with replay/reordering protection.

reducing the lifetime of the virtual circuit. For this reason, a 48-bit sequence number was specified. For an OC-192 link carrying 64-byte SDUs back-to-back at line rate, the sequence number would wrap after 14.5 million seconds, or 167 days. For connections (especially PVCs) that persist longer than 167 days, this is not a concern because the sequence number is reset after each integrity session key update (which is described in Chapter 8), and key updates should occur more frequently than 167 days.

Sometimes, replay/reordering protection is not needed. If higher-layer protocols or applications (e.g., TCP/IP) can detect or tolerate out-of-sequence delivery and packet duplication, then the added overhead associated with replay/reordering protection is not necessary. The procedure for implementing AAL SDU integrity without replay/reordering protection is shown in Figure 7.2. When the AAL SDU is generated, the sender calculates a MAC using the secret key it shares with the receiver, appends the MAC to the AAL SDU, and transmits the augmented SDU. When the AAL SDU reaches its destination, the receiver validates the MAC by recalculating it and comparing this value with the MAC included in the SDU. If the MAC values do not match, then the SDU should be discarded, and an error should be reported or recorded in a counter, depending on the implementation.

The data origin authentication service is specified at the AAL level because adding the MAC to an AAL SDU is more straightforward than ATM cell-level integrity. During development of the Security Specification 1.1, a cell-level integrity mechanism was also considered, which included a special ATM cell to carry the MAC that was calculated over a given number of cells that preceded it. The mechanism, however, required the receiver to buffer ATM cells until the MAC cell is received—If the MAC failed, then all of the cells would be dropped. This mechanism is more complicated than the AAL-based mechanism, and so the AAL mechanism was selected.

7.3 Keyed MACs

The ATM Security Specification defines two classes of algorithms for the integrity service: the HMAC algorithm, and the block cipher/CBC mode MAC. Both of these algorithms are symmetric algorithms; that is, they use shared secret keys to generate the MAC. Although asymmetric (public key) algorithms could be used for this service, their performance for data stream integrity is limited.

In general, a keyed hash function (e.g., keyed MD5 or HMAC) takes a message M, augments it with a key K, and generates a hash value across the augmented message. This hash value is used as the MAC. Since only the sender and receiver know K, when the receiver validates the MAC (by performing the same operation as the sender), the receiver is assured that the sender generated the message and that the message was not modified in

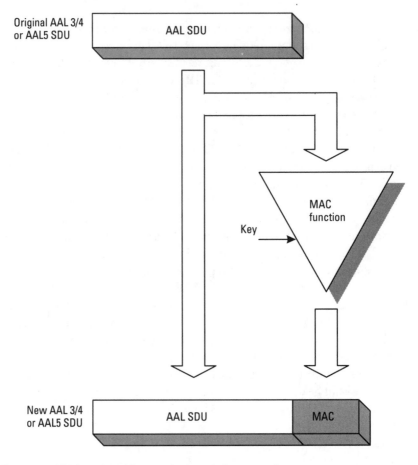

Figure 7.2 AAL integrity without replay/reordering protection.

transit. For HMAC, if H is the hash function (e.g., SHA-1, MD5, or RIPEMD), then the sender calculates the MAC as follows [1]:

1. Pad the end of K with 0x00 until the padded length is the block length of the hash function, B (in octets). This produces the value Kpad;

2. Calculate MAC = H(Kpad $\oplus$ Opad, H(Kpad $\oplus$ Ipad, M));

where $\oplus$ is the exclusive or (XOR) operator, Opad is the outer padding, which is the value 0x36 replicated to a length of B octets, and Ipad is the inner pad, which is the value 0x5c replicated to a length of B octets.

The HMAC algorithm is a powerful algorithm because it works with a variety of hash algorithms. This provides considerable flexibility for the implementer because the hash algorithm can be selected according to technical criteria such as the security and computational complexity of the algorithm. For example, as Dobbertin describes in [2], MD5 may have undesirable collision properties. However, MD5's performance may lead an implementer or end-user to select it for high-bandwidth applications, especially where there is little concern for a concerted malicious modification attack. However, if hash throughput is not much of a concern but malicious modification attacks are a significant concern, then other hash algorithms such as SHA-1 or RIPEMD may be selected. In addition, the hash-independent property of HMAC allows it to be easily upgraded in the future, as stronger and/or faster hash algorithms are developed. In keeping with the theme of flexibility, ATM Security 1.1 defines the use of the HMAC algorithm for all three algorithms: MD5, SHA-1, and RIPEMD.

Another method for generating MACs is the block cipher/CBC mode MAC. Recall that this MAC, which is described in more detail in Chapter 6, takes a message M and uses a block algorithm in CBC mode with shared secret key K to encrypt the message. The last block of this encrypted message is postprocessed to produce the resulting MAC. This MAC algorithm is useful for two reasons: (1) encryption algorithms, particularly those that are implemented in special-purpose silicon, are faster than message digest algorithms, and (2) ATM adapters and drivers that implement encryption can also implement AAL integrity without adding a new cryptographic algorithm implementation. The block algorithms that are specified for use with the CBC MAC include DES, Triple DES, and FEAL.

7.4 SME and Data Origin Authentication

The data origin authentication service is performed on an active virtual circuit, which is established via signaling (SVCs) or via management (PVCs). The particular algorithm and integrity options (i.e., the replay/reordering protection option), as well as the shared secret master and initial session keys, may be configured manually or via the SME protocol.

When the SME initiator wishes to negotiate the integrity service, it must specify in the security service options (see Section 7.2.2 of Security 1.1) whether it requires the integrity service, and if so, if it requires replay/reordering protection. If the initiator requires replay/reordering protection, it specifies "required, with replay/reordering protection" in the data integrity service options octet group. If the initiator requires integrity but does not want replay/reordering protection applied, then it specifies "required, without replay/reordering protection." If the initiator requires integrity protection but does not care whether replay/reordering protection is provided, then it specifies "required, with or without replay/reordering protection." In this case, the responder chooses whether replay/reordering protection is to be applied and communicates this choice to the initiator in the data integrity service options in FLOW-2 by specifying "required, with replay/reordering protection" or "required, without replay/reordering protection."

SME is also used to exchange master and initial session keys. The procedure for exchanging these keys is the same as the procedure used for exchanging encryption keys. This procedure is described in detail in Chapter 5.

The SKU service is used to change integrity keys without tearing-down and negotiating a new security association. As with SKU for the confidentiality service (described in Chapter 8), SKU for integrity keys works in two phases: an SKE phase and an SKC phase. The SKE phase uses non-real-time OAM cells with a security function identifier of 2 (data integrity session key exchange) to transfer the next integrity key from the source to the destination. This new integrity key is encrypted with the master key that is developed during SME negotiation. (Note, however, that this is the same master key that is used to encrypt *confidentiality* session keys, if encryption is also provided in the same security association.)

Once SKE is completed, the new key is enacted by sending real-time SKC OAM cells that contain the key number for the new key. Since the integrity service is performed at the AAL SDU level, the key changeover can only occur on an SDU boundary (rather than at an arbitrary cell boundary for the confidentiality service).

7.5 Control Plane Authentication and Integrity

Security Specification 1.1 also provides a mechanism for implementing data origin authentication/integrity on control plane virtual circuits. The purpose of this mechanism is to protect against malicious modification of UNI or NNI signaling messages, particularly those that traverse multiple physical hops (e.g., through a VPC).

The control plane authentication mechanism is the same mechanism that is specified for user plane integrity except that it works on signaling AAL

SDUs rather than user plane AAL SDUs. In addition, the following restrictions apply:

- Control plane authentication parameters are not negotiated. Rather, they are configured manually.

- The control plane authentication mechanism requires master and initial session keys to be preplaced via management (however, SKU is still allowed).

- The control plane authentication service uses the "replay/reordering protection" integrity service option.

This mechanism has a number of limitations, not the least of which is that it only supports hop-by-hop control plane authentication (i.e., authentication of signaling messages between two devices that are physically or logically adjacent). Protection of signaling messages across multiple hops is not provided here. This is due to the problems associated with the handling of information fields that change along an end-to-end path (described further in Chapter 12).

The other limitations associated with this mechanism relate to the fact that the Security 1.1 control plane approach requires the security association to be configured manually. Therefore, this approach does not apply when signaling channels are established dynamically (e.g., PNNI routing control channels). This problem is addressed in a new, but separate, control plane security specification, which is described in Chapter 10.

7.6 Summary

Data origin authentication is an ATM Security 1.1 service that allows a receiving security agent to verify the integrity and source of an AAL service data unit. Depending on the requirements of the security association, additional mechanisms for protection from replay and reordering of AAL SDUs may also be used. The selection of the antireplay option is performed during SME and is typically selected by policy if similar functions are not provided by higher-level protocols. Data origin authentication at the ATM cell level is not provided in the Security 1.1 Specification.

Two algorithms are used for generating MACs: the keyed hash function and block cipher/CBC. The keyed hash approach incorporates a shared secret key into the message that requires protection and uses a hash function on the keyed message to generate a MAC. The receiving end takes similar steps with the same key to verify the message. The block cipher/CBC method, however, uses an encryption algorithm (with a shared secret key) to generate the MAC for the message. SME is used to negotiate which algorithm is used. Implementers may choose either approach, based on such factors as performance (e.g., hash function performance versus performance of block cipher in CBC mode) and/or cost (e.g., reuse of cryptographic hardware).

References

[1]   Krawczyk, H., M. Bellare, and R. Canetti, "HMAC: Keyed-Hashing for Message Authentication," Internet Engineering Task Force RFC 2104, February 1997.

[2]   Dobbertin, H., "The Status of MD5 After a Recent Attack," *CryptoBytes*, Vol. 2, No. 2, RSA Labs, Summer 1996.

8

Encryption

This chapter describes some of the cryptographic algorithms and modes of operation defined in ATM Security Specification Version 1.1 for providing confidentiality services. It also discusses some encryption issues in the context of ATM communications.

As described in Chapter 2, the basic unit of ATM data is the cell, which consists of a 5-byte header and a 48-byte payload. The payload can be encrypted, but the header is left in the clear to allow end-to-end switching. When implementing cell encryption, careful attention to the proper bit ordering (numbering from left to right, or right to left) is crucial for correct cryptographic processing. By convention in the ATM Security Specification 1.1 [1], each of the 48 bytes in an ATM cell payload are numbered 1 to 48, and within each byte, bits are numbered 8 to 1 (left to right), as shown in Figure 8.1. These bytes are grouped into blocks of 8 bytes (64 bits), which are encrypted at once by the DES or FEAL encryption algorithm.

The bits within the 64-bit blocks used by the DES and FEAL symmetric key block encipherment algorithms are numbered, from left to right, from 1 to 64 as shown in Figure 8.2. For modes of operation (described in Section 8.3) involving feedback (e.g., CBC), the leftmost ciphertext bit (bit 1) is XORed with the leftmost bit in the cell payload (bit 8 of payload octets 1, 9, 17, 25, 33, and 41). The result is encrypted by DES or FEAL in the leftmost bit position (bit 1). For the counter mode of operation, the leftmost bit of the keystream from the DES or FEAL algorithm (bit 1) is XORed with the leftmost bit in the cell payload (bit 8 of

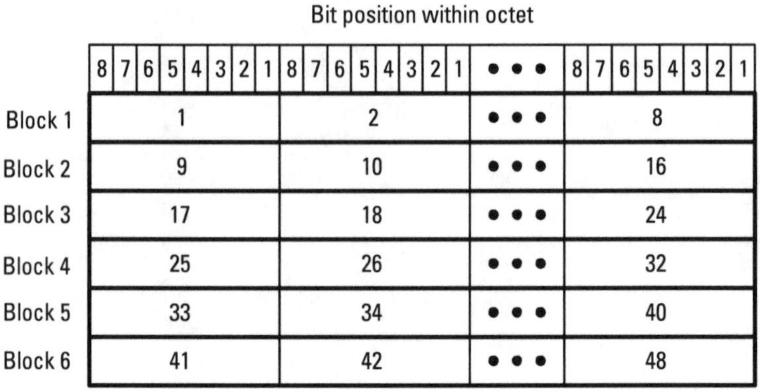

Bit position within octet

8 7 6 5 4 3 2 1	8 7 6 5 4 3 2 1	• • •	8 7 6 5 4 3 2 1
Block 1 1	2	• • •	8
Block 2 9	10	• • •	16
Block 3 17	18	• • •	24
Block 4 25	26	• • •	32
Block 5 33	34	• • •	40
Block 6 41	42	• • •	48

Payload octet number

Figure 8.1 Bit ordering within an ATM cell.

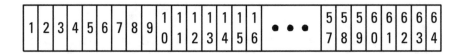

Figure 8.2 Bit ordering within an encryption/decryption block.

payload octets 1, 9, 17, 25, 33, and 41). The result becomes the leftmost payload bit of the encrypted cell. When encrypting the counter mode state vector (the result of which is to be XORed with the cell payload), the leftmost bit (bit 63) of the state vector is encrypted by DES or FEAL at bit position 1, bit 62 of the state vector is encrypted at bit position 2, and so on, with bit 0 of the state vector encrypted at bit position 64.

8.1 Block Algorithms

Cryptographic algorithms fall into two categories: block ciphers and stream ciphers. Stream ciphers, like the One Time Pad (where the key is as long or longer than the message to be encrypted/decrypted) operate on successive bits of the message with successive (and corresponding) bits of the key or key stream. Block ciphers, on the other hand, break the message up into blocks (8, 32, 64, 128, etc. bits in length) and operate on each block with the same key. These two categories of ciphers are illustrated in Figures 8.3 and 8.4.

The focus in this book is block ciphers, as those are the kinds of cryptographic algorithms specified by Security 1.1. Block ciphers can use public-key or secret-key algorithms.

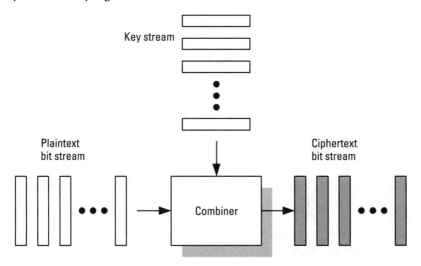

Figure 8.3 Stream encipherment.

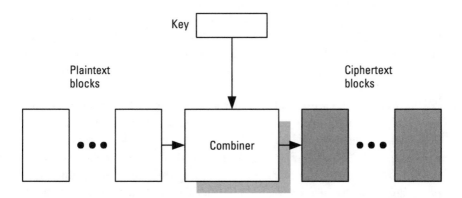

Figure 8.4 Block encipherment.

8.2 Public-Key Versus Secret-Key Algorithms

Public-key algorithms use two keys; one key is kept private and one key is made public. When using secret-key algorithms, both (or all) parties share a common encryption/decryption key, which must be kept secret. As stated in Chapter 1, public-key encryption provides nonrepudiation and scales better with regard to key management but is much more computationally intensive than secret-key encryption. There are two public-key algorithms specified for use by Security 1.1. There are also two secret-key algorithms (and several variants of them) specified for use by Security 1.1.

8.2.1 RSA

RSA is a public-key cryptography algorithm named for the three men (Ronald Rivest, Adi Shamir, and Leonard Adleman) who developed it. Security 1.1 allows RSA for digital signatures and key exchange.

In general terms, when using RSA, one chooses a pair of large prime numbers p and q, and computes their product, n. One must also choose a key, d. The second key, e, is computed using a variant of Euclid's algorithm for computing the greatest common divisor, such that $e \cdot d \mod (p-1)(q-1) = 1$. This way, e and d are multiplicative inverses $(\mod (p-1)(q-1))$ of each other. One (and only one) of the keys (e or d) and the modulus, n, is made public. The remaining key is private and should be protected as such. The strength of RSA public-key encryption resides in the difficulty of factoring large numbers (the modulus, n). If someone is able to factor n into p and q, he could then recover the keys d and e in the same manner as the original calculations.

The RSA algorithm encrypts a block of information by treating that block as a large number and raising it to the other confidant's public key power, $\mod n$. When the other confidant receives the message, he (and only he) can decrypt it by taking the message and raising it to his private key power, $\mod n$.

For digital signatures, the information (such as the hash value produced by the SHA-1 function) is raised to the originator's private key power, $\mod n$. Since he is the only one holding this key, nonrepudiation is provided (that is, he must be the one signing this information). When someone else wishes to verify that the originator was the one signing this information, that other party can raise the message to the originator's public key power, $\mod n$, and recover the information. The verifying party can then compare this recovered value with a hash value computed over the message (by SHA-1). The two values should agree. If not, either the message has been corrupted (intentionally by a malicious party or naturally by bit errors) or it did not originate with the claimed person.

Implementation details for this cryptosystem can be found in [2, 3]. As stated in the original paper [2] and emphasized by Rivest in [4], p and q should be chosen with certain properties: specifically, large prime factors in p - 1 and q - 1. This discourages attacks such as those described by Simmons and Norris [5], where encrypted information can be recovered by repeatedly raising the encrypted value to the power of the encryption exponent. When p and q are chosen as indicated, this attack is sufficiently costly (computationally) that it has been suggested in [4] that the effort would be better spent factoring the modulus, n.

8.2.2 Diffie-Hellman

Although Diffie-Hellman is considered a public-key cryptography algorithm (named for its inventors, Whitfield Diffie and Martin Hellman), it is more rightly termed a key development algorithm. Whereas both communicating parties possess a private and public component, the real encryption/decryption key is developed from pieces supplied by both communicating parties. Security 1.1 allows Diffie-Hellman for key exchange, as described in Chapter 5.

This algorithm, also known as *exponential key distribution*, makes use of the difficulty of computing logarithms over finite fields with a large prime number (p) of elements. The modulus, p, and a base, g, are public parameters of the cryptosystem. In this algorithm, each party (A and B) generates a random number (a and b) greater than 0, but less than p - 1. Party A computes $x = g^a \bmod p$ and publishes x while keeping a private. Party B computes $y = g^b \bmod p$ and publishes y while keeping b private.

When parties A and B wish to communicate privately, such as to exchange symmetric cryptographic keys for bulk encryption, they use a key $z = g^{ab} \bmod p$. Party A computes $z = y^a \bmod p$ (or g^b raised to the a power) and party B computes $z = x^b \bmod p$ (or g^a raised to the b power). This key, z, can now be used with a symmetric encryption algorithm to exchange private information or a session key for another symmetric encryption algorithm. For more details, the reader is referred to the paper by Diffie and Hellman [6].

8.2.3 DES

DES is a symmetric block cipher that operates on 64-bit blocks of data (input and output) and uses a 56-bit key. It is a Feistel-type cipher. Feistel ciphers operate on left and right halves of a block of bits, in multiple rounds. The block halves are exchanged (left for right) from their usual order after the last round. An important property of Feistel ciphers is that the function f, employed by a Feistel cipher to operate on a left or right half-block of data, need not be invertible to allow inversion of the Feistel cipher. In DES, the function f can itself be considered a product cipher (or substitution- permutation cipher), since that function performs both substitutions (to introduce confusion) and permutations (to introduce diffusion).

Another important property of Feistel ciphers is that due to their structure, decryption is performed using the same multiple round process as encryption but uses the subkeys (one required per round) in reverse order. By eliminating the need for two different algorithms (one for encryption and one for decryption), implementation is simplified.

Since DES is a secret key algorithm, the encryption/decryption keys must be shared between communicating parties, either by preplacement or by key exchange protocols (such as those involving RSA or Diffie-Hellman). DES and triple DES (described in Section 8.2.3.2) are specified by Security 1.1 for encryption to provide confidentiality. Further details on DES can be found in U.S. Federal Information Processing Standard 46 [7].

8.2.3.1 DES40

DES40 effectively uses a 40-bit encryption/decryption key instead of the 56-bit key used with DES. Although now DES can be exported from the United States with the full 56-bit key, there was a period of time where only encryption using 40-bit (or smaller) keys could be exported from the United States.

Typically eight octets of key are supplied for use with DES. Since the algorithm only uses 56-bit keys, eight of the bits (k_8, k_{16}, k_{24}, k_{32}, k_{40}, k_{48}, k_{56}, and k_{64}) are ignored. These bits can be used for parity checking within the key. To achieve a 40-bit key for the exportable version of DES, 16 of the bits (k_{1-4}, k_{17-20}, k_{33-36}, and k_{49-52}) are set to zero.

Even though DES40 is listed in Security 1.1, it is now considered deprecated and its use is discouraged.

8.2.3.2 Triple DES

Triple DES employs the DES algorithm in a way sometimes referred to as encrypt-decrypt-encrypt (EDE) mode. EDE mode using two keys was proposed by W. Tuchman and summarized by Schneier in [3]. The incoming plaintext is encrypted with the first key, decrypted with the second key, and then encrypted again with the first key. On the other end, the received ciphertext is decrypted with the first key, encrypted with the second key, and again decrypted with the first key to produce plaintext. This process is shown in Figure 8.5.

Two-key, triple DES schemes (with 56-bit keys) can be cryptanalyzed using a *chosen plaintext* attack with about 2^{56} operations and 2^{56} words of memory [8]. (In terms of work, this is on par with two-key, double DES, which is susceptible to a *known plaintext* attack with 2^{56} operations and 2^{56} words of memory.) Although in theory this is a weakness, Merkle and Hellman [8] state that in practice it is very difficult to mount a chosen plaintext attack against a DES cryptosystem. This makes two-key, triple DES significantly stronger than two-key, double DES, because an attack would now require 2^{112} operations (and no memory).

Although triple DES can be used with two or three keys and in several modes (EDE, EEE, etc.), it is the two-key EDE variant that is specified for use by Security 1.1.

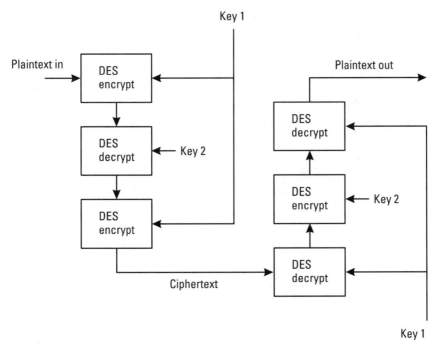

Figure 8.5 Two-key, triple DES.

8.2.4 FEAL

FEAL is also a Feistel cipher, with a variable number of rounds. Designed by Akihiro Shimizu and Shoji Miyaguchi, FEAL operates on 64-bit blocks of data (input and output) with a 64-bit secret key. FEAL was designed for optimal performance in software implementations on 8-bit microprocessors, but 16-round FEAL (FEAL-16) is less secure than DES [9]. To achieve security on the order of that provided by DES, the number of rounds in the FEAL implementation must be increased to 24 or more rounds, which reduces the throughput of software implementations.

Security 1.1 allows 32-round FEAL (FEAL-32) for confidentiality services. Implementation details of FEAL can be found in various cryptography texts [3, 9].

8.3 Modes of Operation

Modes of operation specify how data is encrypted and decrypted by the cryptographic algorithms. Each mode of operation has associated with it three properties, as shown in Table 8.1. These properties include the ability of the mode to self-synchronize in the event of an upset (e.g., cell loss) in the encrypted data stream, the ability of the mode to scale to high speeds, and the mode's ability to protect against dictionary lookup attacks (which can occur when a plaintext symbol always maps to the same ciphertext symbol). This section describes each of these modes in more detail.

The simplest is the ECB mode. With ECB mode, blocks enter the algorithm, are encrypted or decrypted, and exit the process. ECB mode is like using electronic encipherment/decipherment as a manual process, looking

Table 8.1

Properties of Cryptographic Modes of Operation

Mode	Property		
	Self-synchronizing	Scalable	Dictionary lookup protection
ECB	Yes	Yes	No
CBC	Yes	No	Yes
Counter mode	No	Yes	Yes

up each entry in a (electronic) book of codes. Each block (word) encrypted under the same key (code book) will produce the same value.

This mode has several disadvantages. First, one can build a dictionary of plaintext-ciphertext pairs for future use (during that key period), since the same plaintext encrypted by the same key will yield the same ciphertext. A further disadvantage is that ECB mode provides no protection against replay attacks. An adversary could record an encrypted message and later during the same key period (i.e., before the cryptographic keys have been changed), replay the message, which would be properly decrypted and processed.

Security 1.1 defines three modes of operation for use with the secret key cryptographic algorithms for confidentiality services: ECB, CBC, and counter mode. Of these three specified modes of operation, ECB and CBC modes are self-synchronizing; that is, as long as bit count integrity has been maintained and only flipped or stuck bits have been encountered, the crypto-system will come back into synchronization after a block or two. Depending on the implementation, counter mode may need to be resynchronized after any bit errors.

8.3.1 CBC Mode

Cipher block chaining refers to a mode of operation in which data is fed around the cryptographic engine to be combined with unencrypted data. This is depicted in Figure 8.6 and is thoroughly described in U.S. Federal Information Processing Standard 81 [10]. In brief, for encryption, the first plaintext block is XORed with an initial value or initialization vector (IV). The result is then sent through the cryptographic engine to be encrypted. The encrypted block is output down the communication line and a copy is fed back and XORed with the next block of plaintext (instead of an IV) for subsequent processing.

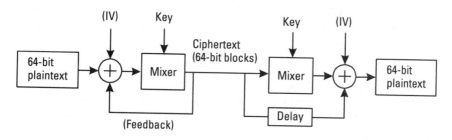

Figure 8.6 CBC mode of operation.

On decryption, the first block of incoming ciphertext is not only decrypted by the cryptographic engine but is also fed ahead (around the crypto engine) for use with the next block. Meanwhile, the decrypted block is XORed with the IV to produce the first block of plaintext. When the next block of ciphertext comes in, it is fed forward (for future use) and sent into the crypto engine for decryption. The decrypted block is then XORed with the previous block of ciphertext to produce plaintext.

Pipelining is a method of implementation whereby an algorithm is broken up into many stages and the output of one stage is fed directly into the next stage. This allows the algorithm, DES for instance (which can be broken into at least 16 stages), to operate on many blocks of data simultaneously, each in various stages. Encryption functions and modes of operation with feedback of key or plaintext/ciphertext (e.g., CBC mode) do not scale well for high speeds. In pipelined implementations of encryption hardware, the pipeline must be flushed or run dry in order to obtain the value to be fed back for the XOR operation with the next block, defeating the gains of pipelining. This limits cryptographic throughput rates. Additionally, modes of operation employing feedback or feed-forward functions do not scale (in a parallel manner) *and* interoperate with versions having different degrees of parallelism.

8.3.2 Counter Mode

Counter mode (also sometimes known as filter generator algorithms) has been found both to scale for high-speed operation and interoperate with unscaled or differently scaled implementations (Figure 8.7). This mode can also take full advantage of pipelined cryptographic hardware. Being efficient and easy to implement, counter mode is well suited for ATM encryption.

Counter mode (CM) is defined as a next-state function (that does not depend on a cryptographic key) and a cryptographic function that makes use of the state (from the next-state function) and the cryptographic key. The resultant output of this cryptographic function is combined with the plaintext or ciphertext. Specifically, one way of implementing CM, shown in Figure 8.8, is by using a linear feedback shift register (LFSR) to generate a sequence of states, with each state feeding into a crypto engine such as DES. Using the (shared) secret key, the state is encrypted and then XORed with the plaintext blocks and sent down the communication line. Decryption uses the same process. The sequence of states is generated and encrypted in the same manner and then XORed with the incoming ciphertext to reclaim plaintext blocks. To recover from synchronization loss, the decryptor must

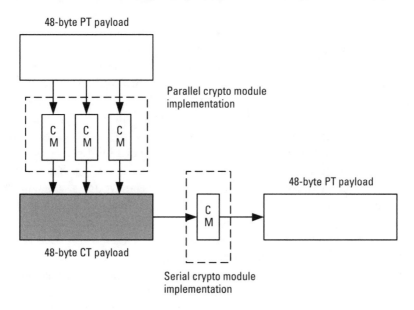

Figure 8.7 Interoperation of differently scaled crypto implementations.

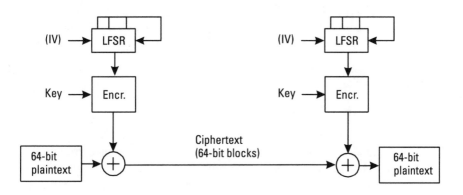

Figure 8.8 CM operation.

be provided with the same element of the sequence that the encryptor used when encrypting that block of data.

There are three points to notice about counter mode. The first is that, as described above, encryption and decryption are exactly the same process. Secondly, the feedback is apart from, and not involving the cryptographic engine (i.e., in the LFSR). As long as efficient LFSRs are used, pipelined cryptographic hardware can operate at full cryptographic rates. The third point is that by having the LFSRs generate decimated sequences [11], cryptographic throughput can be increased by employing multiple sets of encryption engines and LFSRs (with each LFSR generating a different portion of the same sequence) operating in parallel. Encryptors with different quantities of encryption engines (each operating in parallel) will interoperate because the LFSRs feeding the encryption engines will ensure that the entire sequence is generated, whether by one or many parallel LFSRs.

In the context of ATM counter mode encryption, as specified in Security 1.1, the cryptographic functions are fed by a state vector (SV). The SVs (described in Section 8.4.2) consist of various counters and an element of a linear recurring sequence. This ensures that unique key stream values are generated for each block that is encrypted.

Cryptographic resynchronization is accomplished by the encryptor transmitting an OAM cell containing a resynchronization message with a new SV, as described in Section 8.6.2. The encryptor uses the new SV on the next cell that arrives on the virtual circuit. When the decryptor receives the resynchronization OAM cell, it extracts the new SV and uses it to decrypt the next user data cell. Cell sequence integrity ensures that the next cell to arrive at the decryptor on the specified connection will correspond to the new SV. In both the encryptor and the decryptor, the SV is updated and replaced into the internal memory, ready to be used on the next cell for that connection.

8.4 Key Agility

A context-agile encryption system can switch between various cryptographic contexts quickly and easily. Key-agile encryption implementations limit the context parameters to items such as key, initial variable, and present state. (Full context–agility is beyond the scope of Security 1.1 and is discussed thoroughly in [12].)

Key agility provides obvious benefits. Key-agile encryption allows each user, and, indeed, each virtual circuit to use different key material. This cryptographically separates each user's (and each application's) traffic.

Key-agile software implementations of cryptographic algorithms are usually straightforward, but they can have both performance and security concerns. Hardware implementations sport higher performance, but fast and efficient implementation of high-speed context switching in hardware is not always obvious.

8.4.1 Context Lookup

The number of potential ATM contexts (VPI/VCIs) and the amount of information per context may both be large. As shown in Chapter 2, there may be either 2^{24} possible UNI VPI/VCI combinations or 2^{28} possible NNI VPI/VCI combinations. Implementing a cryptographic context lookup with a flat memory structure may be quite costly.

Because the number of simultaneously active cryptographic contexts is likely to be small, an efficient key-agile encryptor could use an associative memory lookup to determine the key and other cryptographic state information associated with each cell stream. Large (both in width and depth) content addressable memories with access times on the order of ATM cell header processing times, which are very small on high-speed links, are currently (circa 2001) quite expensive. Until large, fast, and inexpensive content addressable memories become available, ATM encryptor designs must compromise either the virtual circuit space over which circuits can be encrypted, or the cell processing latency, or both.

8.4.2 Encryption State

In ATM encryption using counter mode, the encryption state is not only made up of the key used to encrypt or decrypt a particular connection, but also the SV associated with that connection. The SV is 64 bits in length and is made up of five fields.

The first field (21 bits in length) is located in bits 63–43 of the SV and is the current element of a linear feedback shift register. Security 1.1 specifies a Galois implementation of the primitive polynomial $x^{21}+x^{2}+1$ for the LFSR.

Next, in bit 42 of the SV, is a 1-bit field that indicates whether this unit is the initiator or responder on a given connection. The value of the I/R bit is 1 for cells flowing away in the initiator to responder direction, and zero for cells flowing in the other direction.

The third field is a 4-bit sequence number located in bits 41–38 of the SV. As described in the Security 1.1 Specification:

For AAL1 connections, the most significant bit of the sequence number (bit 41) is set to zero. The remaining three bits are extracted from the sequence number within the payload of the cell.

For AAL3/4 connections, the sequence number is extracted from the four-bit sequence number in the payload of the cell. For all other connection types, these four bits are set to zero. (Copyright 2001, The ATM Forum.)

The fourth field is a 3-bit segment number in bits 37–35 of the SV. As described in the Security 1.1 Specification:

> The 384-bit ATM cell payload is segmented into six 64-bit segments for encryption and decryption. The LFSR is held constant for the entire cell payload. The segment number is a 3-bit field that defines which 64-bit segment within the payload is being encrypted or decrypted. (Copyright 2001, The ATM Forum.)

Thus, the purpose of the segment number is to provide a unique input to the counter mode encryption engine for each block in the cell. Note that the most significant bit of the segment number is its leftmost bit, bit 37.

The last field, the jump number, is 35 bits in length and occupies bits 34–0 of the SV. This field is initialized to all zeros when the security association is established and is incremented each time an SKC OAM cell is transmitted (indicating either key changeover or resynchronization) or, for AAL 5 connections, each time an end-of-message cell is received. This ensures uniqueness in the SV even after a resynchronization operation. As with the other numeric fields of the SV, the leftmost bit is the most significant and corresponds to bit 34 of the SV. During SKC, the new jump number is communicated to the decryptor within an SKC OAM cell. The process for constructing this OAM cell is described in Security 1.1 as follows:

> When an SKC OAM cell is transmitted, the sender places its current Jump number in [OAM cell] Octets 17–21. The remaining bits (bits 4–8 in Octet 17 and Octets 14–16) are set to zero.

> The receiver copies the Jump number from the SKC OAM cell into the SV for that connection only if the new Jump number is greater than the previous Jump number. SKC OAM cells containing Jump numbers less than or equal to the previous Jump number are rejected and this should be treated as an error condition. (Copyright 2001, The ATM Forum.)

8.5 Encryptor Architecture

A feasible architecture, suitable for ATM encryption/decryption devices, consists of the following major components:

- Physical input/output (I/O) module for input;
- Cell identification and association module;
- Cell router;
- Cryptographic module;
- Key management module;
- Non-real-time control module;
- Physical I/O module for output.

These modules or functions can be broken down into real-time and non-real-time services. The separation of real-time and non-real-time traffic is critical to the overall system design. Specifically, the system must be designed to accommodate all real-time traffic in a very efficient manner such that excessive delays are not experienced. All user data and some OAM cell traffic is handled in real-time through the physical I/O, identification and association, cell routing, and if necessary, cryptographic services. The non-real-time services consist of network management functions, SME protocol processing (see Chapter 5), and non-real-time OAM processes. The real-time data path is referred to as the high-speed path, and the non-real-time data path is referred to as the lower-speed path. A distinction is also made between general ATM functions and security services. The ATM-specific functions can be implemented in a *shell*, which surrounds the security services. The purpose of the shell is to provide a generic, nonproprietary definition for a large portion of the encryptor. The trusted components can then be concentrated into a controllable module. This may lead to commercially available devices into which a generic or custom (e.g., proprietary) security module may be inserted. Figure 8.9 shows the functional blocks, the shell boundaries, and the separation of real-time and non-real-time functions.

The primary data path (the path that carries user data cells) through the shell is from the physical I/O through the identification and association function to the cell router. User traffic continues through the cryptographic module (beyond or outside of the shell), and is returned to the shell, where the physical I/O output port provides output data. Additional support data paths include interaction between the non-real-time control and the identification and association function for the purpose of maintaining connection and association information. Additionally, non-real-time cells such as signaling cells are diverted from the real-time path at the cell router to the non-real-time control for processing. Similarly, the non-real-time control may

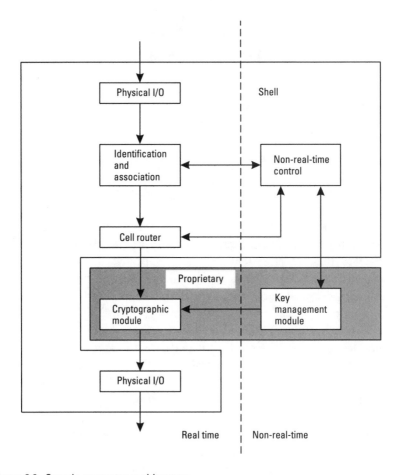

Figure 8.9 Sample encryptor architecture.

insert cells via the cell router. Each functional block is discussed in the following section.

8.5.1   Component Modules

The physical I/O module is the link between the physical transmission of data across a network and the ATM encryptor. On the encryption side, the plaintext input is coming from the host system or network, and the encrypted output is sent as ciphertext to an ATM network. Conversely, the receiving end accepts encrypted data from the ATM network and provides decrypted plaintext to the host system or network. It is assumed that the physical layer for high-speed communications will be SONET (Synchronous Optical NETwork). Hence, the physical I/O modules in this example will be SONET interfaces.

The first function that the encryptor must perform is identification and association of ATM cells. In this architecture, the encryptor takes advantage of the connection-oriented properties of ATM by using connection information to specify parameters in the cryptographic context. Therefore, the ATM-specific VPI/VCI is used not only for connection information, but also to determine the cryptographic processing of the cell. ATM cells can be handled in one of three ways: encrypted, bypassed, or blocked.

As described earlier, one of the approaches for the identification and association function is to perform a table lookup using conventional memory (RAM). Some current encryptors such as FASTLANE [12] use this approach. For tomorrow's encryptors, however, the memory that would be accessed for a context lookup table must be considerably faster than in FASTLANE, which currently supports the OC-12 data rate (622 Mbps). For OC-192c (concatenated), the minimum cell period is only 42.6 ns (424 bits per cell / 9.95 10^9 bps) in order to sustain full cell rate [12]. Read accesses to the connection table must be performed during this period. Additionally, all maintenance of this table must also be performed without interfering with normal traffic. That is, when connections are initiated and/or terminated, the table must be updated appropriately and promptly. The table maintenance is a non-real-time function. Therefore, these memory accesses will occur at unspecified times. One possibility is to allow the maintenance access during idle cell times only. However, given high traffic volume and frequent connection setup/teardown, this approach may be unacceptable, as it would create a backlog of required maintenance accesses. An alternate approach is to increase the memory access rate to allow for both a connection lookup and a maintenance access to be performed within a single cell period. For OC-192c (10 Gbps), this requires the memory to be capable of both a read and write access within 42.6 ns (as calculated earlier) in order to complete the table maintenance without degrading throughput.

Another approach identified in Section 8.4.1 for connection table lookup is to use a content addressable memory (CAM). This associative memory may be the most efficient method to perform the table lookup function because the CAM needs to be only as deep as the number of connections to be identified, plus a select set of generic cells common to all connections such as cryptographic resynchronization cells. CAM is used by loading the search VPI and VCI fields into any unused location in CAM. At this time, the appropriate association information is loaded into a RAM corresponding to the now-filled CAM location. (The CAM finds the correct location when a cell's VPI and VCI are presented. The corresponding RAM then outputs the appropriate association information.)

CAM memory associations limit the number of connections because of limitations in CAM depth. Conventional SRAM can be designed to support all possible connections but in practice must restrict the range of the VPI and VCI fields to keep the amount of memory manageable. In short, CAM is optimal for very wide associative lookups, whereas RAM is preferred for narrower, deeper lookup tables. On the surface, the advantage of the CAM approach may not be obvious. However, consider that each connection (fixed VPI/VCI) contains user data as well as OAM cells. The OAM cells require very different processing than the user data cells. The use of a ternary (1, 0, "don't care") CAM is more efficient at identifying specific types of cells on a given connection than a conventional RAM approach. Using CAM, there may be a single CAM entry identifying a cryptographic resynchronization cell (for all connections) and a single entry for each specific connection. When the CAM matches on both entries, it has identified the cell as being associated with a given connection as well as a specific cell type. Using a RAM approach, either a resynchronization entry is required for every connection (dramatically increasing memory size and address width requirements), or a secondary cell type lookup would be necessary.

Although a CAM implementation may be more efficient, currently, off-the-shelf CAM devices that will support operation at high speeds (10 Gbps and above) are not readily available. Therefore, although architecturally CAM would be the preferred technology, encryptor implementations would likely use synchronous RAM and a reduced VPI/VCI table lookup for the identification and association function until fast, wide, inexpensive CAMs become available.

The primary purpose of the non-real-time control (NRTC) is to provide control functions for the encryptor that do not need to be performed in real-time (e.g., connection management and maintenance, SME, and encryptor "housekeeping" functions). After identification of a cell, non-real-time cells (such as SME cells) are diverted to the NRTC. This requires that the cells be moved from the high-speed data path to the lower-speed data path. The coupling between the two paths is performed using first in, first out (FIFO) buffering. Given the high-speed nature of the real-time path, the FIFO must be able to accept data at full rate. In addition, it must be deep enough to provide enough storage given the relatively slow access from the NRTC. The NRTC must process assembled messages rather than ATM cells. Therefore, a segmentation and reassembly (SAR) function must be performed prior to the NRTC processing.

Once a cell has been properly identified and associated with a given connection and cell type, this information is used to route the cell to the proper destination, the NRTC or the cryptopath. All non-real-time cells are destined for the NRTC; all real-time cells are destined for the cryptographic algorithm.

The cryptographic module must provide real-time processing on a per-cell basis. Fundamentally, the cryptographic module must perform one of two functions for each cell. Real-time cells are categorized as security-related OAM cells (e.g., resynchronization cells) or user data cells. The cryptographic module must process the cell differently based on the cell type. If it is a user cell, the cryptographic module must provide data appropriately for proper encryption/decryption. If the cell is a resynchronization cell, OAM cell processing must be performed. The processing of the resynchronization cells is described in Security 1.1 and is addressed in Section 8.6 of this book.

As stated earlier, in order to effectively encrypt or decrypt data at very high speeds, a nonfeedback mode of operation is desired. The following discussion assumes counter mode, as ECB mode does not protect against dictionary lookup or replay attacks.

User data cells are placed in a FIFO buffer while the key stream is generated. First, the cell processor fetches the current SV from memory. The correct SV is selected based on the context information, which was passed to the cryptographic module along with the cell header. Then, the SV is written to the key generator, updated and written back to SV memory. Assuming a 128-bit word-width interface to the key generator, the cryptographic module must update and write the local SV a minimum of three times to cover the length of an ATM cell payload. (If a 64-bit wide interface to the key generator was used, the cell processor would need to update and write the local SV at least six times to cover a 384-bit ATM cell payload.) Only the final value of SV is written back to SV memory. Cell headers are not modified, as the network requires them to be intact for proper switching.

The cryptovariable or key is fed directly to the key generator. The keystream generated by the key generator is passed to the key/plaintext mixer along with the user data cell payload, which was buffered in a FIFO. The resultant mixer output is ciphertext, which is appended to the original, unmodified cell header (replacing the plaintext payload) to form the encrypted ATM cell.

As with the non-real-time control, the key management module provides non-real-time support services to the encryptor. The primary purpose of the key management module to the encryptor is to generate traffic encryption keys (TEK) for each connection. Context management between virtual circuits (e.g., keys and state vectors) is performed within the cryptographic module (in local memory for the state vectors) or in the identification and association module (in the RAM or CAM described earlier). It should be noted that the communication path between the key management module and the cryptographic module needs to be protected physically or cryptographically.

8.5.2 Resynchronization Processing for the Sample Architecture

In addition to user cell processing, the cryptomodule is required to process cryptographic information. Specifically, cryptographic resync cells must be extracted from and inserted into the cell stream and processed accordingly. All resync cell processing must be performed within a single cell period, 42.6 ns for OC-192 data rates (10 Gbps). Furthermore, the cryptomodule must process two types of resync cells: those destined for the cryptomodule (cell reception) and those originating from within the encryptor (cell insertion).

The insertion of resync cells requires stepping the current SV to the new value and writing the new SV to memory and into the resync cell. Stepping the SV is described in Security 1.1. It involves incrementing the jump number, setting the I/R (initiator/responder) bit accordingly, resetting the sequence number and segment number to all zeros and the LFSR to its preset value. The new SV is then written to the appropriate SV memory location and to the resync cell. In addition, a CRC-10 is computed and inserted at the end of the cell. The new SV stored in memory is used on the next cell arriving on the given connection.

The reception of resync cells requires verification of the CRC-10. Similarly, the jump number is checked to verify that it is greater than the current jump number. If the CRC-10 value or jump number is invalid (not greater than the previously received jump number), the cell is ignored and no resynchronization occurs. If both values are valid, the jump number is extracted and the other SV fields are reset. The new SV is stored in SV memory and is ready for use by the next cell on the given connection.

8.6 State Maintenance Using OAM Cells

As described in Chapter 5, security agents use signaling-based or in-band SME to establish a security association and to provide initial security services such as authentication and key exchange. If data security services (i.e., user plane confidentiality and integrity) are implemented on a connection, however, then another message exchange mechanism is required to allow SAs to maintain the security association. Specifically, a message-passing mechanism is required to allow security agents to maintain cryptographic synchronization (to ensure that the decrypting SA does not continue to improperly decrypt ATM data if a cell is lost) and to allow SAs to occasionally change keys.

Although a number of mechanisms can be designed to allow SAs to communicate at any time, the functions described above place special requirements on this mechanism. For example, if integrity or confidentiality keys are changed, then both SAs must enact the new keys on the same cell. Otherwise, the downstream SA will use the old key to incorrectly decrypt a cell or improperly verify the MAC (and discard an AAL 5 SDU). Likewise, when cryptographic resynchronization is performed, the decrypting SA must use the new counter mode state vector on the correct cell; otherwise, cryptographic synchronization is never regained.

These requirements imply the need for a tight coupling between the security association maintenance messages and the data security service. In fact, the user data stream and the inter-SA messaging mechanism must maintain *cell sequence integrity;* that is, the user data cells and the security association maintenance cells must be received in the same relative order in which they were sent. Although ATM switches are required to maintain cell sequence integrity *within* each VCC or VPC that they switch, this is not true *between* VCC/VPCs. Thus, if a separate virtual circuit is used to carry inter-SA messaging traffic, there is no guarantee that the maintenance messages will arrive in the same relative order with respect to the user data cells. Therefore, the security association maintenance mechanism must pass cells within the VCC or VPC.

ATM Security 1.1 uses OAM cells to implement the required mechanism. OAM cells are defined for VCCs (F5 OAM cells) and VPCs (F4 OAM cells) and are used to exchange ATM management information directly between VCC/VPC switches (segment OAM cells) or between VCC/VPC endpoints (end-to-end OAM cells). For VPCs, end-to-end OAM cells are sent within the VPC on VCI = 4 and, therefore, maintain cell sequence integrity with other cells on the VPC. Likewise, for VCCs, end-to-end OAM cells are sent within the VCC (using PTI = 101 to distinguish them as OAM cells) and, therefore, maintain cell sequence integrity with other cells in the VCC.

Because end-to-end OAM cells maintain cell sequence integrity, they are used by SAs to maintain the security association for the confidentiality and integrity services. As described in Section 5.1.7 of Security 1.1, all security OAM cells use the "System Management" OAM cell type, with either the "Security, Non-Real-time" or the "Security, Real-time" function types. The non-real-time function type is used in cases where the control message does not need to be processed by the receiving SA before the next cell arrival. (Such OAM cells processed by the non-real-time components were described earlier.) The real-time function type, however, is used when the OAM cell must be processed before the next cell arrival. (These OAM cells are processed by the real-time components described earlier.) The distinction between the two OAM cell types is clearly shown in the session key update (SKU) service, described in Section 8.6.1. In this service, the session key exchange phase is performed in advance of the actual changeover in order to prepare the new keys for later use. Because this phase of SKU is not time-sensitive, it is performed using the non-real-time security OAM cells. During the session key changeover phase, however, the new key is used immediately after notification. Therefore, this phase is implemented using the real-time security OAM cells.

Because end-to-end OAM cells are transferred within the user plane VCC or VPC, they are considered by the network to be part of the connection and are subject to the connection's traffic contract. Therefore, these cells may be "policed" by the switches and can be marked as "nonconformant" or dropped if they cause the VPC/VCC to exceed its contract. If this is the case, then the traffic contract for secured VPC/VCCs may need to be adjusted to handle the overhead associated with security OAM cell traffic.

Even if the traffic contract is properly adjusted, however, loss of security OAM cells may still occur. The SKU and resynchronization mechanisms in Security 1.1 recognize this possibility and specify that multiple copies of the OAM cells should be sent to reduce the probability of message loss.

As with SME, security OAM cells can be used when security associations are nested. For this reason, OAM cells are required to be passed in the clear (i.e., they are not encrypted with the rest of the VPC/VCC data traffic) to allow processing by intermediate SAs. In addition, security OAM cells contain a relative ID field to allow SAs to determine if they are required to process them (see Section 5.1.7.3 of Security 1.1). Like the relative ID of the

SSIE SAS, the security OAM cell's relative ID indicates the nesting level for involved SAs. However, the security OAM cell's RID is distinct from the SSIE SAS RID; that is, there is no relationship between these two relative identifiers.

The processing of the security OAM cell RID is shown in Figures 8.10 and 8.11. In Figure 8.10, encryption security agents $SA_{2,E}$ and $SA_{3,E}$ are nested within other encryption security agents $SA_{1,E}$ and $SA_{4,E}$. In Figure 8.11, encryption security agents $SA_{2,E}$ and $SA_{3,E}$ are nested within integrity security agents $SA_{1,I}$ and $SA_{4,I}$. In all cases, when an SA (regardless of its nesting level) sends an OAM cell, it encodes the OAM RID as zero. If this OAM cell is received by another security agent on its plaintext interface, it checks the function ID to determine if it matches the service (confidentiality or integrity) provided by the SA. If the function ID matches, then it increments the RID as shown in Figure 8.10, and the cell is forwarded. If the function ID does not match, then the SA forwards the OAM cell without modifying the RID, as shown in Figure 8.11.

When an SA receives a security OAM cell on its ciphertext interface, it checks the function ID, and if it matches the SA's service, it checks if the RID is zero. If so, it removes the cell and processes it. If the function ID matches and the RID is not zero, the RID is decremented and the OAM cell is forwarded. If the function ID does not match, the OAM cell is forwarded unmodified.

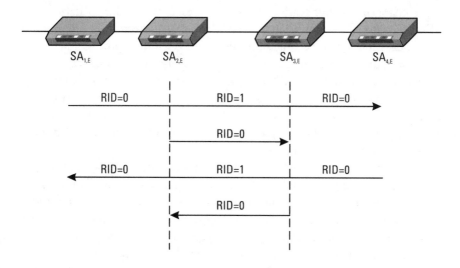

Figure 8.10 OAM relative ID processing for identical nested services (FID = C).

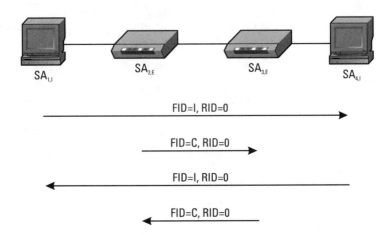

Figure 8.11 OAM relative ID processing for different nested services.

In all cases, the cell is not encrypted or included in the AAL integrity check (although the OAM CRC is recomputed). Furthermore, the SA must preserve cell sequence integrity within the VPC or VCC.

8.6.1   SKU

The SKU service in Security 1.1 allows traffic encryption keys (session keys) to be changed without tearing down and reestablishing the virtual circuit. SKU increases the strength of the confidentiality protection provided on a virtual circuit because it changes the keystream generation process and it limits the amount of data that can be decrypted by a compromised session key. New keys exchanged by SKU are generated at random and are encrypted using the master key developed under the key exchange process that occurs during SME. Because the new session keys are generated at random, if one session key is broken, then past and future session keys are not revealed (providing perfect forward secrecy).

The frequency at which the SKU process is performed depends on site policy and should be configurable. More "paranoid" installations may require session keys to be changed frequently to limit exposure of data under a given key value. These sites, however, must accept the additional overhead associated with frequent key changes. In addition, the method used to trigger a new session key update (i.e., time-based or volume-based) is also configurable. This allows a site to trigger a new SKU when a given amount of data has been processed or when a key has been active for a given period of time.

The SKU process is unidirectional; that is, each direction of a bidirectional virtual circuit is rekeyed separately. The process is divided into two phases: an SKE phase and an SKC phase. During SKE, the source (or key update initiator) generates a new session key at random and encrypts it using a pseudorandom mask developed using the master key and a hash algorithm (MD5, SHA-1, or RIPEMD-160). A "bank ID," which is 4 bits of 1 or 0, is assigned to this key by taking the old key's bank ID and complementing it. Finally, a key number is assigned to the new key by taking the old key's key number, incrementing it, and checking it to ensure the key number did not wrap to 0. The encrypted key, bank ID, and key number are encapsulated into an SKE OAM cell (a non-real-time OAM cell), and the OAM cell is sent multiple times to increase the probability of successful transfer if cell loss should occur.

When the destination (key update responder) receives the SKE OAM cell, it checks the key number to verify that it is larger than the key number of the currently active session key. If so, it then decrypts the session key using the master key and pseudorandom mask generation algorithm and stores the session key, key number, and bank ID in high-speed memory for later SKC.

After a period of time (at least 1 second), the key update initiator performs SKC by inserting the key number and bank ID of the new session key into an SKC OAM cell (a real-time OAM cell). In addition, if counter mode is used, the key update initiator also includes the new state vector. Once constructed, the OAM cell is transmitted multiple times to increase the probability of reception. At this point, the key update initiator starts encrypting VC data using the new session key.

When the key update responder receives the SKC cell, it extracts the key number, bank ID, and state vector from the OAM cell and uses the key number or bank ID to select the new session key that was previously stored in high-speed memory. If counter mode is used, then the state vector is also extracted and readied. Once the SKC OAM cell is processed, the new key and state vector are used to decrypt subsequent data. Since user data can immediately follow the SKC OAM cell, it is important that the OAM cell processing be accomplished within one cell time.

8.6.2 Cryptographic Resynchronization

As described earlier, the counter mode of operation is readily implemented in parallel and facilitates fast encryption of ATM cell data. This mode of operation, however, requires the encrypting and decrypting processes to be synchronized, and if one or more data cells are lost, then the two processes lose synchronization, resulting in improper decryption (garbled data). Therefore, if counter mode is used, then the encryption and decryption processes must be periodically synchronized. As with the SKU service, crypto-resynchronization is unidirectional, is performed at a configured interval, and can be time-based or volume-based, depending on policy. In this case, though, the issue is performance versus overhead (rather than security versus overhead). That is, higher resynchronization frequencies result in better decryption performance, but they add overhead.

The resynchronization process uses the SKC OAM cell (a real-time OAM) cell described earlier. In this case, the bank ID and key number for this session key are inserted in the OAM cell, along with the new counter mode state vector to be used. This OAM cell is sent multiple times, again, to increase the probability of reception, and the new state vector is used on subsequent user cell traffic by the encryptor and decryptor.

8.7   Performance Considerations

Encryption will impact the performance of an ATM communication link by adding latency to that link. If the encryption or decryption process cannot keep up with the maximum cell arrival rate, then the cell traffic throughput on that virtual circuit must be throttled in some way to avoid cell loss. If the cryptographic processing cannot be completed within one cell time, this throttling can be done via CAC at virtual circuit setup time (for constant, variable, and unspecified bit rate traffic) or by participation in the flow control after virtual circuit setup (for available bit rate traffic). In either case, the cryptographic devices must participate in the establishment and/or control of the virtual circuit, making it no longer "transparent" to the switching network [12].

To minimize impact on performance, care should be exercised in the design of cryptographic hardware. This includes pipelined algorithms to allow high clock rates, parallel processing, and possibly high-performance integrated circuit materials (e.g., silicon germanium, gallium arsenide). Also to be considered on circuit boards are controlled impedance clock and signal lines, as well as the intricacies of clock distribution to ensure clock signals arrive at all necessary components simultaneously.

These issues become increasingly important as the line rates of ATM links increase. It is imperative that the performance of cryptographic hardware be matched to the line rates (and cell processing times) of the associated ATM links in order to avoid cell loss and quality of service problems.

References

[1] The ATM Forum, "ATM Security Specification Version 1.1," af-sec-0100.002, March 2001.

[2] Rivest, R. L., A. Shamir, and L. Adleman, "A Method for Obtaining Digital Signatures and Public-Key Cryptosystems," *Communications of the ACM*, Vol. 21, No. 2, 1978, pp. 120–126.

[3] Schneier, B., *Applied Cryptography*, New York: John Wiley & Sons, 1996.

[4] Rivest, R. L., "Remarks on a Proposed Cryptanalytic Attack on the M.I.T. Public-Key Cryptosystem," *Cryptologia*, Vol. 2, No. 1, 1978, pp. 62–65.

[5] Simmons, G. J., and M. J. Norris, "Preliminary Comments on the M.I.T. Public-Key Cryptosystem," *Cryptologia*, Vol. 1, No. 4, 1977, pp. 406–414.

[6] Diffie, W, and M. E. Hellman, "New Directions in Cryptography," *IEEE Transactions on Information Theory*, Vol. IT-22, No. 6, 1976, pp. 644–654.

[7] National Institute of Standards and Technology, *Data Encryption Standard (FIPS PUB 46-3)*, 1999.

[8] Merkle, R. C., and M. E. Hellman, "On the Security of Multiple Encryption," *Communications of the ACM*, Vol. 24, No. 7, 1981, pp. 465–467.

[9] Menezes, A. J., P. C. van Oorschot, and S. A. Vanstone, *Handbook of Applied Cryptography*, Boca Raton, FL: CRC Press, 1997.

[10] National Bureau of Standards, *DES Modes of Operation (FIPS PUB 81)*, 1980.

[11] Witzke, E. L., and L. G. Pierson, "The Role of Decimated Sequences in Scaling Encryption Speeds Through Parallelism," *Conference Proceedings of the IEEE Fifteenth Annual International Conference on Computers and Communications*, Scottsdale, AZ, March 27–29, 1996, pp. 515–519.

[12] Pierson, L. G., et al., "Context-Agile Encryption for High Speed Communication Networks," *ACM Computer Communication Review*, Vol. 29, No. 1, 1999, pp. 35–49.

9

Access Control

Access control is a decision made by network devices, hosts, or special security devices (e.g., firewalls) to grant access to network and host resources. This decision is made according to site policy and in a manner consistent with the properties of the network or application protocol. For connectionless protocols, each protocol data unit (PDU) is allowed access on an individual basis. For connection-oriented protocols, however, access is granted or denied during the connection request. The trade-offs associated with each approach are the same as those for connectionless/connection-oriented networking in general. That is, for long-lived connections, the overhead associated with connection-oriented access control is amortized over the life of the connection, resulting in less overhead per unit data.

Access control can be based on general attributes associated with the network request. These attributes can be *explicitly* specified protocol parameters such as addresses and upper layer protocol information, or they can be *implicitly* associated with the request and use other information such as the time of day. In addition, access control can be based on the result of a cryptographic authentication protocol, which binds the requesting entity's name to a secret held by that entity. The latter form of access control provides stronger security, particularly if the request traverses an untrusted network, where generic access control parameters are vulnerable to malicious modification.

Access control can also be based on special labels that accompany the access request. These labels specify the sensitivity level and access categories of the accompanying data and are used by trusted network devices or hosts to decide how to handle the request.

This chapter describes access control in ATM networks, including general access control (explicit and implicit) and label-based access control. In addition, the method for transporting labels as defined in the ATM Security Specification Version 1.1. is also described.

9.1 General Access Control

Access control decisions are made according to the attributes of a network service request and the policies of the network that provides the service. In general, access control can be based on any attribute that can be associated with the network service request (i.e., implicit or explicit attributes). Explicit attributes are those that are included in the network packet or connection request, and they can include the following:

- Source and destination addresses;
- Higher-layer protocol information;
- Data sensitivity labels (described in Section 9.2);
- Quality of service information;
- Packet/connection type (e.g., user data, control data, or management information).

In addition, access control decisions may also be made on implicit information regarding the request, including the following:

- Time of request;
- Past history of requests;
- Current network state (such as link availability, congestion, link utilization level, and security *threat condition*).

When explicit parameters are used in the access control decision, these parameters must be reliable. That is, the hosts and network devices must be trusted to generate and process these parameters correctly. Otherwise, attacks such as source address spoofing may be used to circumvent access control mechanisms. Therefore, when access control is performed on entry points from untrusted networks (especially a public network), it should be supplemented with strong authentication (see Chapter 6). The access control and strong authentication functions may be combined in a single ATM security agent, as shown in Figure 9.1.

In connectionless networks, access control decisions are made on a packet-by-packet basis. Therefore, the overhead associated with access control (i.e., extra header fields such as labels and time required for access control processing) is incurred with each packet. For connection-oriented networks such as ATM, however, the access control decision is made only once, during connection establishment, which reduces the per-unit data overhead as the lifetime of the connection increases.

The ATM Security Specification does not define how general access control functions are to be implemented. This decision was made for the following reasons:

- General access control (other than label-based access control and strong authentication) relies on protocol information contained in other specifications (e.g., the UNI specification).

- A complete set of explicit and implicit access control attributes cannot be specified.

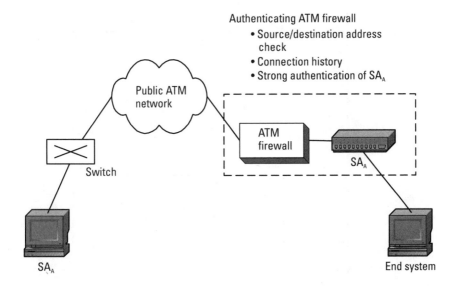

Figure 9.1 General access control with strong authentication.

- General access control (other than strong authentication and label-based access control) does not have interoperability concerns associated with it. Therefore, implementors should be allowed to develop this function as they choose in order to differentiate their products.

9.2 Label-Based Access Control

In some networks, information flows must be further segregated according to the sensitivity of the information they carry. In this case, information sensitivity cannot be determined using the generic access control data described earlier. Rather, a sensitivity *label* must be attached to the information flow.

Sensitivity labels contain two components: a hierarchical component that denotes the sensitivity *level* of the flow and a nonhierarchical component that denotes the information *compartment*. The relationship between levels and compartments is shown by the example in Figure 9.2.

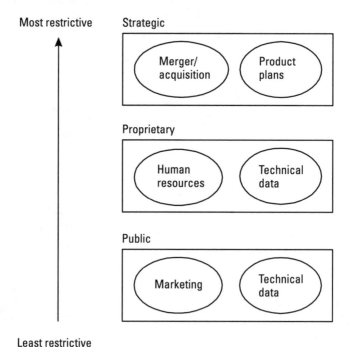

Figure 9.2 Example sensitivity levels and compartments.

In this example, the levels are indicated by "strategic," "proprietary," and "public," and the compartments are indicated by "marketing," "technical data," and so forth. Note that a compartment may belong to more than one level (such as "technical data").

Labels are used to keep connections or packets separated in networks that process multiple levels or compartments. Such networks are called multilevel secure, or MLS networks, because they are trusted to properly label and respect information flows at more than one level. The use of labels in MLS ATM networks is depicted in Figure 9.3.

In this figure, the network on the left is a *system high* network, which operates at a single level and compartment (in this case, proprietary technical data). Therefore, when the ATM SETUP message traverses this part of the network, it is not labeled; the label is implied by the sensitivity of the network.

When the SETUP message crosses SA₁ into the multilevel network, SA₁ labels the SETUP message (and therefore, the connection) as proprietary technical data. As the multilevel network processes the message, it is trusted to maintain the integrity of this label and route the connection appropriately. When the SETUP message reaches the destination, SA₂ checks the label in this message to verify that it is authorized to accept the connection. This check is performed as follows:

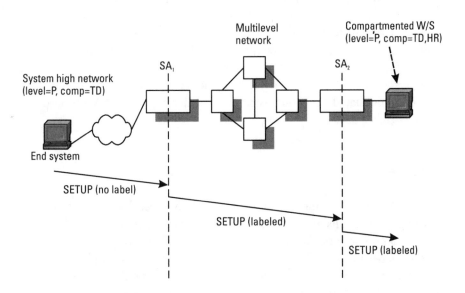

Figure 9.3 Example of an MLS network.

1. SA$_2$ compares the level indicator in the label against the minimum and maximum levels configured on its interface. If the label falls outside the interface range, then the connection is rejected. In this example, the label's level ("proprietary") matches the level of the SA ("proprietary").

2. The SA compares the compartment in the label against the set of compartments its interface is configured to accept. If the label's compartment is not in the set of acceptable compartments, then the connection is rejected. In this example, the label's compartment ("technical data") is a subset of the compartments supported by the SA ("technical data" and "human resources").

3. If both tests pass, then the connection is allowed to proceed.

If the compartmented workstation (which is authorized to process data in multiple compartments) is remote from SA$_2$, then the intervening network is an MLS network and SA$_2$ must keep the sensitivity label affixed to the connection SETUP message. This allows the network and workstation to identify the sensitivity of this flow (because it is not uniquely implied by the network) and protect it accordingly.

Label processing in multilevel networks is predicated on the assumption that the security agents, network devices, and compartmented workstations are trusted to "do the right thing" and not accept connections that are labeled with sensitivity greater than that supported by the device. However, trusting a device to decide correctly can be difficult, depending on the consequences if the device chooses incorrectly. If the consequences are high (e.g., compromise of national security), then the device must be rigorously analyzed and evaluated [1]. For this reason, the development of MLS products in practice has been slow.

9.2.1 FIPS 188

FIPS 188 [2] is the standard used by the ATM Security Specification for labeling connections and extends the specifications developed by the IETF [3]. FIPS 188 defines two label formats: a generic label format and network-specific label format. The generic format is designed for application-level access control and is very flexible. The network-specific label is more streamlined to reduce overhead and facilitate faster processing (because it is designed to be processed on a per-packet basis).

In ATM security, the network-specific label is used to label connections. Any of the network labels allowed by FIPS 188 is supported in ATM, including restrictive labels (which require *all* label attributes to be satisfied before accepting the connection) and permissive labels (which only require at least *one* label attribute to be satisfied).

The format of the FIPS 188 network label is shown in Figure 9.4.

The FIPS 188 label contains the following fields in its header:

- *ID:* A 1-byte value that identifies this label as a FIPS 188 label;

- *Length:* A 1-byte value that specifies the length of label, including all header fields;

- *Tag set name:* A 4-byte value that identifies the domain of interpretation for the label (which defines how the tags are decoded).

Following the header is a list of tags that are to be applied to the connection. Each tag contains a tag type identifier, length, and data, with the tag data depending on the tag type. The FIPS 188 tag types are shown in Table 9.1.

The format for each of these tag types (except tag type 7) is specified in FIPS 188 [2], but the meanings for the level and compartment fields are

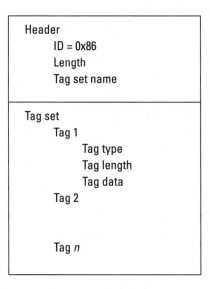

Figure 9.4 FIPS 188 label format.

Table 9.1
FIPS 188 Tag Types

Tag Type	Description	Level Designator	Compartment Designator
1	Restrictive bit map	Integer	Bit map (each bit corresponds to restrictive compartment)
2	Enumerated tag type	Integer	List of integer values
5	Range tag type	Integer	Two integers (min. and max. compartments)
6	Permissive bit map	Integer	Bit map (each bit corresponds to release type)
7	Free form tag type	User-defined	User-defined

specified when the tag set name is registered with the U.S. National Institute for Standards and Technology (NIST).

As shown in Figure 9.4, multiple tags may be included in the label. This provides the flexibility to allow label specifications using multiple tag types. For example, a restrictive tag (e.g., tag type 1) and a permissive tag (e.g., tag type 6) may be included simultaneously for a connection. As specified in FIPS 188, if both tag types are present, then the restrictive tag is processed first, followed by the permissive tag.

When an entity receives a connection request with a label that contains a restrictive tag, the connection is allowed if the tag's level falls within the device's range and the compartments specified in the tag are a subset of the compartments supported by the device (logical "AND"). This example is described earlier in the example in Figure 9.3. If the label contains a permissive tag, then the connection is allowed if the following conditions are satisfied:

1. The tag's level falls within the device's range;
2. At least one of the release category markings matches the device's role.

For example, if a connection has a permissive tag with level "proprietary" and release categories "marketing, technical data," then an engineer's workstation that is allowed to access proprietary technical data may accept such a connection.

9.2.2 Label Transport in ATM Security

In general, the labels specified in FIPS 188 can be applied to network packets, application PDUs, and network connections. Since ATM is connection-oriented, the label information is used during connection establishment to specify the sensitivity of the data carried by the connection. When an ATM connection is labeled, the label is carried in the SSIE, which is described in Chapter 5. Specifically, the label is carried in its own SAS, which is separate from any other SASs that may carry information for the SME protocol. Label-based access control SASs are separated from SME SASs because the security labels apply to the entire virtual circuit rather than on individual security associations (which may only cover parts of the virtual circuit).

The format of a label-based access control SAS is shown in Figure 9.5.

The SAS fields are used with label-based access control as follows (header fields not described here are described in Chapter 5):

- *SAS Type—access control SAS:* Label-based access control is a function performed on a virtual circuit and is not performed within SME; therefore, it has its own SAS type.

- *Transport indicator—signaling or in-band:* Label-based access control is performed during the establishment of the connection or security association, and uses either transport method as described in Chapter 5.

- *Flow—no significance:* The label-based access control protocol is unidirectional. That is, the sensitivity of the connection is declared by the SA and is not negotiated. Therefore, there is no need to track flow numbers.

- *Discard—do not discard:* In general, the labeling SA does not know how many SAs will process the security label. For example, in Figure 9.3, SA_1 does not know if other SAs that examine labels exist in the MLS network. To allow all SAs on the connection to examine the label, the label should not be discarded.

- *Scope—do not care:* Since the label applies to the connection and not the security association, all scope fields are coded to zero to indicate that any receiving SA can process this label.

```
┌─────────────────────────────────────────────────────┐
│ SSIE header                                         │
├─────────────────────────────────────────────────────┤
│ Security association section                        │
│                                                     │
│     Type = 0x02 (label-based access control)        │
│     Length                                          │
│     Version = 0x01 (Security 1.1)                   │
│     Transport indicator                             │
│     Flow = 0                                        │
│     Discard = 0                                     │
│     Scope = 0x0000                                  │
│     RID = 0x0000                                    │
│                                                     │
│     Security service data                           │
│         Label ID = 0x28                             │
│         Label length                                │
│         Label type = 0x01 (FIPS 188)                │
│         Label-specific data                         │
├─────────────────────────────────────────────────────┤
│ Other security association sections                 │
│                                                     │
│                                                     │
│                                                     │
└─────────────────────────────────────────────────────┘
```

Figure 9.5 Format of label-based access control SAS .

- *RID—0:* For the same reason, the access control service is not nested (as described in Chapter 5); therefore, this field is coded to zero.

The security service data fields are as follows:

- *Label ID—0x28 (FIPS 188):* In the ATM Security Specification 1.1, the security-specific data for label-based access control is limited to the FIPS-188 label.

- *Label length:* This field contains the length for the entire label-specific data field.

- *Label-specific data:* This field contains the FIPS 188 label data in network format as described in Section 9.2.1.

The label-based access control SAS is part of an SSIE, which may carry additional SASs for the SME protocol. Since the SSIE can be carried in-band or in signaling, it follows that label-based access control can also be performed in-band or in signaling. The trade-offs associated with the selection of the transport mechanism are described in Chapter 4. For label-based access control, however, the signaling-based transport method is preferred because it allows label-based access control to occur in conjunction with establishment of the connection. Furthermore, it allows multiple SAs to examine the label, whereas with the in-band protocol, the label is only visible to the two SAs that perform the protocol.

ATM security agents add label-based access control SASs when the SA connects a single level network or host to a multilevel network, or when the SA is otherwise configured to add such labels. When an SA receives a label, it accepts the connection or security association if its label processing passes the steps described in Section 9.2.1 (and described further in FIPS 188).

9.3 Summary

Label-based access control for ATM uses the standard FIPS 188 label format to specify the sensitivity label and access category for the information contained in the connection. This information is carried in the SSIE; however, it is carried separately from SME protocol data because the label-based access control function is performed on a virtual circuit rather than a security association (which may only span a portion of the virtual circuit).

In addition to sensitivity labels, other information such as protocol information and implicit connection information can also be used to determine whether access should be granted. If spoofing of protocol fields is of concern, then cryptographically strong authentication should also be used.

References

[1]   International Standards Organization, "Information Technology—Security Techniques—Evaluation Criteria for IT Security," ISO/IEC 15408, December 1999.

[2]   U.S. Department of Commerce National Institute of Standards and Technology, "Standard Security Label for Information Transfer," Federal Information Processing Standards Publication 188, September 1994.

[3]   Kent, S., "U.S. Department of Defense Security Options for the Internet Protocol," Internet Engineering Task Force RFC 1108, November 1991.

10

PNNI Routing Security

Recall from Chapter 2 that the PNNI protocol is used to route a switched virtual connection request to the desired destination. PNNI makes its routing determination by tracking the current topological state of the network via the exchange of PNNI topology state elements (PTSEs). When a PNNI node receives a PTSE, it updates its topology database with the contents of the PTSE. Therefore, if the PTSE's contents are bad, then the node's topology database is corrupted, and SVCs may not be properly routed.

Incorrect PTSEs may be inserted directly by a malicious PNNI node that has been attached to the network. Once attached, the malicious node may advertise that it can reach parts of the network, thereby directing other switches to route connections through it, at which point the connections may be dropped (denial of service) or examined (eavesdropping). In any case, generation of false routing data by a switch will cause other switches that are otherwise operating correctly to make incorrect routing decisions and further propagate bad data by distributing routing information that is based on the bogus route data.

To address these threats, the ATM Forum provides a specification for PNNI routing security [1]. This chapter provides a brief description of the security mechanisms defined in this specification, including procedures for marking PNNI information packets, selection of topology database entries, and securing PNNI routing control channels (RCCs).

213

10.1   Approach

The correct operation of PNNI implies a chain of trust. That is, each PNNI node is trusted (e.g., via careful software design processes, certification, and configuration control) to properly originate and process PTSEs. If each node is trusted, then the principal threats to the PNNI network originate elsewhere, either through the malicious introduction or malicious modification of routing information.

In the PNNI security model, each PNNI node (i.e., an ATM switch) that is trusted to participate in the protocol is provided with a shared secret key or a private key and is authenticated using the control plane security (CPS) mechanism described in Section 10.3. Once authenticated, both peers use CPS to provide integrity protection, and optionally confidentiality, on the RCCs to protect PTSEs from malicious modification. Finally, each PNNI node follows specific procedures for indicating the reliability of the information that it is sending to its peer. This process uses "transmit security" and "tagged security" flags that accompany each PTSE. PNNI nodes use the transmit security flag to indicate whether the PTSE was ever received over an insecure link. This flag is set to "secure" when the PTSE is created, and the receiving node sets it to "unsecure" if it is received over a link that does not have CPS protections applied.

The tagged security flag is set by the PTSE originator to indicate the reliability of the information contained in the PTSE. The value of this flag is determined by the reliability of the PTSEs used to construct the new PTSE. The procedure for determining this flag's value is as follows:

1. If any of the PTSEs that are used to form the new PTSE have a tagged security value of "unsecure," then the value of the tagged security flag for the new PTSE is "unsecure."

2. If any of the received PTSEs used to form the new PTSE have a transmit security flag value of "unsecure," then the value of the tagged security flag for the new PTSE is "unsecure."

3. If any other information used to construct the new PTSE is not considered secure, then the tagged security value for the new PTSE is "unsecure."

4. Otherwise, the tagged security value for the new PTSE is "secure."

An example of the use of the tagged security and transmit security flags is shown in Figure 10.1.

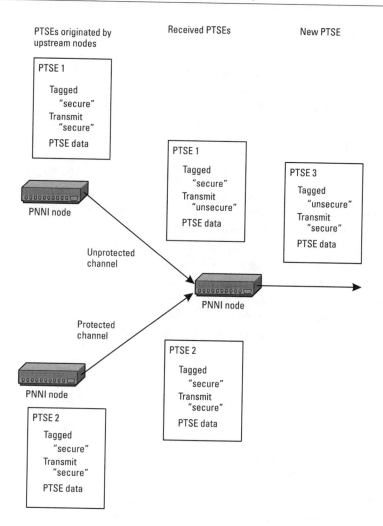

Figure 10.1 PNNI security tagging.

In this example, a PNNI node receives two PTSEs with tagged security flag values of "secure": one over a protected channel and one over an unprotected channel. The node modifies the transmit security flag for PTSE 1 to "unsecure" because it was received over the unprotected channel. The node creates PTSE 3 using information from PTSE 1 and PTSE 2 and sets the transmit security flag to "secure" because it is locally generated. However, it sets the tagged security flag to "unsecure" because PTSE 3 is derived from PTSE 1, which has a transmit security value of "unsecure."

In the example in Figure 10.2, the sending node originates a new PTSE that is derived from secure information, and therefore, the tagged security flag is set to "secure." In addition, the transmit security flag is also set to "secure" because this node originated the PTSE. However, when the receiving node obtains the PTSE over an unprotected link, it sets the transmit security flag to "unsecure" and decides whether this new PTSE should be retained. If so, the node stores the PTSE with the new flag values in its topology database.

The decision to retain a PTSE is based on the PTSE's freshness and security. Freshness and security, however, may be at odds with each other, for example, if a new instance of the PTSE arrives over an unsecured link. In this case, if security is given priority, then the receiving node retains the stale (but secure) PTSE in its topology database. However, if the node accepts the PTSE, then it is susceptible to database corruption by malicious nodes that originate corrupt (but fresh) PTSEs. In addition, the decision to retain only secure PTSEs will result in the node's inability to route to unsecured nodes. Due to these tradeoffs, the decision to give priority to security or freshness is a configuration matter that is guided by the network policy.

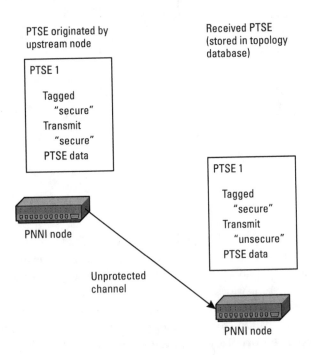

Figure 10.2 PTSE retention in topology database.

10.2 Security Information Group

The flags described in the previous section are carried in a new security information group (IG), which is specified in [1]. The security IG may accompany PNNI hello packets, PNNI topology state packets (PTSPs), and database summary packets [2]. The format of the security IG is shown in Figure 10.3.

The security IG contains the following header fields:

- *Type:* This field indicates the IG type, which is 641 for the security IG.

- *Length:* The length field denotes the length of the entire IG, that is, the IG header and any IGs that may be included in the security IG (when scope = "included," as described below).

- *Scope:* The scope field indicates whether this security IG's flags pertain to the higher-level IG or PNNI packet to which this security IG belongs (scope = 1), or if the security IG's flags pertain to IGs that it includes or encapsulates (scope = 2). The distinction between these two scope options is described later in more detail.

- *Application:* Currently the only application of the security IG is the use of the tagged security and transmit security flags (application = 1). Other applications may be vendor-defined or standardized in the future.

- *Security status:* This value is a bitmap, which contains the transmit security (bit 1) and tagged security (bit 2) flags. These bits are set to

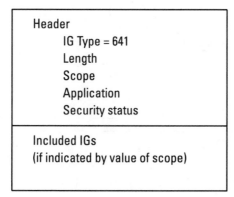

Figure 10.3 Format of security information group.

1 to indicate that the corresponding tagged or transmit security flag is secure, indicating the security status of the higher-level or included IGs. All other security status bits (bits 3–8) are reserved for future applications of the security IG.

The values of the tagged security and transmit security flags may apply to all IGs in the higher-level packet or IG, as indicated when the IG scope is 1. The use of the higher-level scope is shown in Figure 10.4.

In this example, the flags contained in the security IG apply to all other PTSEs contained in the PNNI packet. In other words, it specifies the security status for the higher-level packet that contains it. Thus, the contents of

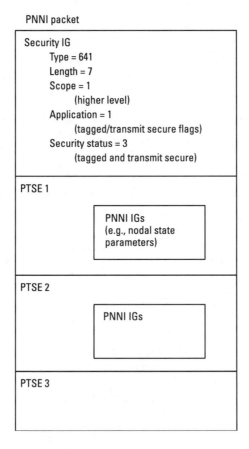

Figure 10.4 Example application of higher-level security IG.

PTSE 1, PTSE 2, and PTSE 3 are all tagged and transmit secure. Since the security IG contains no other IGs, its length reflects the length of the security IG header.

Alternatively, the security IG can be scoped to denote the tagged/transmit security status of IGs that are included by it, as indicated when the IG scope is 2. This is shown in Figure 10.5.

In this example, the flags of the security IG only apply to those PTSEs/IGs that it includes (PTSE 1 and PTSE 2). The included PTSEs are listed immediately after the security IG header, and the length field for the security IG includes the lengths of PTSE 1 and PTSE 2. Therefore, the tagged/transmit security flags apply to PTSE 1 and PTSE 2, but *not* to PTSE 3.

The selection of which scoping mechanism to use (higher level or included IGs) depends on the desired behavior of PNNI nodes that do not implement security when they receive the security IG. If a PNNI node, which does not implement PNNI security, processes a security IG with scope equals "higher level," as shown in Figure 10.4, the security IG will be ignored because it is not recognized. However, the other PTSEs in its scope will be processed using the standard protocol (i.e., without security extensions). This allows a mixed network to continue operating according to the standard PNNI procedures.

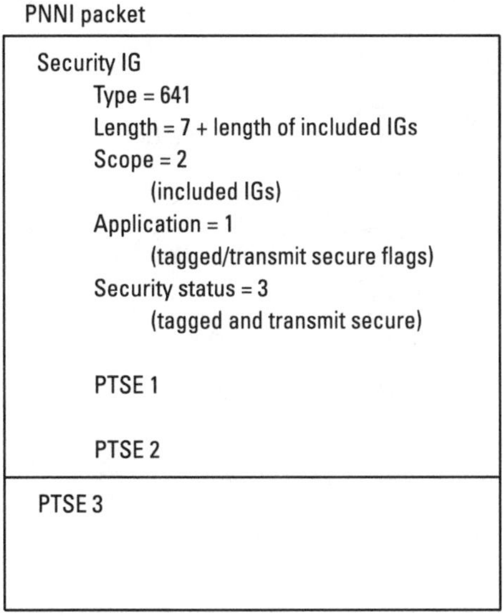

PNNI packet

```
Security IG
      Type = 641
      Length = 7 + length of included IGs
      Scope = 2
            (included IGs)
      Application = 1
            (tagged/transmit secure flags)
      Security status = 3
            (tagged and transmit secure)

      PTSE 1

      PTSE 2

PTSE 3
```

Figure 10.5 Example application of included IGs.

If a nonsecurity PNNI node receives a security IG with scope equals "included IGs," as shown in Figure 10.5, then it will discard the IG and all included PTSEs. This may have a detrimental effect on the network's ability to route connections. However, security considerations may prefer such behavior. Therefore, the selection of the scoping method to be used should be configurable to allow use selection according to site policy.

The possibility exists for a PNNI packet to contain multiple security IGs with conflicting information. In this case, the lowest level security IG specifies the security flags for a given IG. An example of this situation is shown in Figure 10.6

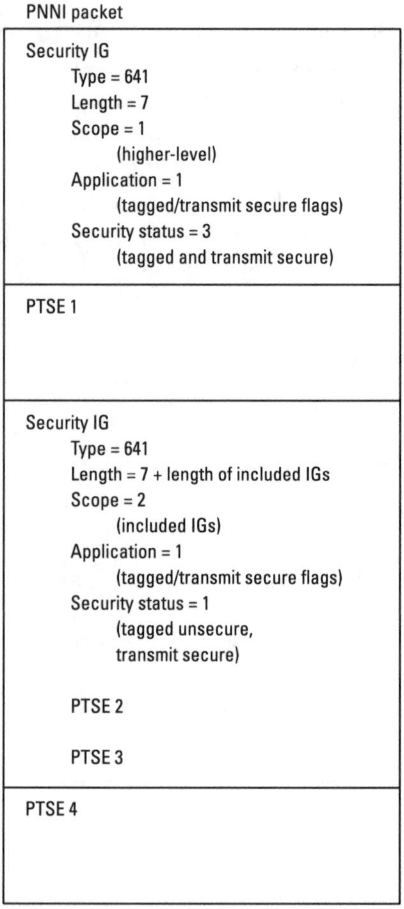

PNNI packet

Security IG
    Type = 641
    Length = 7
    Scope = 1
        (higher-level)
    Application = 1
        (tagged/transmit secure flags)
    Security status = 3
        (tagged and transmit secure)

PTSE 1

Security IG
    Type = 641
    Length = 7 + length of included IGs
    Scope = 2
        (included IGs)
    Application = 1
        (tagged/transmit secure flags)
    Security status = 1
        (tagged unsecure,
        transmit secure)

PTSE 2

PTSE 3

PTSE 4

Figure 10.6 PNNI packet with conflicting security IGs.

In this case, PTSE 1 and PTSE 4 are tagged and transmit secure. However, PTSE 2 and PTSE 3 are tagged unsecure and transmit secure because the security IG that contains them (their lowest level security IG) overrides the packet's security IG.

10.3 Control Plane Security and Link Establishment

The setting of the transmit security flag, which is determined by the receiver, depends on the security services provided on the RCC. These services are provided by the mechanisms specified in the CPS specification [3]. This specification extends the Security 1.1 control plane authentication/integrity service (described in Chapters 4 and 7) by providing additional mechanisms for initial authentication and key exchange when the RCC is established, as well as confidentiality for control plane messages.

The primary enhancement provided by the CPS specification over the Security 1.1 control plane security mechanism is the ability to authenticate and exchange message encryption/integrity keys automatically. This improvement is important for PNNI because RCCs are established dynamically between nodes in a PNNI peer group, making manual key management infeasible. CPS provides two mechanisms for this service: one based on the SME protocol (which is described in Chapter 5) and one based on the Internet Key Exchange (IKE) protocol defined by the IETF in RFC 2409 [4]. Both approaches may use public-key or secret-key algorithms to perform initial authentication and key exchange.

Both protocols are performed in-band, that is, in the control channel at the time it is established but before it is allowed to carry message traffic. When SME is performed, the three-way protocol is used each time a new control plane channel is established (even if multiple channels are established between two peers). With the IKE approach, an IKE phase one exchange is performed once between the peers, and phase two exchanges are performed for each control channel between the peers. Alternatively, the phase one key may be used to secure all control channels between the same two peers. When IKE or SME is performed in-band, a special frame format is used to allow peers to distinguish secured message traffic from standard UNI or PNNI signaling messages.

Once initial authentication and key exchange are complete (via the mechanisms described above or via management using preplaced keys), data origin authentication and encryption are performed on the control plane messages. Regardless of the authentication/key exchange method used (IKE or SME), a common approach is used for message integrity and encryption. This approach is based on the IETF's encapsulating security payload (ESP) specification, RFC 2406 [5]. The format of the CPS message frame is shown in Figure 10.7.

The CPS frame consists of the following fields:

- *Type and subtype:* These values are coded so that they uniquely distinguish this frame from non-CPS control plane messages.

- *Security parameters index (SPI):* The SPI is used to identify individual security associations and is determined by IKE protocol processing. If SME is used instead, then this value is 0.

- *IV:* The IV is used by some encryption modes of operation (e.g., cipher block chaining and counter mode) to synchronize encryption and decryption processes in peer devices (synchronization is described in Chapter 8). Encryption is performed over the fields shown in Figure 10.7.

- *Message:* This is the signaling or PNNI routing message that is to be secured.

- *Sequence number:* The 32-bit sequence number is incremented for each message and is used for replay and reordering protection (similar to the mechanism described in Chapter 7).

- *MAC:* The MAC is computed using the integrity key exchanged during IKE or SME. This allows the receiver to verify the source of the message and whether it was modified in transit. The MAC is computed over the (plaintext) fields shown in Figure 10.7.

- *Pad and pad length:* These fields are used to make the length of the encrypted part of the frame an integer multiple of the encryption algorithm's block size.

When encryption and authentication are performed together on the frame, authentication is performed first, followed by encryption. This allows the receiver to detect if it is decrypting the frame with the wrong key. However, note that although the CPS frame is based on ESP, the order in which authentication and encryption are performed is reversed from the order specified in RFC 2406.

With respect to PNNI security, once the new RCC is authenticated (using IKE, SME, or preplaced keys), the message traffic is secured using

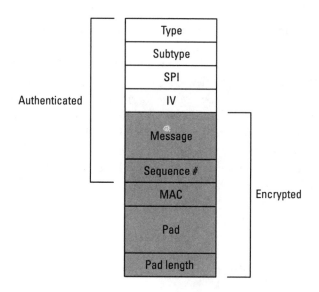

Figure 10.7 CPS frame format.

CPS, and the port is added by the PNNI node as a *secure port* when the RCC reaches the *two-way inside* state. The PNNI Security Addendum [1] allows secured and unsecured links to other nodes to exist simultaneously. Therefore, each peer node must maintain two state machines and data structures when exchanging topology databases using the neighboring peer protocol: one for all unsecured ports and one for all secured ports. When the node sends database summaries, PTSEs, or other PNNI information to its peer, it uses information from the secure port data structure and the secure port state machine, if possible.

As with the standard PNNI protocol, when a secure PNNI RCC leaves the two-way inside state, the secure neighboring peer state machine drops the link from its port list. If this is the last port, then all state information for the neighboring peer is released.

10.4 Summary

To correctly route SVCs, the PNNI nodes must exchange correct routing information. If this information is corrupted via malicious modification or malicious injection of PTSEs, then PNNI routing can become severely degraded. The PNNI security mechanism described in [1] addresses this threat by marking the security status of PTSEs when they are generated and received. These PTSEs are retained in the node's topology database according to these markings and the retention policy that is configured in the node.

PNNI security uses the new CPS mechanism specified in [3] to protect PNNI messages from malicious modification. CPS extends the Security 1.1 control plane security mechanism by providing initial authentication, automatic key exchange, and message encryption in addition to integrity. This mechanism relieves the key management burden associated with the Security 1.1 mechanism, making it more amenable to PNNI security where RCCs are dynamically established and released.

References

[1]   The ATM Forum, "Addendum to PNNI v1.0–Secure Routing," FB-RA-PNNI-RSEC-0171.000, May 2001.

[2]   The ATM Forum, "Private Network-Network Interface Specification, Version 1.0," af-pnni-0055.000, March 1996.

[3]   The ATM Forum, "Control Plane Security Baseline," FB-SEC-CPS-0172.000, May 2001.

[4]   Harkins, D., and D. Carrel, "The Internet Key Exchange (IKE)," Internet Engineering Task Force RFC 2409, November 1998.

[5]   Kent, S., and R. Atkinson, "IP Encapsulating Security Payload (ESP)," Internet Engineering Task Force RFC 2406, November 1998.

Part IV:
Additional Topics in ATM Security

11

Future Standards Development Topics

The ATM Security Specification Version 1.1 is an important specification for ATM security because it provides the fundamental mechanisms required for cryptographic security services and initiation of security associations. This specification provides a solid foundation upon which other security mechanisms can be built, allowing consideration of additional ATM security standardization areas for making security more manageable and flexible. This chapter describes some of these proposed mechanisms.

11.1 Security-Based Routing and Discovery

The network-based ATM security services described in the Security 1.1 Specification [1] (especially encryption, network authentication, and access control) assume that the connection requiring these services will be routed through the necessary devices. This assumption is valid as long as the following conditions hold:

1. The network topology is designed so as to constrain the route of the virtual circuit and cause it to pass through required security devices;

2. The security devices along the virtual circuit's path implement the required services, algorithms, etc.

Constraining the network topology and the location of security services, however, is overly restrictive, especially given the enormous amount of flexibility provided by the SME protocol. Because the SME protocol allows end systems to request security services of the network, and because it allows security agents to specify and negotiate detailed parameters for the security association, it would make sense to augment SME to allow connections to be routed to appropriate SAs during call setup according to the security requirements for the virtual circuit and the security capabilities of the network. If such a mechanism existed, then security devices can be located at arbitrary locations in the network, where appropriate, providing flexibility to the end user or network management to select the security services. (However, in networks where a high degree of administrative control is desired, the distribution of security services throughout a network might provide too much flexibility.)

An example of security-based routing is shown in Figure 11.1.

In this example, the calling party (which contains an SA that implements the integrity service) requires triple DES encryption on the virtual circuit that it is trying to establish, but it does not need the network authentication services provided by SA_A. Since the network security services are distributed throughout the local network, a mechanism is required to ensure that the call is routed through the SA_E that implements triple DES, but not through SA_A.

Although this example may seem contrived, security services may be distributed throughout a network for a number of valid reasons. These reasons include the following:

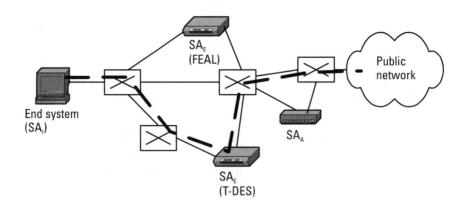

Figure 11.1 Security-based virtual circuit routing.

- It is unreasonable to expect a single security device to implement all the possible algorithms that may be required. Therefore, multiple security devices implementing the same security service, but different algorithms, may be found in various locations in a network.

- When a new security device is added to the network, connecting the device to some location other than the public network attachment point would minimize network downtime.

- Deploying security services in a distributed fashion allows high-performance connections that do not require security to bypass security devices altogether rather than pass through them (albeit without security protections applied). This distributed approach removes potential bottlenecks.

- A network may attach to multiple service providers with different security postures, requiring application of different encryption algorithms (e.g., strong encryption over a public carrier or weaker encryption when using a trusted carrier). This need is described further in [2].

- By not constraining topology to support security devices, the network architect is provided with more flexibility to design the network to his needs (e.g., parallel links for load balancing, replication of security services for reliability, etc.).

Ideally, a mechanism for security-based virtual circuit routing would consider the information regarding the security requirements in the connection request, as well as the security state of the network (i.e., the availability of security services and their locations). In a way, this is very much like the QoS-based routing provided by the PNNI, except that in this case we are dealing with security QoS, or the quality of security service.

A few methods for implementing security-based routing are described in an ATM Forum member contribution [3]. The most straightforward way to implement this feature is to do so within the PNNI protocol. This method would require new PTSEs to encode the security state of an ATM node that provides security services (e.g., the service provided, the algorithms supported, etc.). These PTSEs would be flooded to all other nodes in the PNNI network, and the switches would use this topology information along with the security requirements information in the virtual circuit request to determine how to route the connection.

The problem with this approach is that it requires *all* PNNI nodes in a network to be trusted to properly route connections to the required security devices. This requires extensive testing and cooperation from equipment vendors and providers to ascertain the level of trust that can be placed in the PNNI implementations. In addition, this requires careful network configuration control to prevent introduction of switches from untrusted sources, which can destroy the "chain of trust" required to properly route connections.

Another approach described in [3] is a *security overlay network* approach. This method confines the security-based routing decisions to the network SAs, which form an overlay network over the physical ATM network, as shown in Figure 11.2.

With this approach, the SAs establish security associations with each other, creating the security overlay network, and the network topology is slightly constrained to allow a request for security services to be directed by default to any SA. When the first SA (e.g., SA$_1$) receives the connection request, it examines the request to determine if the call needs to be routed to another SA (in this example, if the connection requires FEAL encryption). If so, then SA$_1$ loosely source-routes the connection (e.g., through PNNI designated transit lists) to route the call to SA$_2$.

The advantage of this approach is that the trust is mostly concentrated in the SAs, which are presumably already trustworthy. Some trust, however, is still required of the network to properly process loosely source-routed connection requests.

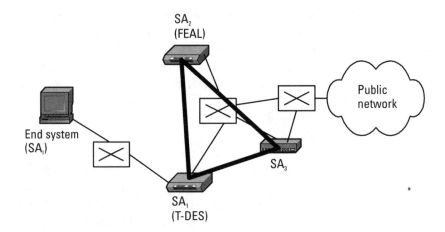

Figure 11.2 Security overlay network.

Both methods (the PNNI-based and security overlay network–based methods) require a mechanism for discovering the location of security services in an ATM network. With the PNNI approach, this information is flooded to all the other PNNI nodes along with standard topology information. With the security overlay network, this information may also be flooded but only between participating SAs. In addition to the flooding approach, other approaches also exist for security overlay networks. These approaches include using an ATM directory service to act as a security service locator, using the PNNI anycast mechanism to connect to any security agent that implements a service, adding integrated layer management interface (ILMI) objects that provide a security agent with location information for other SAs when it connects to a network, or some other service location protocol.

As with standard QoS-based routing, routing based on security QoS requires the network elements (PNNI nodes or security agents) to be aware of the current *security state* for the network. This allows a call to be routed so that the services applied to the connection match the security requirements, even when the security state of the network changes due to link failure, introduction of new SAs, etc. This requires a mechanism for accurately specifying (encoding) the user security requirements and the current security posture of the network. One method for encoding this information is described in [2]. However, as with standard QoS-based routing, the mechanism for encoding security state must also support summarization of security QoS and aggregation of SAs and protected links, which allows this architecture to scale to large networks.

Although this mechanism has been discussed in the ATM Forum, its specification is not expected in the near future because of the number of technical issues (possibly requiring additional research) associated with this mechanism.

11.2 Renegotiation of Security Associations

In the Security Specification 1.1, all parameters for a security association remain constant during the lifetime of the security association (except for session keys, which can be changed using the SKU protocol, as described in Chapter 8). If these constant parameters (e.g., encryption algorithm, length of keys, and master keys) need to be changed, then the existing security association must be torn down and reestablished, which results in interruption of service. For high-bandwidth connections that persist over many months, the need for renegotiation of master keys and other algorithm attributes increases with the lifetime of the security association, and even a short outage due to security association release and reestablishment results in a significant loss of data.

To address this concern, a contribution was brought to the ATM Forum that described one project's implementation of the ATM Security Specification and a mechanism that renegotiated security parameters without interrupting service [4]. This mechanism is similar to the SKU mechanism already defined in Security 1.1, but it supports all of the services provided by the SME protocol.

Like the SKU service, the security renegotiation mechanism uses OAM cells to carry renegotiation messages. However, unlike the SKU protocol, which defines its own protocol and message format to perform a specific function, the security renegotiation mechanism uses the existing SME protocol and message format and defines mechanisms for reliable message delivery and encapsulation of SME messages into an OAM cell stream. The operation of the security renegotiation mechanism at the initiator is shown in Figure 11.3.

When the *renegotiation initiator* (not necessarily the original *SME* initiator) decides that it wishes to change one or more parameters of the security association, its SME protocol process creates an SSIE that contains a FLOW-1 SME message. This message is segmented into 40-byte fragments by the security renegotiation process, which encapsulates the fragments into F5 OAM cells and sends them to the OAM cell scheduler, where each OAM cell is scheduled for transmission within the user data cell stream. When the responder receives each OAM cell (SSIE fragment), it places its contents into a reassembly buffer, and once the entire SME message is received, it is passed to the responder's SME protocol handler.

Since the network can discard SSIE fragments (OAM cells), the security renegotiation mechanism uses a reliable delivery protocol to ensure that the receiving security agent can recover a complete SME protocol message. This reliable delivery protocol uses a sliding window acknowledgement mechanism (similar to Transmission Control Protocol (TCP)) to allow the receiver to indicate to the sender when it has received a contiguous sequence of segments, or when it has detected a missing fragment.

When the responder finishes processing the received FLOW-1 SSIE, it sends a FLOW-2 SSIE using the same segmentation and reliable delivery mechanisms. The initiator processes the received FLOW-2 SSIE, and sends a FLOW-3 SSIE to complete the SME protocol. After sending the FLOW-3

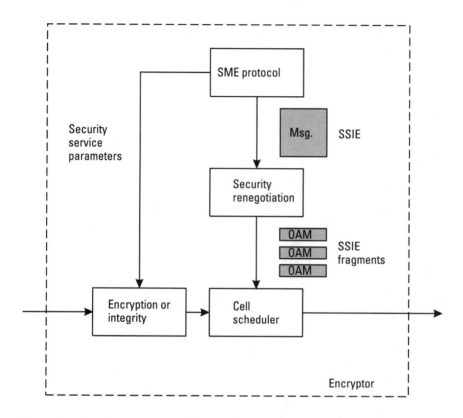

Figure 11.3 Security renegotiation processing at the initiator.

SSIE, the initiator waits until it receives an acknowledgment from the responder that indicates that it has successfully received the FLOW-3 SSIE.

At this point, the initiator and responder have used SME to negotiate the new parameters for the security association, but they are still using the old parameters for the security association. To coordinate the changeover, the initiator inserts a series of F5 OAM cells into the user cell stream to indicate that the new security association parameters are to be used on the next user cell on the protected virtual circuit. At this point, the initiator begins to use the new parameters for the security service, and when the responder receives this OAM cell, it also begins to use the new parameters, completing the security renegotiation process.

Members of the Secure Communications over ATM Networks (SCAN) project in Europe proposed this mechanism to the ATM Forum.

This mechanism, which was based on their implementation, is currently being developed as a specification.

11.3   In-Band SME for Simplex Connections

Recall from Chapter 5 that in Security 1.1, the in-band protocol for SME message transport is only specified for Pt-Pt, bidirectional virtual circuits. The reason for the restriction is the fact that the SME protocol requires a bidirectional channel in which to communicate, and if the channel is the user plane virtual circuit, then the virtual circuit must be bidirectional.

However, if the in-band SME channel is decoupled from the user plane virtual circuit, then the in-band protocol can be used to perform SME for a simplex or multipoint virtual circuit. (In this case, the protocol is not really performed in-band, but rather, in a special virtual circuit that is momentarily established for SME exchanges.) This is the goal of a mechanism that was described in another ATM Forum member contribution [5]. The operation of this mechanism is shown in Figure 11.4.

When a calling end system requests a simplex connection, the SETUP message contains traffic parameters that indicate that the bandwidth in one direction is zero. When the initiator receives this message, it holds the simplex SETUP message and sends a duplex SETUP message (with traffic parameters encoded to request sufficient bidirectional bandwidth to complete the SME protocol in a reasonable period of time). This message contains a special SSIE SAS, which includes a relative ID to allow nested SAs to determine if they should respond.

When the initiator SA sends the duplex SETUP, it does not know the ATM address of the desired responder SA. Therefore, it uses the original called party (end system) address that was contained in the received simplex SETUP message, and the network routes the connection toward the called party. When the duplex SETUP is received by the responder SA (on the way to the called party), the responder intercepts the duplex connection request, and if the SSIE contains only one SAS (and its relative ID is zero), then it remembers the called party's address and accepts the duplex connection.

When the initiator receives the CONNECT message for the duplex connection, it initiates the in-band SME protocol with the responder. Once SME is completed, the initiator releases the duplex connection that was established for SME.

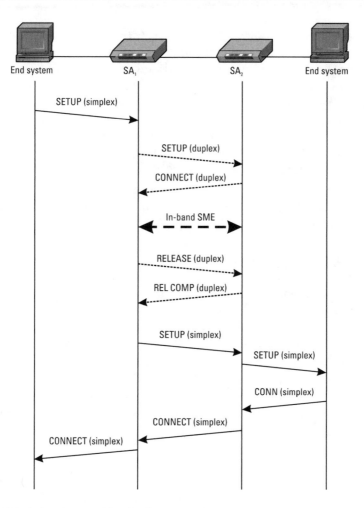

Figure 11.4 In-band protocol for simplex connections.

At this point, the initiator sends the SETUP message for the original simplex connection, and this message is augmented with an SSIE. The initiator, however, must modify this message to ensure that:

1. The simplex connection request is routed through the security agent with which it just completed SME;

2. The remote SA (responder) can correlate the simplex connection request with the correct SME exchange and resultant security association.

Depending on the layout of the ATM network, when the simplex connection request resumes, the network may route the connection around the responder for the recently completed SME exchange. To force the routing of the virtual circuit to the proper responder, the initiator uses the responder's ATM address (which was obtained during the SME exchange) in the called party information element. When the responder receives the (simplex) SETUP, it replaces its address in the called party information element with the address of the intended destination (which was remembered earlier from the duplex SETUP or included in the SSIE by the initiator).

To correlate the SME protocol exchange with the simplex SETUP request, a special identifier is exchanged during SME, and the same identifier is contained in the SSIE that is carried by the (simplex) SETUP request.

While this protocol is a straightforward extension to the Security 1.1 in-band approach, it is complicated by the possibility of nested security associations on a simplex virtual circuit, as shown in Figure 11.5. (Nesting of security associations is described in Chapters 4 and 5.)

When this protocol is applied in this nested situation, three SME exchanges are performed. The first exchange occurs between SA_2 and SA_3 in response to the establishment of the duplex channel for SME communications between SA_1 and SA_4. The second SME exchange is performed on this new duplex channel between SA_1 and SA_4. After this exchange is completed, the duplex channel is released and the simplex SETUP proceeds to SA_2, where another duplex channel is established with SA_3. At this point, the third SME is performed, the duplex channel is released, and the simplex SETUP propagates to the called party.

The complication with this approach is that for a nesting level of n, the number of SME exchanges performed is $n(n+1)/2$, and the number of duplex VC connections (with associated latencies) is n. Therefore, the simplex circuit establishment latency grows quickly with the number of nested security associations.

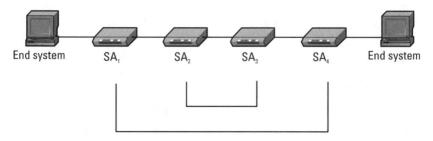

End system SA_1 SA_2 SA_3 SA_4 End system

Figure 11.5 Nested security associations.

Because this mechanism provides an important extension to the existing in-band protocol, it is currently under active development and is expected to become a specification in the near future.

11.4 Wireless ATM Security

Since the wireless communications channel behaves differently than point-to-point copper wires or optical fibers, different attacks are possible. Denial of service attacks based on the hidden node problem, power capture, or plain radio frequency (RF) jamming are all possible.

The hidden node problem is illustrated in Figure 11.6. Nodes A and B are both within receiving range of node C, but not within receiving range of each other. If nodes A and B both attempt to transmit at the same time, a collision will occur at node C. Because of the interference between nodes A and B, node C will not be able to receive either message. Carrier sensing is useless in this situation, since with nodes A and B being outside of each other's range, neither one will sense that the other is attempting to transmit.

This problem could be exploited to perform a denial of service attack on the link between node A and node C by bringing a rogue node into position B. If rogue node B made repeated attempts to connect to node C (even

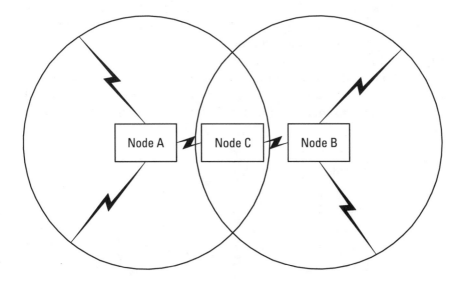

Figure 11.6 Hidden node problem.

if the attempts were refused by node C), they could tie up the airwaves and deny service between nodes A and C. The basic hidden node problem is more thoroughly described in the book by Bing [6].

A power capture situation can arise when a powerful node (more powerful either by virtue of closer proximity or higher RF output) is transmitting at the same time and to the same destination as a weaker node. In Figure 11.7, the transmissions from node B are being received with greater signal strength at node A than those from node C, causing node A to listen to node B rather than node C. Bing describes this situation in greater detail in [6].

Power capture can also be employed as a denial of service attack. A rogue node B could position itself such that its signal, as heard by node A, is many times greater than the strength of the signal from node C as measured by node A. Again, if rogue node B made repeated connection attempts to node A (even if they were refused by node A), they could congest the airwaves and deny service between nodes A and C.

To deny service, an adversary may also jam some of the wireless communication links by transmitting powerful signals designed to intentionally cause destructive interference. This is shown in Figure 11.8.

The attacks described above, and others based on the shared nature of radio waves propagating through the air (such as eavesdropping), are not unique to wireless ATM networks. These attacks can be a problem to any wireless network. Some of them, such as jamming and eavesdropping, have possible countermeasures (spread spectrum techniques and steerable null antennas to counter jamming, and encryption to counter eavesdropping). In addition, unintentional hidden node and power capture problems caused by friendly nodes can be reduced by configuration control and sound wireless network design. Solutions to counteract malicious use of hidden node and power capture situations to cause denial of service attacks remain research

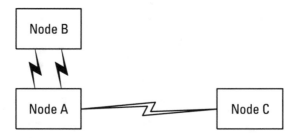

Figure 11.7 Power capture situation.

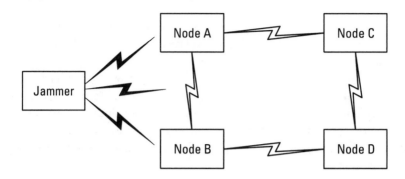

Figure 11.8 Signal jamming.

efforts and are far from standardization. (It should be noted that infrared (IR) communications will probably not suffer from hidden node attacks and will be much less susceptible to power capture, jamming, and eavesdropping attacks than RF communications. IR communications depend on having a clear line-of-site between the transmitter and the receiver. Therefore, building and room walls can be used to keep interlopers out and contain the IR waves. IR, however, forces other trade-offs in versatility and distance.)

11.4.1 Shared Media Access Security

In a sense, wireless ATM networks present the worst of all worlds! They require additional traffic and overhead to establish ATM connections, yet they behave much like a shared Ethernet. Because both Ethernet and wireless ATM are broadcast over shared media, both are subject to collisions, eavesdropping, and message injection by rogue nodes. This environment is very different from wired ATM networks, where links between adjacent nodes are not shared and physical access to the communication links is more restricted. Messages transmitted over shared media (e.g., hybrid fiber-coax segments, and especially free space via radio waves) most likely will require encryption and message authentication codes to provide authenticity, confidentiality, and nonrepudiation.

11.4.2 Security Standards Support for Wireless ATM

The ATM Forum has a wireless (WATM) working group whose charter is to develop recommendations intended to extend the use of ATM technologies to a broad range of wireless services. Their vision is to enable ATM connectivity anytime, anywhere.

Much of the work thus far in the WATM working group has dealt with mobile wireless ATM. Although there are security issues involved with location management, mobility management, and handoffs, no specification has emerged (as of July 2001) from this working group for ATM Forum approval. Mobile wireless–specific security topics such as terminal identity confidentiality, terminal identity authentication, signaling information confidentiality and authentication of security related mobile network entities have been discussed at times in the WATM working group but have not yet been included in a specification.

The security mechanisms provided by the Security 1.1 Specification, however, can be used to address some of the security requirements of wireless networks. As stated in Section 11.4.1, messages sent over radio waves likely need to be encrypted. Security 1.1 supports the various scenarios for data encryption over the wireless segment. One scenario, involving a wireless tail circuit, is shown in Figure 11.9. This could be a connection where no encryption would be required if the entire path was fiber optic media. However, due to the higher vulnerability of the wireless segment, encryption is needed for that portion of the circuit. Another scenario is depicted in Figure 11.10 with a wireless segment in the middle of the circuit. This connection could negotiate encryption over the entire circuit, with additional encryption (super encryption) or a stronger cryptographic algorithm for the wireless segment of the circuit.

The first scenario would roughly correspond to one of the lower security association nesting diagrams in Figure 5.7 in Chapter 5 (especially if security nesting level 0 used the null cryptographic algorithm). The second scenario would correspond to the upper nesting diagrams in Figure 5.7 as either a nested security association or as several disjoint security associations. As shown there, all of these conditions are possible and supported by security mechanisms included in Security 1.1.

A potential problem exists in the second scenario when choosing a path that includes a wireless segment that needs additional or stronger encryption on that segment. In this case, the additional overhead imposed by encryption may cause deterioration of the quality of service. During connection setup, negotiations will need to balance the additional encryption overhead due to the wireless segment with the requested quality of service.

Another (albeit less flexible) possibility is that encryption, which is most likely implemented in hardware, could be included at the physical level of wireless segments. Automatically encrypting these links would increase the latency (and possibly decrease the throughput) by a fixed amount. Because this encryption would always be in place and it is not changing cryptographic

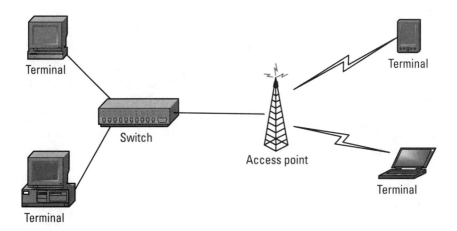

Figure 11.9 Wireless segment at the end of the circuit.

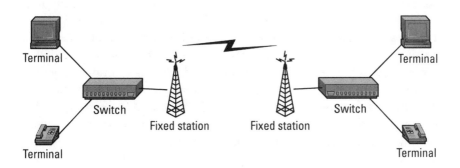

Figure 11.10 Wireless segment in the middle of the circuit.

algorithms on a virtual circuit by virtual circuit basis, the (permanently) modified link parameters must be taken into account during QoS negotiations.

A malicious node could combine a conventional masquerade attack [7] with a power capture attack. By impersonating an authorized terminal and transmitting at a higher power level, the malicious node could trick the network into accepting messages from it. This underscores the importance of using encryption for the wireless links in the circuit. Although not yet in the ATM Forum standards, terminal identity authentication, which verifies that the terminal identity transmitted over the radio waves is the one claimed by the terminal, may also help to defeat this attack.

Wireless ATM networks are also more susceptible to replay attacks (where a message is recorded and replayed at a later time) than wired (fiber, copper) ATM networks. The ATM Forum Security Specification provides several mechanisms to deter this attack. When using counter mode encryption, as discussed in Chapter 8, the state vector described in Security 1.1 contains several fields (sequence number, segment number, and linear feedback shift register value) to thwart replay attacks. In addition, there are user plane and control plane mechanisms in Security 1.1 that work to defeat these attacks.

11.5 Summary

This chapter describes additional security mechanisms that have been proposed in the ATM Forum. Some mechanisms address some of the current shortcomings in the Security Specification 1.1, while others provide new capabilities that take advantage of its flexibility. One should note, however, that these mechanisms are in various stages of completion at the time of this writing and may or may not become approved specifications. Specifically, there is currently considerable activity in standards and implementations for security renegotiation and in-band SME for simplex connections. In addition, there is also some activity in the development of ATM wireless specifications, which may address security issues. However, work on security-based routing and discovery is still in the early concept phase.

References

[1]   The ATM Forum, "ATM Security Specification Version 1.1," af-sec-0100.002, March 2001.

[2]   Schumacher, H. J., S. Ghosh, and T. S. Lee, "Top Secret Traffic and the Public ATM Network Infrastructure," *Information Systems Security*, Vol. 7, No. 4, Winter 1999, pp. 27–45.

[3]   Tarman, T. D., and P. E. Sholander, "Issues in Security Service Discovery and Routing," ATM Forum contribution ATMF/99-0181, April 1999.

[4]   Laurent, M., C. Delahaye, and M. Achemlal, "Security Services Negotiation Through OAM Cells," ATM Forum contribution ATMF/99-0335, July 1999.

[5] Altman, A., "In-Band Security for Simplex Connections," ATM Forum contribution ATMF/99-0568, November 1999.

[6] Bing, B., *High-Speed Wireless ATM and LANs*, Norwood, MA: Artech House, 2000.

[7] Cooper, J. A., *Computer & Communications Security*, New York: McGraw-Hill, 1989.

12

Research Topics

The ATM security mechanisms described in the preceding chapters have been implemented, standardized, or can be readily standardized with a little effort. Some ATM security techniques, however, require additional research before they can reach a similar level of maturity. Hardware-based algorithm-agile encryption at high speed presents interesting challenges in terms of encryptor design and the effect the architectural approach has on ATM virtual circuits. In addition, intrusion detection on ATM layer protocols (e.g., virtual circuit establishment signaling and routing protocols) is a novel concept that has not been the subject of much research. Other issues, such as authentication and confidentiality of control plane signaling messages, present unacceptable trade-offs in their current forms, which has prompted the ATM Forum to defer further development of standard mechanisms until these problems are resolved.

12.1 Algorithm- and Robustness-Agile Encryption

Different users and applications (manifested by different virtual circuits) can have different security requirements for data privacy, integrity, and authentication. In Chapter 8, the key-agility aspects of context-agile encryption were discussed. In this chapter, several other aspects of context-agile encryption are discussed, which at the time of this writing remain fertile research areas.

12.1.1 Robustness Agility

The term "robustness" in this circumstance refers to *cryptographic* robustness or strength. A robustness-agile encryption system can quickly and easily change the confidentiality services offered (e.g., to an ATM virtual circuit) to an arbitrary level of strength or cryptographic robustness. To do this, robustness-agile encryptors must switch rapidly (within a cell time) between contexts of different cryptographic strength.

This switching has at least three forms. The first is between different cryptographic algorithms. The second is between variants of the same algorithm implementing different modes of operation with different protection characteristics. The third form is between variants of the same algorithm, which may utilize a different key, and other cryptographic state variable, lengths. Other variables relating to cryptographic algorithms and their implementation may also be varied as part of the cryptographic context. Thus, robustness-agility requires even more information in the cryptographic context associated with each virtual circuit than encryptors that are only key-agile. This implies that larger context memories are required to contain this extra information. The first and second methods of varying the cryptographic robustness are discussed in the next section.

Each encryption algorithm specified for use in Security 1.1 has a fixed or specified key length. (Even the now deprecated DES40 is treated as a separate algorithm from DES and triple DES.) However, future work in this area may also permit the use of algorithms with variable-length keys [e.g., the Advanced Encryption Standard (AES)]. NIST has selected Rijndael as the algorithm for its AES, which supports key lengths of (at least) 128, 192, and 256 bits. With an algorithm such as this, cryptographic robustness can be varied from one virtual circuit to another by changing the length of the key, as appropriate. Reference [1] provides a general treatment of both robustness agility and algorithm agility.

12.1.2 Algorithm Agility

Encryptors that contain multiple algorithms (or variants of algorithms) and can switch between them quickly enough to service adjacent cells in a high-speed data stream are said to be algorithm-agile. An algorithm-agile encryptor can also implement different modes of operation of the same encryption algorithm, such as the DES feedback modes, as separate algorithms.

Algorithm-agile encryption provides advantages in addition to variable cryptographic strength. It also allows for compatibility between a broader range of devices. Each may implement various different algorithms because of a wide variety of application and policy requirements. For example, a workstation may contain an encryption/decryption module supporting algorithms *A* and *B*. This allows that workstation to engage in both a secure file transfer session with a server that only supports algorithm *A* and a video conference to a system that only supports algorithm *B*.

As stated in Chapter 8, some commonly used encryption algorithms and modes do not scale well for high speeds. This includes the class of encryption functions with feedback based on a combination of key and plaintext or ciphertext. In networks containing various kinds of application traffic, it is important for an encryptor to be agile between widely used algorithms and scalable, high-performance algorithms. The various aspects of context agility are summarized in Table 12.1.

Agility between various encryption algorithms can also satisfy requirements that could vary from one communication session to another, such as error magnification and ATM QoS parameters. Several of these QoS parameters—CTD and cell delay variation (CDV, the difference between best-case and worst-case CTD)—are affected by algorithm-agile encryption. The differing latencies through different encryption algorithms can affect both CTD and CDV, which in turn affects the performance of interactive, real-time applications such as voice and video.

Robustness- and algorithm-agile encryptors can indirectly affect the ATM QoS, since different algorithms, modes, and key lengths may affect delay, delay variation, throughput, error magnification, and/or sensitivity to synchronization upset. For this reason, the encryptors (incorporating knowledge of the encryption methods used) must participate in the ATM QoS negotiation that occurs at connection setup. One interesting effect is the CDV due to the different relative latencies of each algorithm. Algorithm-agile encryption preserves cell order within an individual virtual circuit and among virtual circuits that use the same encryption algorithm. Depending on the architecture of the encryptor, however, an algorithm-agile encryptor

Table 12.1
Context-Agility Aspects and Attributes

Key-Agile	Robustness-Agile	Algorithm-Agile
Can change cryptovariables (key, IV, etc.) for each cell stream	Can change cryptographic parameters (key length, etc.) for each cell stream	Can change cryptographic algorithms or modes of operation for each cell stream

may cause reordering of cells that use different encryption algorithms. As these differently delayed streams are queued and recombined into a single cell stream, this may also introduce additional CDV among cells of the same virtual circuit that use the same encryption algorithm. A paper by Sholander and others [2] addresses this topic in detail. Their research indicates that encryptors should participate in the QoS negotiation, and that algorithm-agile encryptors may need to append output buffering to low latency algorithms in order to minimize CDV. With the higher latency algorithms, this delay-equalization method trades lowered CDV for increased CTD. When algorithm-agile encryptors participate in QoS negotiations, the set of available algorithms may be dynamically restricted to maintain a previously negotiated CDV bound.

As an example, Sandia National Laboratories developed and produced a limited quantity of DES ASICs [3], an integrated circuit implementing the Data Encryption Standard. This chip, which is implemented as an 18-stage pipeline, operates at a clock frequency that easily supports OC-48 (2.488 Gbps) communications. If an encryptor is built using three of these DES ASICs concatenated in series to implement triple DES, and clocked at 40 MHz, it would have a throughput of over 2.5 Gbps. It would also have latency through the encryption algorithm of 1,350 ns (3 chips × 18 stages/chip × 25 ns delay/stage). This will increase the CTD on any circuit employing this algorithm.

Another cryptographic algorithm would likely have a different delay. (A trivial example is the *null* algorithm, which could add no delay.) Because cell streams using different cryptographic algorithms that are not buffered out to equal delays will not remain marching in lock-step with each other, one stream can cause the other to be delayed by a fraction of a cell. This delay increases the CDV on the affected circuit. (The paper by Selvakumar and Venkateshwaran [4] does an excellent job of illustrating this concept.)

Recent research by Selvakumar and Venkateshwaran [4] indicates that a middle ground between the two extremes (no increase in CDV with longer CTD, and minimal increase in CTD with greater CDV) can be achieved. If the latencies of the algorithms in the pool of available cryptographic algorithms can be characterized, along with the transmission times of the cells through the cryptographic equipment (including any added delay) and the sustained cell rate for each circuit, then analysis can be performed to determine the optimal trade-off between increased CTD and CDV. By grouping cryptographic algorithms according to their latencies into several partitions, output buffering can be applied incrementally.

As an example, if an encryptor supports four algorithms with latencies of 3, 6, 7, and 10, the algorithms could be grouped into some of the following sets of partitions:

1. {3, 6; built out to 6}, {7, 10; built out to 10};
2. {3; no extra buffering}, {6, 7; built out to 7}, {10; no extra buffering};
3. {3, 6, 7; built out to 7}, {10; no extra buffering}.

Using CTD-cost and CDV-cost equations developed in [4], one can select the optimal grouping of algorithms and corresponding delay equalizations. The partition sets could be defined at the time of encryptor design, when the selection of cryptographic algorithms has been decided. As long as only several cryptographic algorithms are supported, and hence the number of partition sets is limited, the trade-off analysis could be performed in real-time, at circuit setup.

12.2 Control Plane Confidentiality

In situations where traffic analysis is considered a threat, the information contained in ATM signaling messages must be considered sensitive. The information elements contained in Q.2931 messages contain valuable information for traffic analysts, including called and (optionally) calling party identifiers, and information about higher-layer protocols as contained in the AAL parameters and broadband higher-layer information (BHLI) information elements. If a site considers this information sensitive, then a mechanism is required to protect the confidentiality of control plane messages.

Two approaches are possible for control plane confidentiality, as shown in Figure 12.1. The *hop-by-hop* approach uses encrypted channels to transfer control plane information between logically adjacent switches. This approach is implemented in two ways: using the CPS method (described in Chapter 10 and specified in [5]), and using the Security 1.1 user plane confidentiality service (described in Chapter 7 and specified in [6]) on the signaling virtual circuit or the virtual path connection carrying the signaling VC. The hop-by-hop approach, however, requires all switches that receive encrypted signaling messages to decrypt the message before processing it. This is a realistic scenario across the public network if two switches terminate a VPC tunnel through the public network. These methods do not work, however, if the public network must process protected messages.

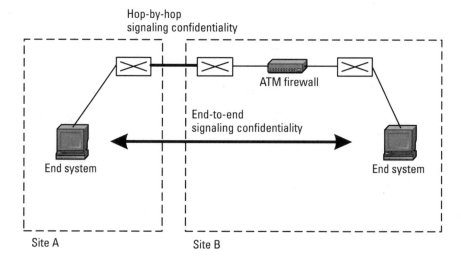

Figure 12.1 Control plane confidentiality approaches.

Another approach to signaling confidentiality is the *end-to-end* approach. This method encrypts some of the information elements in the message, and allows other information elements that are required for call processing by the network to be left in the clear. Two options exist for end-to-end confidentiality. The first approach is to encrypt in place the IEs that only have end-to-end significance. Of course, the selection of information elements to be encrypted must be performed carefully. For example, IEs that only have relevance in the end systems (e.g., BHLI) may be encrypted, but other information elements such as the called party identifier cannot be encrypted in place because intermediate switches must examine them. The advantage of this approach is that it does not result in much expansion in the signaling message (a small amount of expansion may be required to identify the intended decrypting switch and to pad the IE to a multiple of the encryption algorithm's block size).

The second approach would have an SA encapsulate the protected IEs in the signaling message, encrypt the encapsulated IEs, and include substitute IEs in the plaintext portion of the message. Therefore, as shown in Figure 12.2, IEs that are normally processed by the network (e.g., called party IE) may be encapsulated in an SSIE and encrypted, with a replacement IE (e.g., a called party IE for a remote gateway security agent) in the plaintext portion of the message. At the remote end, the gateway security agent would

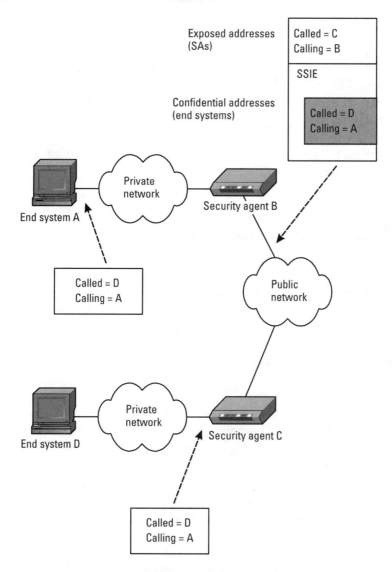

Figure 12.2 Encapsulation and encryption of information elements.

decrypt the information elements and use them in the completion of the connection request.

This method, which was proposed in [7], was discussed in the ATM Forum Security Working Group and deferred until a later version of the specification. The SSIE defined in [6], however, can be readily extended with a new octet group to support encapsulation and encryption of IEs.

The problem with the encapsulation approach to end-to-end control plane confidentiality is that it causes the signaling message to grow. The SSIE is currently constrained to 512 bytes, which could be exceeded if many IEs are encapsulated or if the control plane confidentiality service is nested. The encapsulation of IEs, however, is a straightforward approach to control plane confidentiality and it achieves the desired result of masking signaling parameters from ATM traffic analysis.

12.3   Control Plane Authentication

Like the control plane confidentiality approaches described in the previous section, control plane authentication can also be applied on a hop-by-hop basis or end-to-end basis. With hop-by-hop authentication, the contents of the signaling message are protected as they travel between logically adjacent switches, providing protection from unauthorized introduction and modification of signaling messages. However, hop-by-hop authentication has the following problems:

1. To protect signaling messages end-to-end, all links between ATM endpoints must have this protection. This increases the scope of trust that is required, and presents a difficult key management problem if the number of intervening switches is large.

2. If any link in the chain is not protected (e.g., in the public network), the subsequent switches and the receiving end system have no way of knowing if the message was maliciously injected or modified.

The CPS specification [5] and the ATM Security Specification 1.1 [6] provide mechanisms for hop-by-hop signaling authentication and integrity. In the Security 1.1 mechanism, the user plane integrity mechanism (with replay protection) is applied to the signaling AAL service data unit that contains the message, as described in Chapter 7. The message authentication code is applied using a shared secret key, and the receiving device verifies the MAC with the same key. The initial shared secret keys are distributed via management, and may be updated periodically using the Security 1.1 session key update mechanism.

The mechanism specified in the CPS specification also provides hop-by-hop authentication, but it enhances the Security 1.1 method by allowing algorithm negotiation and exchange of initial MAC keys before the signaling channel is activated, as described in Chapter 10. Negotiation and key exchange is performed using the IKE protocol [8] or the SME three-way exchange protocol specified in [6]. After negotiation and key exchange, CPS-protected signaling messages are encapsulated in a special signaling AAL SDU, a MAC is generated over its contents, and the SDU is optionally encrypted.

Hop-by-hop control plane authentication is best applied on interswitch links that are not physically secured. In particular, control plane authentication should be considered for interswitch control plane channels that are tunneled through a virtual path that traverses the public network.

However, hop-by-hop authentication does not provide complete protection. Unless the security configuration of the network is carefully controlled end-to-end, a destination network or end system cannot assume that the signaling information elements were properly processed or not maliciously modified. For this reason, end-to-end authentication is required.

With end-to-end authentication based on digital signatures, the destination network or end system must be able to reconstruct the signaling message to exactly match the message that was originated at the source. This requirement is complicated by the fact that signaling information elements may be legitimately reordered or modified by intermediate switches during their processing of the message.

One approach for digital signature-based, end-to-end control plane authentication, shown in Figure 12.3, is to copy the information elements to be authenticated, encapsulate the IEs within the SSIE, and sign the SSIE contents. When an end system or switch receives the SSIE, it verifies the digital signature of the encapsulated IEs, examines the contents of these IEs, and decides whether to allow the connection to proceed, based on local policy.

This approach is analogous to the encapsulation method for control plane confidentiality described earlier, and it shares the same trade-offs. Specifically, the encapsulation method is simple, but results in expansion of the message, which may be unnecessary if the network does not modify the authenticated IEs.

A second approach, which is described in [7] and was seriously considered in the ATM Forum, does not duplicate the authenticated IEs. Rather, the digital signature is generated directly over the IEs in place in the message. To manage the possibility that the IEs could be reordered during the network's call processing, an IE list is used to denote the original ordering of the

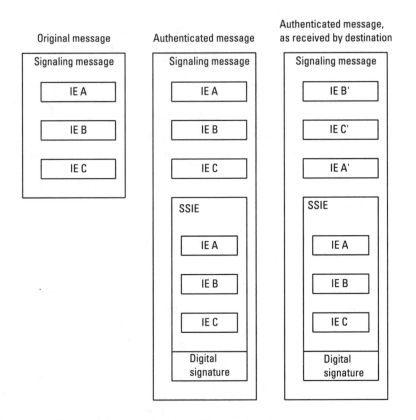

Figure 12.3 Encapsulation of authenticated information elements.

IEs when they were signed. This is shown in Figure 12.4. When an end system or switch receives this message, it rearranges the information elements according to the order specified in the IE list, validates the digital signature, and allows the connection to proceed according to local policy.

This method results in more processing to reorder IEs, but since it replaces encapsulated IEs with a short IE list, this approach results in less message expansion. This method, however, assumes that the IEs will not be modified in transit (otherwise, the signature will fail). For some IEs (e.g., the BHLI), this is a valid assumption. The trick, however, is to identify these IEs and hope that all security-relevant IEs are in this set (which is not a good assumption).

Another problem is that digital signatures are all-or-nothing—If one byte in an IE is changed, the digital signature fails, period. A desirable

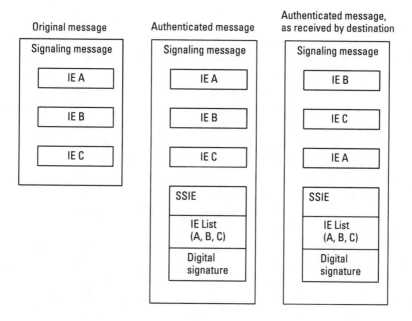

Figure 12.4 In-place authentication of information elements.

solution to the IE modification problem (without resorting to the encapsulation approach) would have the signature validation step indicate which bytes of the IE(s) were modified. Then, the receiving device would have the choice whether to allow the connection to proceed given the knowledge of what fields were modified in transit. However, no techniques that implement this feature were available during the development of the Security Specification 1.1, so the ATM Forum decided to defer work in end-to-end control plane authentication.

12.4 ATM Intrusion Detection

Many security methodologies, especially those used for physical security, follow a detect-delay-respond (DDR) model. To prevent an attack from succeeding, they first detect an activity, then the attacker or intruder must be delayed while the nature of the attack is determined and a response is dispatched. Similarly, in cyberspace, the first action of an intrusion detection system is to detect an intruder or that an unauthorized activity is taking place. Delaying actions typically need to be implemented as part of the network security package but are usually outside of the intrusion detection system. Once the intrusion detection system has determined the nature of the intrusion or attack, a response is generated. An intrusion detection system can thus sense and correlate events, assess or aid in determining what is occurring, and initiate countermeasures.

In general, intrusion detection systems can be real-time systems or after-the-fact systems. Real-time intrusion detection systems operate, as the name implies, in real time, sensing events, making assessments, and taking actions very quickly. After-the-fact systems automatically scrutinize logs and audit trails, looking for evidence indicating a break-in or some other unusual occurrence has taken place.

Intrusion detection systems can also be categorized in two ways, misuse detection (typically based on attack signatures) and anomaly detection systems. Signature-based systems look for misuse in the form of a series or group of events that signify a known attack. A disadvantage of this style system is that the types of attacks to be detected must be known in advance. Because new attacks are invented daily, intrusion detection systems based on signature databases are always somewhat out of date. This is akin to the problem of keeping virus-checking programs up to date. Anomaly-based systems develop metrics and heuristics about the networks in which they are installed. These systems examine activities in the network to see if they conform to established profiles of normal usage. Anomaly-based intrusion detection systems are more flexible than signature-based systems because they can perform range and bounds checking involving parameters, rather than only existence checking of various known events. These systems, however, are typically slower in reaching a decision, and are more prone to signaling false positives.

Intrusion detection systems can also be host-based or network-based. Network-based systems rely heavily on network "sniffers" (for links using broadcast media) and sensors (for point-to-point links) placed in the network communication links, analyzing traffic flowing over these links. Host-based systems can employ a wide range of tactics including examining events on (and within protocol stacks of) switches, routers, and end systems, and monitoring traffic at network interfaces. Host-based systems can also scan host-generated log entries, examine processes (including results of processes, process runtime statistics, and other process actions) executing on the host, and monitor user input for hosts of interest, on which they are installed. This is depicted in Figure 12.5.

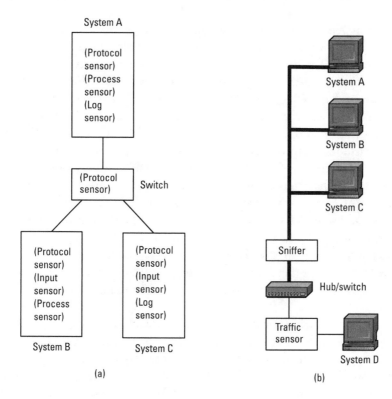

Figure 12.5 Sensor placement in (a) host-based and (b) network-based intrusion detection systems.

12.4.1 Switched Network Intrusion Detection

Intrusion detection systems must operate differently in switched networks than in broadcast or shared media networks. In networks where traffic is broadcast over shared media, sensors can be placed directly on that shared media where they can "sniff" the passing traffic for all hosts on that subnet, and ascertain much of what is happening on the network. Switched networks do not allow this luxury. Since all traffic is not passed over common links, sensors must be distributed throughout the network at strategic points (i.e., switches, critical end systems, or trunk connections) to gain knowledge of network events.

Switched networks in general, and specifically ATM networks, pose special challenges for network intrusion detection. Point-to-point data flows can only be viewed at end systems and switches along the path, and other nodes may require network configuration changes to view traffic. More and more often, however, switched networks are the basis for enterprise and public networks. ATM provides the backbone for telephone networks and much of the Internet. Furthermore, as voice, video, and data traffic converge into one network, the effects of a disruption can lead to a total fiasco. Today, most intrusion detection systems operate at the IP layer and are blind to network attacks or component failures at the layer 2 level and below. (Layer 2, which includes protocols such as ATM and Ethernet, is the data link layer of the OSI Reference Model and is responsible for transferring information units such as characters or bytes, from one node to another. This layer also includes conversion to and from bit streams, and buffering issues.)

In addition, ATM networks have special control protocols that affect network state and availability. Furthermore, native ATM applications such as telephone and video services use adaptation layers to interface to the ATM network, bypassing the IP layer. Therefore, intrusion detection in ATM networks must be performed below layer 3, and must examine control and data flows.

ATM networks scale very well and can therefore grow quite large. As a result, the intrusion detection system (described in the next section) can become overwhelmed. Because these networks have a wide range of link rates, from T1 (1.5 Mbps) to OC-192 (10 Gbps) and higher, ATM intrusion detection systems may use many varieties of sensor types. For example, sensors that examine events at the edges of the network may be implemented in software, while speedy, hardware-based sensors examine events in the core of the network.

12.4.2 Anatomy of Intrusion Detection Systems

At a minimum, switched network intrusion detection systems can have three types of communicating components: sensors, intrusion assessment engine(s), and response agents. There may be additional components, depending on the design of the specific intrusion detection system (see Figure 12.6).

The sensors detect network events and report them to one or more assessment engines. The assessment engine evaluates and correlates the sensor information and may initiate responses. Response agents carry out some action based on the evaluation of what was detected.

Additional components that may optionally be part of an ATM intrusion detection system include a rule editor and a user interface. If the assessment engine is driven by a set of rules, a rule editor may be necessary to

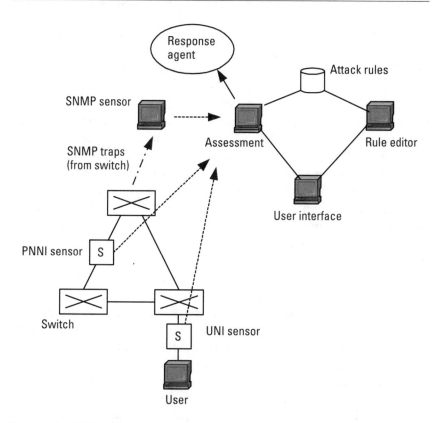

Figure 12.6 ATM intrusion detection system architecture.

construct the rule database. Depending on the intended user of the system and its design, a user interface may be provided. The relationship of all these components is depicted in Figure 12.6.

Sensors, distributed throughout the network, report events that result from ATM protocol or other operations (e.g., configuration). These network events could include new connections, new switches joining the PNNI peer group, and peer group leader elections. Sensors can be placed between switches (for traffic in the network core) and between workstations and switches (for monitoring the edges of the network).

A possible design may include direct sensors and indirect sensors. Direct sensors monitor ATM protocols directly, whereas indirect sensors monitor the *effects* of ATM protocol operations via SNMP traps, as shown in Figure 12.6. An event on an ATM switch (e.g., configuration, link status, signaling change) would initiate an SNMP *trap* operation, which would send a message to an SNMP trap daemon on a host system, where the message is filtered and reformatted, and sent to an assessment engine.

Direct sensors can be further divided into two groups: active direct and passive direct sensors. Active direct sensors are sensors that actively participate in the ATM protocols to detect events resulting from ATM protocol operations. An example of such a sensor would be one whose function is to participate in PNNI protocol activities (e.g., new node events and peer group leader elections) and send filtered events to an assessment engine for analysis. Passive direct sensors monitor ATM protocol operations but do not participate in the protocols. An example of a passive direct sensor would be a sensor that taps a connection between an end system and a switch and observes UNI protocol activities (e.g., connection setup and release requests). These UNI protocol activities are filtered, formatted, and passed to an assessment engine as an event.

Sensors can be implemented in software or hardware. Software-based sensors may be appropriate at the edges of the network, where performance is not held at a premium, but their low cost enables widespread distribution. On the other hand, hardware-based sensors, although costing more to produce, are expected to operate at much higher communication rates. This makes them suitable for placement in the core of the network where fewer sensors are required, but where high performance is demanded.

The assessment engine is responsible for receiving messages from sensors, combining this new information with previously acquired information, evaluating the information, and initiating a response. Assessment engines can vary widely in design—from using a simple word or register to store a static attack signature, to using sophisticated artificial intelligence techniques. The real power and flexibility of intrusion detection systems lies in the assessment engine, how it handles the data and decides what constitutes an attack.

If the assessment engine is rule driven (i.e., if it loads a set of rules describing events and their relationships that constitute an attack, and measures for responding to that attack), a rule editor is needed. Creating a rule database comprehensive enough to cover multiple, complex attacks is an arcane and tedious process. A rule editor, particularly a graphical rule editor can greatly simplify this process for a user or administrator. A clearer, simpler process helps to prevent or reveal errors in the rules.

Some intrusion detection systems have a user interface, which is a central point of control and status for the system. This might display overall system status, status of specific sensors (active, bypassed, tripped, etc.), alarms (when the assessment engine has decided enough events have occurred to constitute an attack), and responses initiated. It could also give the system operator a way to load new rule sets into the assessment engine, take sensors off-line (bypass mode), and perform other control functions.

Responses are actions carried out by response agents. The assessment engine activates response agents when an attack is sensed. Any attack (defined to the assessment engine) may have multiple responses. Examples of a response could be:

- A telephone page to the network administrator;

- An e-mail message to the network administrator (or security officer);

- Disabling a port on an ATM switch;

- Increasing the sensitivity of a sensor (by decreasing its threshold for triggering).

12.4.3 Example Attack

One possible attack illustrated here, is the *peer group leader take-over attack*. This is an attack where a rogue node takes over leadership of an ATM PNNI peer group. This can be done by an insider penetrating the PGL, or by a node outside of the peer group joining the group and getting elected PGL. At that point the corrupt PGL can adjust QoS parameters and disseminate the modified information, effectively cutting off communication to portions of the network. Smith, Hill, and Robinson describe this type of attack in [9].

This example focuses on the outsider forcing a PGL election. For this attack to be successful, three things must happen:

1. A new member should join the PNNI peer group;

2. A PGL election should be held;

3. A new peer group leader should be announced.

If these events occur (possibly within a specified time), and the newly elected PGL is the same as the new node who recently joined the peer group, then the PGL take-over attack is assumed to have occurred. An appropriate response when this attack is sensed may be to disable the switch port to which the rogue node is connected and then logging the action to a file.

12.4.4 Advanced Issues

Because ATM networks scale well, both in size and speed, ATM intrusion detection systems must also scale. There are several ways this can be achieved.

As networks grow, an increasing number of sensors will need to communicate with the assessment engine. One way to prevent "sensor overload" in the assessment engine is to use multiple assessment engines, arranged hierarchically for scalability. This is illustrated in Figure 12.7.

In this model, various sensors report to certain assessment engines. By assigning sensors to specific assessment engines, the load of any given assessment engine is kept manageable. Assessment engines may also act as response agents (for assessment engines below them) and as sensors (to assessment engines above them). In this way, the lower level assessment engines can take tactical actions and report up to a higher level. The high-level assessment engine can then view the overall picture, develop strategy, and send commands regarding specific actions, down to the lower level assessment engines. The lower level assessment engines may also communicate with each other on a peer-to-peer basis, exchanging information about events detected and actions taken.

This parallels some of the work done by Drs. Sumit Ghosh and Tony Lee [10] in simulating centralized versus decentralized military command and control. They found from their simulations that decentralized command, control, and communication functions allowed faster reaction times, resulting in faster convergence on the enemy and higher kill rates, with fewer casualties. Similarly, it is hoped that hierarchical assessment and allowing communication between peer assessment engines can provide rapid detection and accurate evaluation of attacks, as well as timely responses to isolate and limit network damage, while preventing the highest echelon of command from being swamped with excessive information. Because of the size and communication rates to which ATM networks can scale, the attributes of rapid detection, timely response, and preventing assessment engine overload become ever more important.

Another method of preventing sensor overload in assessment engines may be to use smart sensors. Smart sensors would not only detect events, but also be able to generate limited responses. With sensors taking autonomous action (thereby minimizing message traffic to the assessment engine), and possibly communicating with each other, more sensors could report to an assessment engine without causing an overload. The disadvantage of this method is that the assessment engine might not receive the event information that it needs to obtain a global view of an attack.

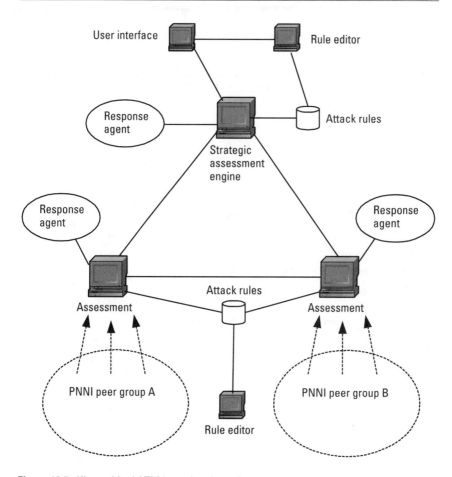

Figure 12.7 Hierarchical ATM intrusion detection system.

References

[1] Pierson, L. G., et al., "Context-Agile Encryption for High Speed Communication Networks," *ACM Computer Communication Review*, Vol. 29, No. 1, 1999, pp. 35–49.

[2] Sholander, P., et al., "The Effect of Algorithm-Agile Encryption on ATM Quality of Service," *Global Telecommunications Conference, IEEE GLOBECOM '97*, Phoenix, AZ, November 3, 1997, Vol. 1, Conference collection, pp. 470–474.

[3] Wilcox, D. C., et al., "A DES ASIC Suitable for Network Encryption at 10 Gbps and Beyond," in *Cryptographic Hardware and Embedded Systems*, C. K. Koc and C. Paar

(Eds.), Lecture Notes in Computer Science, Vol. 1717, Berlin: Springer-Verlag, 1999, pp. 37–48.

[4] Selvakumr, S., and V. Venkateshwaran, "Partition Equalizer: A Scheduler for Algorithm-Agile-Encryptor ATM Networks," *Computer Communications*, Vol. 24, No. 7–8, 2001, pp. 631–640.

[5] The ATM Forum, "Control Plane Security Baseline," FB-SEC-CPS-0172.000, May 2001.

[6] The ATM Forum, "ATM Security Specification Version 1.1," af-sec-0100.002, March 2001.

[7] Laurent, M., O. Paul, and P. Rolin, "Securing Communications over ATM Networks," *Proceedings 1997 IFIPSEC 13th International Information Security Conference*, Copenhagen, Denmark, May 1997.

[8] Harkins, D., and D. Carrel, "The Internet Key Exchange (IKE)," Internet Engineering Task Force RFC 2409, November 1998.

[9] Smith, R. N., D. W. Hill, and N. P. Robinson, "ATM Peer Group Leader Attack and Mitigation," *IEEE Military Communications Conference (MILCOM) Proceedings, Volume 1*, Atlantic City, NJ, October 31–November 3, 1999, pp. 729–733.

[10] Lee, T., and S. Ghosh, "Simulating Asynchronous, Decentralized Military Command and Control," *IEEE Computational Science & Engineering*, Vol. 3, No. 4, 1996, pp. 69–79.

Acronyms and Abbreviations

AAL   ATM adaptation layer

ABR   available bit rate

ACL   access control list

AES   Advanced Encryption Standard

AESA   ATM end system address

AFO   annual frequency of occurrence

AINI   ATM internetwork interface

ALE   annual loss expectancy

ARP   Address Resolution Protocol

ASIC   application-specific integrated circuit

ASP   ATM service provider

ATM   asynchronous transfer mode

BHLI   broadband higher layer information

BICI   broadband intercarrier interface

B-ISDN   broadband integrated services digital network

BUS   broadcast and unknown server

CA   certificate authority

CAM   content-addressable memory

CBC   cipher block chaining

CDV   cell delay variation

CLIP   classical IP over ATM

CLP   cell loss priority

CM   counter mode

CPS   control plane security

CRL   certificate revocation list

CTD   cell transfer delay

DES   Data Encryption Standard

DSA   Digital Signature Algorithm

DTL   designated transit list

ECB   electronic codebook

ELAN   emulated LAN

EMP   electromagnetic pulse

ESI   end system identifier

ESP   encapsulating security payload

FDDI   fiber distributed data interface

FEAL   Fast Data Encipherment Algorithm

FIFO   first in, first out

FIPS   Federal Information Processing Standard

GFC   generic flow control

GMT   Greenwich mean time

HEC   header error check

HMAC   hashed message authentication code

ID   identifier

IDN   initiator distinguished name

IE   information element

IEEE   Institute of Electrical and Electronics Engineers

IETF   Internet Engineering Task Force

IG   information group

IKE   Internet key exchange

IKEK   initial key exchange key

ILMI   integrated layer management interface

I/O   input/output

IP   Internet Protocol

IPSec   IP security

IR   infrared

ISK   initial session key

IV   initialization vector

LAN   local area network

LANE   local area network emulation

LE-ARP   LAN emulation address resolution protocol

LEC   LAN emulation client

LECS   LAN emulation configuration server

LES   LAN emulation server

LFSR   linear feedback shift register

LGN   logical group node

LIJ   leaf-initiated join

LIS   logical IP subnet

LRS   linear recurring sequence

MAC   message authentication code

MD5   Message Digest 5

MDC   manipulation detection code

MIB   management information base

MK   master key

MLS   multilevel security

MPC   MPOA client

MPOA   multiprotocol over ATM

MPS   MPOA server

NHRP   Next Hop Resolution Protocol

NIC   Network Interface Card

NIST   National Institute of Standards and Technology

NNI   network-network interface

NRTC   non-real-time control

NSAP   network service access point

NTK   need to know

NTP   Network Time Protocol

OAM   operations and management

OSPF   open shortest path first

OUI   organizationally unique identifier

PGL   peer group leader

PGP   Pretty Good Privacy

PNNI   private network-to-network interface

PTI   payload type identifier

Pt-Mpt   point-to-multipoint

Pt-Pt   point-to-point

PTSE   PNNI topology state element

PTSP   PNNI topology state packet

PVC   permanent virtual connection

PVP   permanent virtual path

QoS   quality of service

RAM   random access memory

RCC   routing control channel

RDN   responder distinguished name

RF   radio frequency

RFC   Request for Comments

RID   relative identifier

RM   rate management

RSA   Rivest, Shamir, Adelman (a cryptographic algorithm)

SA   security agent

SAAL   signaling ATM adaptation layer

SAID   security association identifier

SAR   segmentation and reassembly

SAS security association section

SDU service data unit

SHA Secure Hash Algorithm

SK session key

SKC session key changeover

SKE session key exchange

SKU session key update

SME Security Message Exchange protocol

SNMP Simple Network Management Protocol

SONET synchronous optical network

SSCOP Service Specific Connection Oriented Protocol

SSIE security services information element

SSL Secure Sockets Layer

SV state vector

SVC switched virtual circuit

TCP Transmission Control Protocol

TEK traffic encryption key

TLV type-length-value

TSAID target security agent identifier

UBR unspecified bit rate

UNI   user-to-network interface

UPC   usage parameter control

VC   virtual connection

VCC   virtual channel connection

VCI   virtual channel identifier

VP   virtual path

VPC   virtual path connection

VPI   virtual path identifier

Selected Bibliography

Altman, A., "In-Band Security for Simplex Connections," ATM Forum contribution ATMF/99-0568, November 1999.

American National Standards Institute, *Triple Data Encryption Algorithm Modes of Operation (ANS X9.52)*, American Bankers Association, 1998.

Amoroso, E. G., *Intrusion Detection*, Sparta, NJ: Intrusion.Net Books, 1999.

The ATM Forum, "Addendum to PNNI v1.0—Secure Routing," FB-RA-PNNI-RSEC-0171.000, May 2001.

The ATM Forum, "ATM Name System, Version 2.0," af-dans-0152.000, July 2000.

The ATM Forum, "ATM Security Specification Version 1.1," af-sec-0100.002, March 2001.

The ATM Forum, "Control Plane Security Baseline," FB-SEC-CPS-0172.000, May 2001.

The ATM Forum, "Integrated Local Management Interface (ILMI) Version 4.0," af-ilmi-0065.000, September 1996.

The ATM Forum, "Methods for Securely Managing ATM Network Elements—Implementation Agreement Version 1.0 (draft)," BTD-SEC-MPS-00.04, April 2001.

The ATM Forum, "PNNI Version 1.0 Security Signaling Addendum," af-cs-0116.000, May 1999.

The ATM Forum, "Private Network-Network Interface Specification, Version 1.0," af-pnni-0055.000, March 1996.

The ATM Forum, "Traffic Management Specification, Version 4.0," af-tm-0056.000, April 1996.

The ATM Forum, "UNI Signaling 4.0 Security Addendum," af-cs-0117.000, May 1999.

The ATM Forum, "User-Network Interface (UNI) Signalling Specification, Version 4.0," af-sig-0061.000, July 1996.

The ATM Forum, "User-Network Interface (UNI) Specification, Version 3.1," af-uni-0010.002, September 1994.

Bautz, G., and K. S. Wrona, "Security Requirements for Wireless ATM Systems," ATM Forum contribution ATMF/96-1216, October 1996.

Berube, M. S., *The American Heritage Dictionary, 2nd College Edition*, Boston: Houghton Mifflin, 1982.

Bilar, D., and D. Burroughs, "Introduction to State-of-the-Art Intrusion Detection Technologies," in *Enabling Technologies for Law Enforcement and Security*, S. K. Bramble, E. M. Carapezza, and L. I. Rudin (Eds.), *Proceedings of SPIE*, Vol. 4232, 2001, pp. 123–133.

Bing, B., *High-Speed Wireless ATM and LANs*, Norwood, MA: Artech House, 2000.

Bird, R. et al., "The KryptoKnight Family of Light-Weight Protocols for Authentication and Key Distribution," *IEEE Transactions on Networking*, Vol. 3, No. 1, February 1995, pp. 31–41.

Cohen, F. B., *Protection and Security on the Information Superhighway*, New York: John Wiley & Sons, 1995.

Cooper, J. A., *Computer and Communications Security*, New York: McGraw-Hill, 1989.

Cooper, J. A., *Computer Security Technology*, Lexington, MA: D. C. Heath, 1984.

Denning, D. E. R., *Cryptography and Data Security*, Reading, MA: Addison-Wesley, 1982.

de Prycker, M., *Asynchronous Transfer Mode*, New York: Ellis Horwood, 1993.

Deutsch, M. S., *Software Verification and Validation*, Englewood Cliffs, NJ: Prentice-Hall, 1982.

Diffie, W, and M. E. Hellman, "New Directions in Cryptography," *IEEE Transactions on Information Theory*, Vol. IT-22, No. 6, 1976, pp. 644–654.

Dobbertin, H., "The Status of MD5 After a Recent Attack," *CryptoBytes*, Vol. 2, No. 2, RSA Labs, Summer 1996.

Freier, A. O., P. Karlton, and P. C. Kocher, "The SSL Protocol Version 3.0," available at http://www.netscape.com/eng/ssl3/, November 1996.

Graft, D., M. Pabrai, and U. Pabrai, "Methodology for Network Security Design," *IEEE Communications*, Vol. 28, No. 11, 1990, pp. 52–58.

Händel, R., M. Huber, and S. Schröder, *ATM Networks—Concepts, Protocols, Applications*, Reading, MA: Addison-Wesley, 1998.

Hetzel, W. C., *Program Test Methods*, Englewood Cliffs, NJ: Prentice-Hall, 1973.

International Standards Organization, "Hash Functions—Part 3: Dedicated Hash Functions," ISO/IEC 10118-3, 1997.

International Standards Organization, "Information Technology—Open Systems Interconnection—The Directory: Authentication Framework," ISO/IEC 9594-8, 1995.

International Standards Organization, "Information Technology—Security Techniques—Data Integrity Mechanism Using a Cryptographic Check Function Employing a Block Cipher Algorithm," ISO/IEC 9797, 1994.

International Standards Organization, "Information Technology—Security Techniques—Evaluation Criteria for IT Security," ISO/IEC 15408, 1999.

International Standards Organization, "Information Technology—Security Techniques—Key Management—Part 2: Mechanisms Using Symmetric Techniques," ISO/IEC 11770-2, 1996.

Internet Engineering Task Force, "Classical IP and ARP over ATM," RFC 2225, April 1998.

Internet Engineering Task Force, "Definitions for Managed Objects for ATM Management," RFC 2515, February 1999.

Internet Engineering Task Force, "HMAC: Keyed-Hashing for Message Authentication," RFC 2104, February 1997.

Internet Engineering Task Force, "The Internet Key Exchange (IKE)," RFC 2409, November 1998.

Internet Engineering Task Force, "IP Encapsulating Security Payload (ESP)," RFC 2406, November 1998.

Internet Engineering Task Force, "The Kerberos Network Authentication Service (V5)," RFC 1510, September 1993.

Internet Engineering Task Force, "The MD5 Message Digest Algorithm," RFC 1321, 1992.

Internet Engineering Task Force, "Multiprotocol Encapsulation over ATM Adaptation Layer 5," RFC 1483, July 1993.

Internet Engineering Task Force, "NBMA Next Hop Resolution Protocol (NHRP)," RFC 2332, April 1998.

Internet Engineering Task Force, "Network Time Protocol (Version 3) Specification, Implementation, and Analysis," RFC 1305, March 1992.

Internet Engineering Task Force, "OSPF Version 2," RFC 2328, 1998.

Internet Engineering Task Force, "PKCS #1: RSA Cryptography Specifications Version 2.0," RFC 2437, October 1998.

Internet Engineering Task Force, "S/MIME Version 3 Message Specification," RFC 2633, June 1999.

Internet Engineering Task Force, "U.S. Department of Defense Security Options for the Internet Protocol," RFC 1108, November 1991.

ITU-T, "B-ISDN DSS2 User-Network Interface (UNI) Layer 3 Specification for Basic Call/Connection Control," Recommendation Q.2931, February 1995.

ITU-T, "The Directory: Authentication Framework," Recommendation X.509, 1997.

Jueneman, R. R., "Electronic Document Authentication," *IEEE Network Magazine*, Vol. 1, No. 2, 1987, pp. 17–23.

Kwok, T., *ATM—The New Paradigm for Internet, Intranet, and Residential Broadband Services and Applications*, Englewood Cliffs, NJ: Prentice Hall, 1997.

Landwehr, C. E., "The Best Available Technologies for Computer Security," *Computer*, Vol. 16, No. 7, 1983, pp. 88–100.

Laurent, M., C. Delahaye, and M. Achemlal, "Security Services Negotiation Through OAM Cells," ATM Forum contribution ATMF/99-0335, July 1999.

Laurent, M., O. Paul, and P. Rolin, "Securing Communications over ATM Networks," *Proceedings 1997 IFIPSEC 13th International Information Security Conference*, Copenhagen, Denmark, May 1997.

Lee, T., and S. Ghosh, "Simulating Asynchronous, Decentralized Military Command and Control," *IEEE Computational Science & Engineering*, Vol. 3, No. 4, 1996, pp. 69–79.

Menezes, A. J., P. C. van Oorschot, and S. A. Vanstone, *Handbook of Applied Cryptography*, Boca Raton, FL: CRC Press, 1997.

Merkle, R. C., and M. E. Hellman, "On the Security of Multiple Encryption," *Communications of the ACM*, Vol. 24, No. 7, 1981, pp. 465–467.

National Bureau of Standards, *DES Modes of Operation (FIPS PUB 81)*, 1980.

National Bureau of Standards, *Guidelines for Automatic Data Processing Risk Analysis (FIPS PUB 65)*, 1979.

National Institute of Standards and Technology, *Advanced Encryption Standard (Draft)*, 2001.

National Institute of Standards and Technology, *Data Encryption Standard (FIPS PUB 46-3)*, 1999.

National Institute of Standards and Technology, *Digital Signature Standard (FIPS PUB 186-1)*, 1998.

National Institute of Standards and Technology, *Secure Hash Standard (FIPS PUB 180-1)*, 1995.

National Institute of Standards and Technology, *Standard Security Label for Information Transfer (FIPS PUB 188)*, 1994.

Pandya, A., and E. Sen, *ATM Technology for Broadband Telecommunications Networks*, Boca Raton, FL: CRC Press, 1999.

Patiyoot, D., and S. J. Shepherd, "Security Issues for Wireless ATM Networks," *Proceedings of IEEE 1988 International Conference on Universal Personal Communications*, Vol. 2, Florence, Italy, October 5–9, 1998, pp. 1359–1363.

Pettit, R. H., *ECM and ECCM Techniques for Digital Communication Systems*, Belmont, CA: Lifetime Learning Publications, 1982.

Pierson, L. G., and E. L. Witzke, "Data Encryption and the ISO Model for Open Systems Interconnection," *Joint Proceedings, Ideas in Science and Electronics (ISE'84)*, Albuquerque, NM, May 2–4, 1984, pp. 32–40.

Pierson, L. G., and E. L. Witzke, "A Security Methodology for Computer Networks," *AT&T Technical Journal*, Vol. 67, No. 3, 1988, pp. 28–36.

Pierson, L. G., et al., "Context-Agile Encryption for High Speed Communication Networks," *ACM Computer Communication Review*, Vol. 29, No. 1, 1999, pp. 35–49.

Rivest, R. L., "Remarks on a Proposed Cryptanalytic Attack on the M.I.T. Public-Key Cryptosystem," *Cryptologia*, Vol. 2, No. 1, 1978, pp. 62–65.

Rivest, R. L., A. Shamir, and L. Adleman, "A Method for Obtaining Digital Signatures and Public-Key Cryptosystems," *Communications of the ACM*, Vol. 21, No. 2, 1978, pp. 120–126.

Rueppel, R. A., "Stream Ciphers," in *Contemporary Cryptology*, G. J. Simmons (Ed.), Piscataway, NJ: IEEE Press, 1992, pp. 65–134.

Schneier, B., *Applied Cryptography*, Second Edition, New York: John Wiley & Sons, 1996.

Schneier, B., "Attack Trees," *Dr. Dobb's Journal*, Vol. 24, No. 12, 1999, pp. 21–29.

Schumacher, H. J., S. Ghosh, and T. S. Lee, "Top Secret Traffic and the Public ATM Network Infrastructure," *Information Systems Security*, Vol. 7, No. 4, 1999, pp. 27–45.

Selvakumar, S., and V. Venkateshwaran, "Partition Equalizer: A Scheduler for Algorithm-Agile-Encryptor ATM Networks," *Computer Communications*, Vol. 24, No. 7–8, 2001, pp. 631–640.

Shimizu, A., "The FEAL Cipher Family," in *Advances in Cryptology—CRYPTO '90*, Lecture Notes in Computer Science, Vol. 537, Berlin: Springer-Verlag, 1991, pp. 627–638.

Shimizu, A., and S. Miyaguchi, "Fast Data Encipherment Algorithm FEAL," in *Advances in Cryptology—EUROCRYPT '87*, Lecture Notes in Computer Science, Vol. 304, Berlin: Springer-Verlag, 1988, pp. 267–278.

Sholander, P., et al., "The Effect of Algorithm-Agile Encryption on ATM Quality of Service," *Global Telecommunications Conference, IEEE GLOBECOM 97*, Vol. 1, conference collection, Phoenix, AZ, November 3, 1997, pp. 470–474.

Simmons, G. J., and M. J. Norris, "Preliminary Comments on the M.I.T. Public-Key Cryptosystem," *Cryptologia*, Vol. 1, No. 4, 1977, pp. 406–414.

Smith, R. N., D. W. Hill, and N. P. Robinson, "ATM Peer Group Leader Attack and Mitigation," *IEEE Military Communications Conference (MILCOM) Proceedings, Volume 1*, Atlantic City, NJ, October 31–November 3, 1999, pp. 729–733.

Tarman, T. D., and E. L. Witzke, "Intrusion Detection Considerations for Switched Networks," in *Enabling Technologies for Law Enforcement and Security*, S. K. Bramble, E. M. Carapezza, and L. I. Rudin (Eds.), *Proceedings of SPIE*, Vol. 4232, 2001, pp. 85–92.

Tarman, T. D., and P. E. Sholander, "Issues in Security Service Discovery and Routing," ATM Forum contribution ATMF/99-0181, April 1999.

Tuchman, W., "Hellman Presents no Shortcut Solutions to the DES," *IEEE Spectrum*, Vol. 16, No. 7, 1979, pp. 40–41.

Wilcox, D. C., et al., "A DES ASIC Suitable for Network Encryption at 10 Gbps and Beyond," in *Cryptographic Hardware and Embedded Systems*, C. K. Koc and C. Paar (Eds.), Lecture Notes in Computer Science, Vol. 1717, Berlin: Springer-Verlag, 1999, pp. 37–48.

Witzke, E. L., "Tools for Computer Network Security," *Conference Proceedings of the Fifth Annual International Conference on Computers and Communications*, Scottsdale, AZ, March 26–28, 1986, pp. 252–256.

Witzke, E. L., and L. G. Pierson, "Key Management for Large Scale End-to-End Encryption," *Proceedings, 28th Annual International Carnahan Conference on Security Technology*, Albuquerque, NM, October 12–14, 1994, pp. 76–79.

Witzke, E. L., and L. G. Pierson, "The Role of Decimated Sequences in Scaling Encryption Speeds Through Parallelism," *Conference Proceedings of the IEEE Fifteenth Annual International Conference on Computers and Communications*, Scottsdale, AZ, March 27–29, 1996, pp. 515–519.

About the Authors

Thomas D. Tarman is a distinguished member of the technical staff at Sandia National Laboratories in Albuquerque, New Mexico, where he leads research projects in the areas of ATM security (especially security protocols), switched network intrusion detection, network modeling and simulation, and real-time networking applications (including multimedia and distributed multiprocessing). Mr. Tarman has been actively involved in the ATM Forum's Security Working Group and was editor of its ATM Security Specification, Version 1.1. He received the ATM Forum Spotlight Award in July 2000 for his contributions to the development of the specification and promotion of ATM security. In addition, he was a corecipient of a 1996 *R&D 100* award for the development of a scalable ATM encryptor.

Mr. Tarman holds a B.S. in computer and electrical engineering and an M.S. in electrical engineering, both from Purdue University in West Lafayette, Indiana. He is a member of the IEEE.

Edward L. Witzke is a senior member of the technical staff at Sandia National Laboratories. He has more than 24 years of experience spanning analysis, hardware design, software design and development, project management, and administrative functions. His project experience includes implementation of public-key and secret-key cryptographic algorithms, encryptor architecture design and review, security methodology development, system penetration testing, and design of network intrusion detection systems.

Mr. Witzke was a corecipient of a 1996 *R&D 100* award for the development of a scalable ATM encryptor.

Mr. Witzke holds a Bachelor of University Studies degree with a concentration in computer science, from the University of New Mexico. His research interests include high-performance communication networks, wireless networks, network security, high-speed encryption, and information warfare. He is a member of the ACM and IEEE, and participates in ATM Forum activities. On the rare occasions he has time for outside interests, they include amateur radio, public service and utility frequency scanning, and shortwave listening.

Index

Recent Titles in the Artech House Computing Library

Advanced ANSI SQL Data Modeling and Structure Processing, Michael M. David

Advanced Database Technology and Design, Mario Piattini and Oscar Díaz, editors

Business Process Implementation for IT Professionals and Managers, Robert B. Walford

Configuration Management: The Missing Link in Web Engineering, Susan Dart

Data Modeling and Design for Today's Architectures, Angelo Bobak

Future Codes: Essays in Advanced Computer Technology and the Law, Curtis E. A. Karnow

Global Distributed Applications with Windows® DNA, Enrique Madrona

A Guide to Software Configuration Management, Alexis Leon

Guide to Standards and Specifications for Designing Web Software, Stan Magee and Leonard L. Tripp

Internet Commerce Development, Craig Standing

Knowledge Management Strategy and Technology, Richard F. Bellaver and John M. Lusa, editos

Managing Computer Networks: A Case-Based Reasoning Approach, Lundy Lewis

Metadata Management for Information Control and Business Success, Guy Tozer

Multimedia Database Management Systems, Guojun Lu

Practical Guide to Software Quality Management, John W. Horch

Practical Process Simulation Using Object-Oriented Techniques and C++, José Garrido